Unless Recalled Early

 **Essays in History**

Essays in History
Financial, Economic, Personal

Charles P. Kindleberger

Foreword by Peter Temin

Ann Arbor

THE UNIVERSITY OF MICHIGAN PRESS

Copyright © by the University of Michigan 1999
All rights reserved
Published in the United States of America by
The University of Michigan Press
Manufactured in the United States of America
⊗ Printed on acid-free paper

2002   2001   2000   1999   4   3   2   1

*A CIP catalog record for this book is available
from the British Library.*

Library of Congress Cataloging-in-Publication Data

Kindleberger, Charles Poor, 1910–
    Essays in history : financial, economic, personal / Charles P.
Kindleberger.
        p.   cm. — (Studies in international economics)
    Includes bibliographical references and index.
    ISBN 0-472-11002-0 (cloth : alk. paper)
    1. International finance — History.   2. Economic history.
3. Kindleberger, Charles Poor, 1910–   .   I. Title.   II. Series:
Studies in international economics (Ann Arbor, Mich.)
HG3881.K489   1999
332 — dc21   98-46616
                                                                        CIP

In memory of
Emile Despres, Alvin H. Hansen,
Edward S. Mason, and Willard L. Thorp

Contents

Foreword

Peter Temin

Essays by Charlie Kindleberger! They are a treat for all who read them. Charlie's blend of historical information, acute insight, and lively wit makes for instructive and enjoyable reading. These new essays continue explorations done in previous work.

The essays in this volume cover three broad areas. The first topic Charlie discusses is current events in the 1990s. As always, international financial aspects attract Charlie, and he has insightful comments on many international events of the past decade. The second topic is economic history, ranging from the sixteenth century to World War II. Again, financial history is the center of Charlie's attention. The final group of essays adds to Charlie's reminiscences of his role in the formulation of the Marshall Plan.

One of the personal essays explains how Charlie came to MIT. He had promised his wife that he would leave government service if his weight fell 20 pounds below normal. To paraphrase Charlie's exposition, it did and he did. He looked around for an academic job, and he found one at MIT, where he taught from 1948 until his retirement — and for several years thereafter.

This essay explains how Charlie came to be first my teacher and then my colleague at MIT, along the lines described in the last essay of this volume on Carlos F. Díaz-Alejandro. I remember his classes in international economics vividly through the fog of the intervening 30 years. Charlie ran one of the most open and engaging classes I remember. There was lots of discussion of models and events, with Charlie explaining the theory underlying our views. He adopted the practice of providing only sketchy outlines of the theory. He even was fond of making bold statements that looked consistent with the theory but sometimes were not. The result was that we students left class in a high state of agitation and interest. We continued discussing the theory to sort out what it indicated and what we believed. Of all my classes at MIT, Charlie's was the most "extended" in time by its constant postclass discussions.

As a colleague, Charlie was the same ebullient personality. We have shared a research interest for many years in the Great Depression, and I have had many conversations with him about it. His fine book on *The World in Depression* swiftly became a classic. He and I have jousted in and out of print about many aspects of the Great Depression. Twenty years ago I thought that the depression in the United States could be understood largely in national terms. I now agree with Charlie that its roots were in the international arena.

One essay in this collection revisits a mechanism in the transmission of the Great Depression. Charlie always has noted prominently that the stock market crash of 1929 was followed immediately by a sharp fall in the price of raw materials in international trade. The resulting deflation was one of the factors intensifying the economic contraction. Unclear in earlier expositions was the connection between the stock market and raw-material prices.

The essay here makes the connection clear. In the context of thinking about the current stock market and analyzing the 1987 stock market crash, Charlie discusses 1929. He notes that the Federal Reserve Bank increased liquidity after 1987 and eased the impact of the decline of stock prices on the rest of the economy. In 1929, the Fed expanded but not enough. The crash seized up credit in the economy as a whole, and firms trying to finance inventories could not renew their loans. They sold some of their inventories to raise cash, forcing down the price.

This is a clear story. And, as so often with Charlie's stories, it raises other questions for future research. This story is about credit rationing. Loans were hard to get on any terms. But it also is true that interest rates fell sharply after the stock market crash. There are two possibilities. One, the listed interest rates did not apply to the mass of borrowers. They were only for a few preferred customers. All others found the effective price of capital to be higher, not lower, than before. Two, the restriction of capital was very short lived. In this case, a swift shock to the credit market was enough to destabilize importers and exporters. Even though the credit market recovered its liquidity in short order, the traders did not. I hope that this essay will stimulate economists and historians to track down this story and explore its ramifications.

This is the form of these essays. Charlie is opening a conversation — or many conversations in the many essays. He is an engaging conversational partner, and his opening gambits cry out for responses. As mentioned previously, each story raises new questions and invites responses of all sorts. I will respond here to Charlie's reminiscences about the

Marshall Plan, the great public policy after World War II, to suggest how an ongoing discussion might progress.

Charlie leads readers into the microhistory of postwar policies, the debates about the Marshall Plan and the rooms in which it was debated. I want to back up from this detailed examination to inquire into the context of these plans for reconstruction. I then will return to Charlie's gambits. I first contrast the postwar actions after World Wars I and II. The first postwar economy led to the Great Depression; the second, to what has been called the golden age of economic growth. Then I inquire into the U.S. government's motivation in extending aid to Western Europe in the 1940s. I try to supply some context for Charlie's more detailed accounts.

Recovery from World War II was followed by prosperity and economic growth, while recovery from the smaller World War I was economic chaos, conflict, and depression. Current thought attributes the Great Depression to the inability of policymakers to deal with the shock of World War I. Their solution to the immediate postwar chaos represented by hyperinflations in Eastern Europe was to revive the gold standard. But this solution froze the major industrial economies into insupportable positions and allowed little flexibility to deal with strain. The inability of policymakers to abandon the gold standard then produced the Great Depression.

Charlie agrees with the thrust of this argument, although he shades it differently. He emphasized the role of the missing hegemon in international finance: no longer London, not yet New York. But why was a hegemon needed? It was to manage the gold standard as it had been managed from London before World War I. One therefore can argue either that the gold standard itself or the absence of a manager of the gold standard was the cause of the Great Depression. Charlie's formulation of this point, with its focus on national hegemonic powers, has set the agenda for other scholars in history, economic history, and political science. The topics analyzed by Charlie in his many publications and very briefly here — international aspects of the Great Depression, the Marshall Plan, the golden age of European growth after World War II — are the central topics on everyone's research agenda. We stand on the shoulders of giants.

World War II was an even bigger shock to the world economy than World War I. This can be seen by comparing the maximum share of national output devoted to the war effort in the two wars. (The data are drawn from 1917 for World War I and from 1943 for World War II for European countries and from 1944 for the United States.) The United States devoted 45 percent of its output to the war effort at the high point of expenditures in World War II, compared to only 13 percent at the similar point in World War I. For Britain, the maximum shares of output in the two wars were 57 percent in World War II and 38 percent in World War I. For Germany, the most heavily involved in both wars, the comparable numbers are 76 percent and 53 percent. In addition to devoting a great share of production to war in the second global conflict, these countries also maintained high war expenditures longer.

Yet the larger shock of World War II was not followed by the same economic strains as the interwar period. World War I followed the economically tranquil Victorian and Edwardian periods; there was no expectation of and no preparation for the forces unleashed by the war. World War II, by contrast, followed the Russian Revolution, the Great Depression, and the Nazi domination of Europe. Policymakers had ample warning — if they cared to learn from history — that the world economy would not heal itself from the injury of the war quickly or smoothly without help.

The United Nations, the International Monetary Fund (IMF), and the World Bank were all planned while the war was still going on. But it became apparent by 1947 that these new institutions were not going to be sufficient to guarantee economic — and therefore political — stability in Europe. President Truman, in one of the great actions of an international leader in our century, extended aid to Europe in the form of the Marshall Plan.

The Truman administration needed to work hard to extend this aid because Congress feared that the cost of aid would be large, added to the already large cost of the war itself, as Charlie recalls. The congressional point of view is hard to recapture in light of the great postwar boom that followed. But we must remember that the boom was still in the future. History was not that hopeful. A little thought might have enabled Congress to realize that the costs of aid to Europe would be small, but who could be expected to foresee the future when it was so different from the recent past and so dependent on current actions? Congress consequently delayed and discussed in the rooms Charlie describes.

This train of thought raises an important question. If the expected cost of the aid was large, why was the Truman administration so intent on overriding congressional caution? Was the administration's motive to promote the interests of the United States or was it simply altruism? Economic and political conditions in Europe were very unstable in the late 1940s. In particular, the communists were taking power in Eastern Europe and seemed ready to take Western Europe as well. Having just vanquished Nazi domination of Western Europe, Truman did not relish repeating the experience with Soviet domination. Foreign aid was a way to tip the political balance in favor of democracy and ensure a measure of political tranquility. What was in this for the United States?

Charlie discusses all this in his matchless narrative fashion. But members of a younger generation would approach this question in a more formal manner. The grace lost by this formalism, we young 'uns argue, is offset by the gains in clarity. In the spirit of continuing the conversation begun by Charlie's essays, follow me in a very small formal exercise.

Consider as a game the choice facing the United States after World War II of whether or not to give aid to Europe — that is, as an example of the kind of interaction between people or countries analyzed by game theory. More specifically, think of it as a particular, well-known game: the Prisoner's Dilemma. There are two players in this game: the United States (US) and Western Europe (WE). There are two possible actions: cooperation (the policy stance that Charlie describes following World War II) and "finking" (the policy of continued aggression by nonmilitary means that followed World War I so disastrously).

Cooperation in this game means that US gives aid to Europe and that WE stays democratic and trades with US. Finking means that US does not give aid to Europe and that WE goes communist. The hostile action of Europe is given in its 1940s context, not its 1920s version. While the game can describe choices after each war, the current discussion I am having with Charlie is about the aftermath of World War II. In the formal representation of the game, let US be the column player and WE be the row player.

Assume that aid consists of US giving and loaning a dollars to WE. In the language of the game, aid transfers a dollars from US to WE. Assume also that by going communist, WE gains b dollars and exacts c dollars from US. These magnitudes should be understood as the monetary equivalent of the expected gain to European workers and the expected loss to the United States of having communists on Europe's Atlantic coast. I do not deal here with the now apparent fact that the workers at least would have been grievously disappointed in this expectation.

In order to make this game a Prisoner's Dilemma, I assume that $a < c$. In other words, the expected cost to US of WE going communist (finking) is larger than the cost of aid. If not, if there were no fear in the postwar United States of the consequence of communist expansion, then the Marshall Plan is inexplicable as U.S. self-interest. It could be only altruism.

The game looks like this in the formalism of elementary game theory:

United States

		Aid	No Aid
Europe	Dem.	$a, -a$	$0, 0$
	Com.	$a + b, -a - c$	$b, -c$

It should be noted that b, the gain to Europeans from going communist, has to be positive and small to make this a Prisoner's Dilemma. Specifically, $0 < b < a$. If $b < 0$, then the Europeans expect to lose from going communist and WE stays democratic no matter what US does. If $b > a$, then the Europeans anticipate such a marvelous transformation from going communist that WE goes communist independent of US's actions. Only if b is positive and small does US action make a difference. In all other cases, the Marshall Plan again was altruistic.

Assuming b is positive but small captures the perception in the United States after World War II that there was a chance that Western Europe would go communist but that the pull toward communism was not so strong that it could not be influenced by U.S. aid. It reflects the deep divisions in the parliaments in France and Italy, the sense that Western Europe was balanced on a knife-edge and could go either way. If the United States thought that Western Europe had no reason to go communist with or without aid, or would go communist despite U.S. aid, there was no self-interested motive for extending aid.

This game then is a Prisoner's Dilemma for appropriate values of the parameters. Both parties prefer giving and receiving aid to the alternative of having no aid and having communists in WE. But there is a problem in getting there. Each party has an incentive to cheat in this position — the upper left-hand cell of the matrix. US is even better off if WE stays democratic without aid. And WE would prefer to receive aid and still go communist. In the language of game theory, this solution is not a Nash equilibrium.

It is well known that if this Prisoner's Dilemma game is played only once, then the Nash equilibrium is no aid and the presence of communists. On the other hand, if the game is played infinitely many times, a Tit-for-Tat strategy will enable the parties to get to the better position of aid and democracy. Both parties in this strategy choose aid and democracy as long as the other does the same, but they threaten to go to the one-shot Nash equilibrium forever if the other player once finks. This treat promotes cooperation. (Conditions can be derived under which repeated players will opt for this policy and outcome.)

This theory is a problem for the deliberations about the Marshall Plan. Postwar conditions were changing rapidly; there were not many opportunities to go back and replay the same choices. The United States had to choose between the policies taken after World War I — and by the Soviets after World War II — of extracting reparations from the losers and the policies taken after World War II of extending aid to friend and former foe alike. Congress had to decide on the Marshall Plan without knowing what Western European countries would do.

If WE is rational (in the game-theoretic sense), it will go communist and enjoy the gains, *b,* whether or not US gives aid. But there is a probability that WE will play Tit-for-Tat. In other words, it will stay democratic and reciprocate US policy; it will respond to aid by staying democratic but go communist without aid. In this case, even though WE does not envisage replaying this game over again, it thinks of other kinds of cooperation that will be relevant in the years to come. It chooses to signal US that cooperation will be the norm in whatever future games are to be played. This general expectation transforms a single game into a repeated game.

US, similarly, can think of this decision as part of an ongoing relationship with WE. The Marshall Plan was a discrete episode, but it was also only part of the postwar relations between the United States and Europe. First of all, it was only one part of the aid given to Europe, which ranged from the immediate postwar aid before the Marshall Plan to the support of other measures like the European Payments Union thereafter. Second, we expect the Truman administration to have learned from the Great Depression that the aftermath of world wars stretches out over many years.

The probability that Western Europe was playing Tit-for-Tat must have been big enough to make the cost of having Western Europe be communist loom large even when discounted by the probability that Western Europe would not respond favorably to U.S. actions. The Truman administration was asking Congress to take a gamble. It was not only that the anticipated cost of communism was larger than of the Marshall Plan and other aid. It was also that the Europeans would understand that the Marshall Plan was a signal of what economists now call a policy regime to promote cooperation with Western Europe and between the Western European countries. It was this double estimation that made the argument for the Marshall Plan so complex.

This then is the background for Charlie's recollections of the negotiations leading up to the Marshall Plan. Behind the speeches and the reservations of senators debating the plan, there must have been perceptions that matched the magnitudes of this game if U.S. motives were at least partly self-interested. On the European side, at least in American eyes, there must have been a pull toward communism strong enough to attract some countries but not strong enough to attract them in the presence of U.S. aid. On the American side, there must have been a great fear of communism in Western Europe and a high estimate of the probability that the Europeans would respond well to overtures of co-operation. Charlie tells one part of the story; this response expounds another.

This formal analysis reveals that the arguments for the Marshall Plan from the self-interest of the United States were complex. They were mixed in addition with altruistic impulses toward the recent combatants. The result of this tangle of ideas was complexity in administration and congressional debate. Charlie here contributes to the task of recovering these debates to see if the assumptions of this formal model were valid in 1947. How did Senator Taft, for example, deal with this difficult problem (without the aid of game theory)? Charlie recalls and shares his recollection with us in these essays.

I invite you, gentle reader, to enter into this conversation with Charlie Kindleberger. As you read these essays, enjoy them actively. Allow yourself to be stimulated by the vivid accounts that follow to fill in some of the background — and then to go back to argue, at least in your mind, with Charlie's way of presenting his perceptions and the conclusions he reaches.

Introduction

This is another exercise in tidying up more or less recent work for the benefit of my literary executor. There is rather less coherence perhaps — no, scratch the perhaps — there is rather less coherence in these essays than in earlier collections. History is hardly a strong thread on which to string them. I sometimes accuse myself of having a grasshopper mind, as I and my sisters knew our mother had. Financial and economic history are possibly not excessively disparate, but the personal history is. Moreover, I have written on these subjects before and am acutely aware of the fact that Mark Twain in his later years, according to a biographer, Guy Cardwell, wrote thousands of worthless pages and repeated himself endlessly.

Enough apologizing. In the section on finance, I believe I have a few things that are pretty good and/or worth stating. The first essay on "Asset Inflation and Monetary Policy" came almost two years before Alan Greenspan's cri de coeur about "irrational exuberance" and two and a half years ahead of a leader in the *Economist* of October 4, 1997, which claimed to have discovered this ancient problem. "Caveat Emptor, Investor, Depositor?" for a memorial volume to honor the late Keynesian, Lorie Tarshis, deals with one theme treated in *Manias, Panics and Crashes* (3d ed., 1996) to the effect that policies predicated on assumptions that all economic actors have equal and substantial intelligence, information, and foresight, and that dealers in merchandise and securities are uniformly honorable and law abiding, do not constitute a safe basis for wide-ranging deregulation of financial and economic units. "Free Minting" is another historical protest against the view that markets, left alone, always get it right. They mostly do but not in all cases. The riposte is directed to the proponents of free banking, that would let anyone start a bank without regulation, relying on the inverse of Gresham's law, as they believe that superior banks will flourish and poor ones fail — good money (sound deposits) driving out bad. Minting coins differs from issuing bank notes and deposits, to be sure, and the infection that leads one mint to copy another observed debasing its coinage is stronger than that among "wildcatting" banks, or, more recently, dereg-ulated savings-and-loan associations. Of particular interest in the seven-teenth century is that debasement of coin to earn seignorage to fight the forthcoming Thirty Years' War started a decade before the war broke out in 1618 and was brought to a halt in 1623, only a sixth of the way through the hostilities, when the subsidiary coins became worthless. First blackened with copper, then whitened with paint, children played with them in the street, as in Tolstoy's short story "Ivan the Fool." In the latter case, however, the playthings were made of real gold, which the un-Midas-like Ivan and his neighbors disdained when it became exces-sively abundant.

"Is the Dollar Going the Way of Sterling, the Guilder, the Ducat, and the Bezant?" contains a prognostication that thus far is quite wrong. The comeback of the U.S. economy, the stock market — at least through August 1997 — and the dollar surprised more than one observer. I should perhaps bury my mistakes, but a lingering sense of something — I am not quite sure what — makes me think that confession is good for the soul, if one has a soul. At the same time, the guest appearance of "Should Emerging Markets Climb Back Down?" in Peter L. Bernstein's *Econom-ics and Portfolio Strategy* newsletter in October 1994 drew from him a holographic postscript to a letter of December 1997: "Your piece for us on emerging markets makes good reading at the moment. Classic!" This refers of course to financial influenza among the majority of the Asian Tigers.

The long essay on "Economic and Financial Crises and Transforma-tion in Sixteenth-Century Europe" poses a similar issue of full disclo-sure. The research was undertaken as occupational therapy, to keep busy in retirement so as to stay out of trouble. I called the project "Operation Penelope," hoping to weave by day and unravel by night — though I had no suitors — until the Reaper came to collect. Sadly I finished it, as I thought, sent it off to an economic-history periodical, and got it back with the opinion of the editor that it was insufficiently focused. After some months, I reread it, cut out a few pages of digres-sion and diversion, and sent it off to another outlet. The Institute of International Finance in Princeton has, after deletion of some digressive passages, accepted it, another, doubtless the last, of a series of studies going back in time, starting with the twentieth century and ending in the sixteenth.

I hope it is understandable that compulsive scribblers want to gather their orphans contributed to memorial volumes and Festschriften, even when these are efforts that long have rested, unsought, in a desk drawer. None of these essays, apart from the volunteers like "Asset Inflation" and

"Economic and Financial Crises," came to celebratory symposia out of hiding but were written as closely as possible to the interests of the honoree, given my preoccupations, or, in a new wrinkle, were requested on a particular topic. "Free Minting" combines my interest in financial crises with the late Egon Sohmen's fierce enthusiasm for deregulation. The editors of the Festschriften for Herman van der Wee ("The Merchant as Entrepreneur") and Paul Bairoch ("Types of International Economic History") specified the subjects on which contributions should be produced. The purpose, of course, is a laudable one: to produce a coherent volume rather than the dog's breakfast that usually results. "Historical Economics" again was produced to order for a German volume on the future of economics. It may differ slightly from an exact translation of the German text, as I kept only my first draft and failed to make a photocopy of the English text sent abroad.

A paper commissioned for a particular topic—for example, the diffusion of technology—allows one to accede if interested or decline. In my practice, the rule is to try to accept even though the topic may not square exactly with my research but to tell the editor to reject the submission if it is inadequate or diverges too widely from the assigned topic. They rarely do reject a paper if it is composed as a response to their request: too timid.

The first two items in Part 3 on personal history were commissioned: "Some Economic Lessons From World War II" by the Industrial War College in Arlington, Virginia; "Legislating the Marshall Plan: A Memoir" by *Foreign Affairs,* which put together a symposium to celebrate the fiftieth anniversary of Secretary of State George Marshall's speech at the 1947 Harvard Commencement. Each put the ball slowly over the plate and invited me to knock it out of the park (to use a metaphor from the American national pastime); or, if you prefer, think of the James M. Barrie play, "The General Counts His Medals." Return to the scene of alleged triumphs is irresistible.

As for the essay on "Legislating the Marshall Plan," the original version, used here as essay 14, was much longer than the one that appeared in the *Foreign Affairs* issue of May–June 1997, the latter an amputee, almost a basket case. The editor was of course constrained by limits of space and also by the fact that he had obtained another article on the role of Undersecretary of State William L. Clayton, a hero of mine whose contribution has been sorely neglected, for which neglect my original draft tries to make amends. I am nonetheless reminded of the remark of a witty friend, William N. Parker, who, when I wrote commenting on a letter of his published in the *New York Times Book Review,* sent me the original version, saying, "Now that you have seen the movie, read the book." I may perhaps add that Clayton is one of four gods in my pantheon (far) under whom I have worked, along with, in alphabetical order, General Omar N. Bradley, General George C. Marshall, and Allan Sproul of the Federal Reserve Bank of New York. The dedication of this collection is to another group of heroes that I worked under but closely with, again in alphabetical order: Emile Despres of the Federal Reserve Bank of New York, the Board of Governors, and the Office of Strategic Services, Alvin H. Hansen at the Board and on the Joint Economic Committee of Canada and the United States, Edward S. Mason of the Office of Strategic Services and the Department of State, and Willard L. Thorp at the State Department. Thorp succeeded Mason as assistant secretary of state, intermediate between Clayton and my level.

The eulogy for the late Carlos F. Díaz-Alejandro does not perhaps belong in my personal history although there is a lot of me in academic guise in it, doubtless too much. It does, however, say something about the teaching and learning processes that occupied me for nearly 40 years after 10 years in government, central banking, and the military. It should probably be regarded as sociology, not economics, but I believe that no apologies are needed on that score.

One of the readers for the Press thought that the introduction would give some semblance of coherence to the book if the essays were described along the lines that won Douglass C. North the Nobel Prize for economic science, institutions. I am interested in institutions, implicitly in the essay on technology, "Technological Diffusion: European Experience to 1850," where it is said that technology is only one dimension of the growth process and "matched by comparable profiles in savings, productivity, responsiveness to market stimuli, monopoly formation, consolidation of economic interests, acceptance of risks, etc." (p. 122, this volume). Explicitly, too, the essay describing the establishment of deposit banks as a response to currency debasement, "Currency Debasement in the Early Seventeenth Century and the Establishment of Deposit Banks in Central Europe," can be regarded as a study in institution formation. But institutions wax and wane and do not always promote economic growth and well-being. Guilds were started to train workers and to maintain high standards of workmanship. They ended by resisting technical change and the substitution of less expensive but serviceable goods for those of the highest quality and cost. Private property is generally held to be the crucial institution in economic growth, but one can find examples that run to the contrary: tax farming in early modern Europe was efficient because of limited government staffs, so long as the farms were for prescribed periods, reauctioned when the term ended.

When in France they became private property, held without term and even bequeathable, the system broke down, but it could only be changed by using the guillotine on 28 tax farmers. I prefer not to count myself an institutionalist, a monetarist, a Keynesian, a technologist, a demographer, a financial analyst, and the like but a jack of all trades (and master of none?).

A grasshopper mind? A sign of senescence? Of late I have written slim volumes on sailors in the age of sail and the comparative merits of centralization and pluralism. There is much to be said for depth as opposed to width, for taking one idea, even ideology, and plugging away at it until it gets superseded by another powerful mode of analysis: monetarism and Keynesianism, free markets and regulation, public choice vs. public goods. Ambiguity, the Manichaean attitude, President Truman's objectionable two-armed economist have it right. The answer to the question of what counts most is "it depends," and it depends on the circumstances. In classes in international trade years ago I said that the answer to every question in economics was "it depends" and that it mostly depended on the elasticities.

That answer may suffice for trade theory, but more generally, one can and should extend it. Money should grow at a steady rate, on trend, as a rule, but sometimes boom will be followed by bust, giving rise to the need for a lender of last resort who floods the market with liquidity (and should mop it up afterward). One should continuously bear in mind the remark of Joseph Schumpeter and Joan Robinson that economics is a toolbox. The good economist needs many tools. Choosing the right tool for the given job is partly science, partly art. Exploring economic history widely, as grasshoppers explore, especially in summer, allows one to see and compare how useful the individual tools are.

Part 1

Financial History

Asset Inflation and Monetary Policy

I

Asset inflation, as distinguished from ordinary inflation, the latter referring to rising prices of consumer goods, wholesale commodities, or the national-income deflator, is a phrase not in use in the west, but current in Japan. There are times when assets rise in price in an inflationary way, a boom or even a bubble, while output prices are relatively stable or even declining. Regarding a famous instance in 1928 and 1929, Milton Friedman and Anna Jacobson Schwartz wrote that the monetary authorities should have ignored the rise in the New York stock market, and focused attention on other goals such as the general price level.[1] More recently, at the end of 1989, the Bank of Japan moved to tighten interest rates after ignoring the spectacular rise of the equity Nikkei index from approximately 10,000 in 1984 to 39,000 in 1989, finally fearful that rising asset prices would ultimately provoke inflation at the consumer level, and worried that the spread of inflation from shares to real estate was putting housing out of the reach of the average Japanese and threatening social harmony.[2] This was an instance of international coordination of monetary policy as U.S. and German discount rates were lowered at the same time.

The Governor of the Bank of Japan, Yasuski Mieno, who took office in December 1989, was ambivalent over the change in policy:

> He explained [in an interview with James Sterngold] that steep rises in asset prices could not be given the same emphasis in policy-making as could broader measures of consumer prices. On the other hand, they could not be ignored.[3]

This essay was reprinted with permission from the Banca Nazionale del Lavoro, *Quarterly Review* 48, no. 192 (March 1995): 17–37. I am grateful for comments on the first draft from Peter L. Bernstein, Martin Bronfenbrenner, and Robert M. Solow.

Mikio Wakatsuki, former deputy Governor of the Bank of Japan and in 1994 chairman of the board of councillors of the Japanese research institute, echoed this indecision:

> We still don't know the connection between monetary policy and asset prices . . . what benchmark do you use? Which prices do you follow? We don't know and didn't know then.[4]

The sense of unease felt by Bank of Japan officials was expressed in a different setting in an interview with Paul Volcker:

> *Frederick Smoler:* Wasn't one of the unanticipated consequences of your victory over inflation [in 1979–81] the replacement of speculation in commodities by even more unwelcome speculation in financial instruments?
>
> *Paul Volcker:* You're right . . . the commodities speculation didn't affect the banking system per se; the banks deal in credit instruments, not in commodities, so they avoided most of that. The banks had gone through a speculative real estate boom in the mid-seventies . . . not much compared to what happened since — but we thought it was big then. Then they went through the Latin American lending binge . . . energy speculation in Texas and elsewhere. All that collapsed with high interest rates and severe recession, but within two or three years we were back in a real estate frenzy, with speculation well beyond what we'd had before, and the banking system went through another and even bigger convulsion. I must confess I would not have anticipated it, given the financial hell that everybody had gone through in the early eighties. Could it have been prevented? I don't know.[5]

Work on asset prices in Anglo-Saxon economic circles has concentrated for the most part on how the prices of individual assets are determined, on the relations of the price of one type of asset to that of another — equities, bonds, options, futures, and other derivatives (but not real estate), their connection with general equilibrium, and the theory of efficient markets. The field does not deal with what asset prices and changes in them may mean for inflation. The field is relatively new. In the fall of 1991, the National Bureau of Economic Research established a program in asset prices: "a highly technical field of economics . . . studying a variety of topics . . . including general equilibrium, asset pricing models, international financial integration, derivative securities, and some intriguing microeconomic puzzles."[6] No mention was made of financial bubbles or inflation, or of markets for residential and commercial real estate, the last of which dominate the Bank for International Settlements (BIS) aggregate asset indexes, discussed below. Real estate in such a university as MIT is studied in a separate center not connected with the Finance Department in the Sloan School of Management. Nor do inflation, monetary policy, or real estate appear among the topics discussed at meetings of the NBER Asset Pricing Program in the fall of 1993 or the spring of 1994.[7] John Y. Campbell, director of the NBER program and professor of economics at Princeton University, wrote a review article on the *New Palgrave Dictionary of Money and Finance* (1994b) and a research summary on "What moves the stock market?"[8] again in the narrow context of technical finance rather than macroeconomic behavior and policy. Financial economists "are concerned with interrelationships between the prices of different financial assets. They ignore what seems to many to be the more important problem of what determines the overall level of asset prices."[9] And even Lawrence Summers does not raise the question of what changes in asset prices in general may indicate as guidance for monetary policy.

If American and British investigators tend to ignore asset inflation, the staff of the Bank for International Settlements has paid it attention in recent years, both in annual reports from 1992 forward and in a series of economic studies, of which the most illuminating is *Economic Paper* No. 40 (1994) by C. E. V. Borio, N. Kennedy, and S. D. Prowse, entitled "Exploring aggregate asset price fluctuations across countries: measurements, determinants and monetary policy implications." The present paper begins with a reprise of 1920s views on the subject of Benjamin Strong, Governor of the Federal Reserve Bank of New York, as set forth in Lester Chandler's biography (1956), and of John Maynard Keynes, largely in *A Treatise on Money* (1930). Both men asserted that the primary task of central banks is to stabilize the level of prices, meaning, but without always specifying, the price level of output, wholesale prices including the prices of imports, or the level of consumers' prices. In various asides, qualifications, diversions, however, they looked over their shoulders at the stock market, and speculation in it, at real estate to a lesser extent, and at the dilemma presented when the general price level is steady or falling, but security markets are driven by speculation. I turn next to the work of the BIS staff, and in particular to its indexes of aggregate asset prices, and their problems, generously acknowledged, and finally to the awkwardness of trying to meet two or more goals with basically one instrument — monetary policy — evoking Jan Tinbergen's *Theory of Public Policy* (1965) that government authorities need as many instrumental variables as they have goals, or in more primitive terms, "You can't kill two birds with one stone."

II

In discussion with the Executive Directors of the New York Federal Reserve Bank, describing a meeting he had had with Governor Montagu Norman of the Bank of England at the end of 1924, Strong stated that he had told Norman "his belief . . . shared by all others in the Federal Reserve System, that our whole policy in the future, as in the past, would be directed toward the stability of prices, so far as it was possible for us to influence prices."[10] At other times, Strong set down lists of multiple targets.

> He [Chandler writes] could cooperate in the restoration of stable currencies and the maintenance of favorable monetary conditions abroad only to the extent that the policies necessary for these purposes were not seriously incompatible with domestic objectives, the most important of which were the promotion of price level stability, the maintenance of high levels of business activity, and the prevention of "excessive" speculation, especially in the stock market.[11]

In a letter to Norman in 1925, Strong wrote:

> We have had a dangerous speculation develop in the stock market, with some evidence that it is extending into commodities. There has been a rampaging real estate speculation in some spots, but that is too far away from our influence to be a direct factor . . .
>
> . . . we could better control it as a psychological problem by keeping a sword of Damocles suspended over the speculation, that is, [discount] rates advanced in sequence.[12]

Later in testimony before the 1927 Committee of the Congress on Stabilization, quoted by Keynes with evident approval, Strong said:

> Two months ago there was some concern felt in the country as to the extent of speculation in stocks and the amount of credit which was being employed in support of that speculation. At the same time . . . a decline in the wholesale price level . . . almost entirely due to the decline in the prices of cotton and grain . . . we have this feeling that there is a growth in speculation; possibly a feeling that it ought to be curbed by the Federal Reserve System in some way. On the other hand, we are faced with a clear indication of some decline in the prices of farm commodities. Now, if . . . we felt that the introduction of credit into the market or lowering interest rates might correct the prices of those individual commodities, what might the consequences be for speculation? There you are between the devil and the deep sea.[13]

Chapter 12 of Chandler's biography of Strong reveals a Hamlet-like indecision on Strong's part about the stock market. The Fed was not the arbiter of stock prices. Its concern was only with the use of credit to support speculation. On several occasions, he recommended restriction because of stock speculation, but usually with reluctance and distaste. Overbuilding and real estate speculation in 1925 constituted one of three developments with the possibility of harm. He defended the 1927 reduction in interest rates, despite the well recognized hazard that the country was liable to encounter a big speculation and some expansion of credit, but speculation occurred not in commodities but almost entirely in stocks. If the Federal Reserve System is to be run solely with a view to regulating stock speculation, its policy will degenerate simply to regulating the affairs of gamblers, a view of its role with which he was impatient. The stock market responded not to the volume of credit nor to discount rates but to psychology, and advancing prices reflected the wealth and prosperity of the country. In August 1928, the problem of the monetary authorities was to avoid a calamitous break in the stock market, a panicky feeling about money, and a setback in business because of a change in psychology.[14]

Strong did not consider separate policies to meet multiple objectives when their requirements differed. "We have to spank them all." He was opposed to the type of direct controls then proposed, and to "moral suasion." An attempt to limit credit to banks supplying brokers' loans was futile. "If you block one way, credit will find others." Chandler noted that the direct action proposed to contain stock market speculation bore little resemblance to the later margin requirements introduced by the Securities and Exchange Act of 1934, since it would not have limited loans to brokers by nonbanks, or "others."

In 1928, Strong did propose to Professor O. M. W. Sprague a technique for restricting stock market speculation. The technique, which Chandler says was used in 1925, involved the eleven Federal Reserve Banks outside New York raising their interest rates, in order to draw funds from New York and force the money-center banks there to borrow from the Federal Reserve Bank of New York or call in their brokers' loans. Strong recognized a danger that this might precipitate a stock market crash, but thought the danger "rather slight as there is always a supply of funds at some price."[15]

Strong's rather bizarre proposal to inhibit speculation in stocks in New York by drawing money away from that city is broadly in line with Keynes's distinction in *A Treatise on Money* between the "industrial" and the "financial" circulations of money. The industrial circulation turned over against inputs and outputs, the financial against trade in titles, in speculation, and in providing capital to entrepreneurs.[16] The monetary authorities should seek to stabilize the price of current output, at the same time letting industry and finance have all the money they wanted, but at a rate of interest which, in its effect on the rate of investment (relative to savings), exactly balanced the effect of bullish sentiment. "To diagnose the position precisely . . . and to achieve this exact balance . . . may be beyond the wits of man."[17]

Keynes claimed that in the long run, in which he notoriously did not believe, the value of securities is entirely derivative from the value of consumption goods.[18] Earlier he had noted the investment boom in the United States had produced an enormous rise in the price of securities without any rise at all in the price of current output of new fixed capital.[19] Later he concluded that "a Currency Authority has no *direct* [his emphasis] concern with the level of the value of existing securities, as determined by opinion, but . . . it has an important indirect concern if the level of value of existing securities is calculated to stimulate new investment." No attention should be paid to a boom in land values or a revaluation of the equities of monopolies, entirely disassociated from any excessive stimulus to new investment.[20] "The dilemma is that if the Bank increases the volume of Bank-money so as to avoid any risk of the Financial Circulation stealing resources from the Industrial Circulation, it will encourage the 'bull' market to continue with every probability of a rise value of P' [the price level of new investment] which will lead to over-investment later on; whereas if it refuses to increase the volume of Bank-money, it may diminish the amount of money available for industry or so enhance the rate of interest at which it is available as to have an immediate deflationary effect."[21]

Himself a speculator in securities, Keynes had negative feelings toward speculators. In chapter 12 of *The General Theory,* he writes of the absurd influence of day-to-day fluctuations of the market, the mass psychology of ignorant individuals, likely to change opinions in response to trivia, the fetish of liquidity, the stock market as a game of passing the debased half-crown, or Old Maid, or musical chairs, everyone interested in quick results. It was rare, he stated, for Americans to buy investments to hold for income. Speculation produced no harm as bubbles on a steady stream of income, but became serious when enterprise became a bubble in a whirlpool of speculation. It was usually agreed that casinos should be, in the public interest, inaccessible and expensive, and perhaps the same is true of the Stock Exchange.[22]

Keynes's discussion of the crash in the New York stock market is not very edifying. He observed that wholesale prices were stable or falling, that investment was rising, the stock market booming despite

high short-term interest rates. He suspected that there was profit inflation. In his view, the Federal Reserve caused the crash by trying to curb
the enthusiasm of speculators, but that the depression — only to 1930
when the book was published — was caused by high interest rates.[23] It is
unclear whether he would follow Friedman and Schwartz in believing
that the Federal Reserve should have ignored the stock market boom, in
support of his *obiter dictum* of volume 1 that the duty of the central bank
is to manage money to keep the prices of current output stable.[24]

One can conclude from Chandler's biography of Strong and from
Keynes's writings, mainly *A Treatise on Money,* that the case for ignoring asset prices in the formulation of monetary policy was qualified in a
number of vague ways.

III

Borio, Kennedy, and Prowse hold that "it has now become more widely
accepted that the primary goal of monetary policy should be price stability."[25] At the same time, they recognize that asset prices can affect the
demand for money, may serve as a leading indicator, and that asset
inflation — a term they do not use — can pose problems for monetary
authorities calling for the exercise of judgment.[26] Their particular contribution is to provide aggregate indexes of asset prices, combining price
indexes of residential and commercial real estate with one for equities.
The value of industrial real estate is held to be included in stock market
prices. Bonds are not included though comparison of overall asset prices
with long-term real interest rates pays them some attention.[27] A *New
York Times* story states that the rise in interest rates from February 1994
produced losses for bond holders and mutual funds in bonds "in hundreds of billions of dollars."[28]

The weights for the separate components of the indexes, derived
from their share in total wealth, seem intuitively to overvalue residential real estate, most of which is held as living space, producing a
consumption good, rather than as a financial asset. Like housing, durable consumers' goods are part of household wealth, bought for use and
not for capital gains. Few economists would believe that increases in
the price level of a household's durable goods would so change its
wealth as to have an impact on spending. Residential property accounts for 60 to 75 percent of the weight of the indexes in different
countries, compared with 6 to 20 percent for commercial property, and
10 to 30 percent for equities.[29] It is true that housing bought for living
space during the 1980s in the United States led to a considerable rise in

home-equity mortgages that affected consumer spending and/or investment. A report by Korty Research (1994) contains a graph showing the ratio of mortgage debt to the equity of owner-occupied real estate rising from something on the order of 27.5 percent in 1980 to about 42 percent in 1993, but the source is not given.[30] I regard it as doubtful that homeowners as a class respond to changes in the value of their real estate as do owners of securities, though many of those, too, buy shares for income rather than trading and capital gains. Economic analysis, however, has little choice but to treat owners of a given asset alike when their motives in acquiring an asset may differ substantially. M. C. Reed (1975) observed that in the early days of investment in Britain, securities of a given railroad were bought for at least six different reasons: by landowners to sell real estate on or along the right of way; by manufacturers to improve and cheapen the transport of inputs and outputs; by suppliers of railroad equipment, often buyers of vendor shares; by long-term investors after income, some of whom bought bonds for a steady return, some shares in the hope of growing dividends; by sophisticated speculators seeking short-term capital gains; and by relatively ignorant and greedy latecomers after seeing the profits of the professionals. Today's owners of residential real estate do not cover as wide a spectrum perhaps, but an index that treats them all as professional speculators may well mislead.

The data used by the BIS team also raise questions. The index for residential property in the United States is the median sales price of existing single-family homes, collected by the National Association of Realtors.[31] It seems probable that the boom in capital gains in the 1980s resulted in many newly wealthy households buying second and even third homes, some priced at $1 million or more, as observable in the advertisements in the *New York Times Sunday Magazine* (referred to in the *New Republic* as "porno real estate"). This and speculative building of luxury houses are likely to have skewed the distribution of real estate prices, with the result that the median of the distribution became less representative. Two American economists, Karl Case and Robert Shiller (1988), have produced an index of real estate prices in Greater Boston that deliberately avoids the median, comparing only the prices of houses that have sold for a second time. It is not clear that such a measure can effectively take into account improvements to a particular property — added rooms or garage, redesigned kitchen or bathrooms, a swimming pool, and the like, as the Bureau of Labor Statistics tries in its indexes to separate changes in quality, especially of durable consumers' goods, from "pure" price change. A real estate development, like Levittown on Long Island, New York, started out after World War II with a simple, standardized design, but over the years became highly differentiated through disparate improvements on the part of various owners.

Somewhat puzzling is the fact that the BIS team uses an index for the United Kingdom of house prices (all dwellings) put out by the Department of the Environment, when the *Economist,* later, to be sure, said:

> It is strange that Britain does not already have a reliable indicator of house prices. The Treasury desperately needs this when considering whether interest rates need changing, because house prices are a crucial measure of economic activity.[32]

The *Economist* took note of the house-price indexes of the Halifax and Nationwide building societies, along with that of the Department of the Environment, the last up for scrapping because "no one but economic historians pays attention to it." It regards all three as unrepresentative since they are based on mortgage data when, according to a real estate agency, 28 percent of purchases take place without a mortgage. The agency in question believed that prime properties in London showed a rise from December 1992, 23 percent higher than indicated by the indexes. The *Economist* thought that replacement of existing indexes by an improved one would be a contribution to better informed monetary policy.

In a number of other national indexes, the BIS group was forced to use data for a single city such as Paris, Brussels, Oslo, and Amsterdam, again risking the possibility of a lack of representativeness.

Granted possible deficiencies in their indexes, which Borio and his colleagues make no attempt to conceal, several questions remain: How does monetary policy affect asset prices? How should changes in asset prices affect monetary policy? And are asset prices a leading indicator of changes in inflation in general, of output and/or employment?

On the first score, the authors attempt to demonstrate that rises and declines in asset prices in the 1970s and 1980s were brought about not by changes in the money supply, but by changing credit conditions including, especially on the upside, deregulation of financial restrictions and financial innovation. Deregulation was especially responsible for asset inflation of the Nordic countries — Sweden, Norway, and Finland — and of Japan, in which inflation went far wider than that in the other countries covered (although all were correlated to some degree, with the possible outlier of Germany). They cannot attribute the wide fluctuations to "fundamentals." The Cross report of ten central banks had earlier stated that innovations were typically underpriced and overused.[33] Borio et al. echo this view in saying that lack of familiarity with new conditions led to errors of judgment.[34]

One change, not recognized in either BIS study, was the unintended relaxation of margin requirements for buying stocks in the United States in the development of the Standard and Poor 500-stock index option. Options traded in Chicago by speculators and hedgers required a down payment in cash (margin) of merely 5 percent. With bull speculation in the options market, well-financed arbitrageurs sold forward and bought spot (a limited list of the index's leaders), with the Securities and Exchange-decreed margin of 50 percent. In effect, the margin requirement for speculators was reduced from 50 to 5 percent through the introduction of the option, and supervision of the credit available for speculation was divided between the SEC and the Chicago regulators. Portfolio insurance, using stock options, appeared foolproof, whereas when the options market turned sharply down on October 19, 1987, arbitrage dried up after a surge of selling, and both the spot and forward markets hit air pockets.

Flexibility of credit makes sense of recent bubbles, but deregulation, evident in the 1970s and 1980s, seems not to have loomed too large in the repeated booms and busts of the nineteenth century. How much weight it should bear now is thus something of a puzzle. Equally puzzling is the strong correlation in asset inflation and deflation among the financially developed countries covered in the study. The Nordic countries and Japan are outliers, as noted, but in extent rather than timing. The collapses of equity prices in 1929, in 1991–92, and 1987, with Japan an outlier in the last instance, are well known.[35] This parallel action was a compound of some shares traded in the several markets, some arbitrage, some monetary links among markets, but to a great extent psychological interaction.[36]

It is difficult, however, to explain booms and busts in a dozen different real estate markets when the market for real estate would appear to be largely confined to a given country or even a given locality. The BIS study and annual reports state that real estate booms in the United States were localized, proceeding from the Middle West to New England, to the Southwest and then California.[37] There are leads and lags, to be sure, but the correlation is substantial, both within the United States — though sometimes with differences in vacancy rates and rents between downtown, midtown, and "edge cities" — and from country to country. The 1925 Florida land boom, occurring in an isolated and highly localized area, could safely be ignored. Half a century later, markets for residential mortgages had been integrated nationally, and to some extent internationally, through securitization. An early step was the action of Western savings banks in advertising in the New York press to attract savings by offering interest rates higher than those available in the East. Securitization of mortgages through "Fannie Mae" raised national integration to new heights. Even then puzzles remain. George Akerlof and Paul Romer note that the Houston, Texas, economy, based on oil, had a peak in office construction ahead of Dallas/Fort Worth, but do not understand why construction continued upward in the latter (joint) city for several years after vacancy rates reached 20 and 30 percent.[38]

Strong connections also run between prices in equities and those in real estate. Successful speculation in the stock market encourages that in real estate, both among would-be speculators and among their financiers. Japanese banks have traditionally lent against land as collateral. When their large loans to holders of stocks gained liquidity from the rise in the Nikkei index, this reinforced the banks' readiness to lend to mortgage companies. Much of the connection probably runs less through money flows and credit relaxation than through speculator psychology. A casual look at the national diagrams in the BIS *Economic Study*[39] and the table in the 1993 BIS *Annual Report*[40] shows considerable covariance in the three markets. The historical record left by Governor Strong and Keynes's *Treatise* also indicates that while sometimes asset prices move differently from the level of output prices, posing a dilemma for policy, real estate and share prices tend to move up and down more or less together.

Writing on Chicago real estate more than sixty years ago, Homer Hoyt (1933) observed that building cycles were correlated with the stock market, but behaved somewhat differently in decline than on the upswing. When the stock market collapsed, speculators in real estate were prone to congratulate themselves that they owned physical assets, not mere paper, and that they were financed by intermediate-term credit, not callable day loans. Their satisfaction, however, was short-lived. While the shakeout in shares was relatively speedy, a matter of months or a year, that in real estate proceeded slowly. Real estate buyers moved to the sidelines, waiting for prices to come down. Meanwhile, taxes and interest rates remained high. Leveraged positions in real estate were gradually ground down in a debt/deflation struggle.[41] First the speculators, and then their banks, went bankrupt. Such a process is now going on in Japan where the stock market, after falling from 39,000 to 15,000, has more or less stabilized about 20,000, but the impact on banks and insurance companies is still being felt.[42] Still another two-way connection in Japan runs between real estate and the stock market since many large companies owned (and sometimes sold) large quantities of land.

The 1987 stock market crash in New York differed in effect from that in 1929 not insofar as real estate prices were concerned, but because of the absence of any drastic effect on commodity prices. In 1929, New York banks faced serious liquidity problems over loans to brokers, and rationed credit especially to commodity dealers who needed credit to buy imported primary products shipped to New York and sold on consignment. In 1987, such goods were normally bought abroad. Without credit in 1929, dealers were unable to make their usual purchases, and the prices of imported commodities fell by 10 percent or more in the weeks through December, spreading depression abroad through debt deflation and a negative foreign-trade multiplier.[43] In addition, Alan Greenspan of the Federal Reserve Board and Gerald Corrigan of the New York Federal Reserve Bank acted swiftly in 1987 to provide ample liquidity to New York banks, thereby forestalling a general contraction. The real estate bind was felt in thrift institutions more thoroughly than in commercial banks, but in the manner described by Hoyt almost half a century earlier.

Borio and his colleagues try to measure the extent to which asset price changes are a leading indicator of changes in prices in general.[44] On a priori grounds, they assert, the answer is ambiguous. Asset prices depend on the expected income they produce. But "income" in this sense is also ambiguous. It may reflect rent, interest, or dividends, but it may include a measure, sometimes the entirety, of capital gains. The authors perform a number of econometric tests and conclude that while asset price behavior may contain useful information in many cases, it did not do so for Japan. Put more simply, one would expect the prices of output and assets to move together in an economy dominated by money changes, but if inflation had a strong component of wage increases, the general price level might rise but profits and equity prices fall. In addition, there can be simple bubbles fed by relaxation in credit conditions, an expanded money supply, or by "herd" psychology, which happen not to reach down to the general price level (of output) in the short run. In Sweden share prices tripled from 1985 to 1989 — the BIS aggregate asset index almost doubled — while the price index of "domestic supply" rose only 13 percent (International Monetary Fund 1992). The Bank of Japan felt confident in lowering its discount rate in 1986 and 1987, at the suggestion of the Federal Reserve System,[45] thereby reducing the level of interest rates as a whole, despite the fact that share prices were rising from 200 to 500 percent of the 1985 level, largely because it focused attention on wholesale and consumer prices. Consumer prices inched up only from 100 in 1985 to 101.4 in 1988, while wholesale prices actually fell over the same period from 100 to 91.8.[46]

IV

With output, wholesale, and/or consumer prices moving one way, and asset prices another, monetary authorities with only one string to their bow are in a quandary. The dilemma inherent in conflict between domestic and foreign goals of a central bank is well known, and has given rise in the literature to the "assignment problem."[47] A theoretical solution to the problem is to use monetary policy to meet the international objective, fiscal policy for the domestic. This is a counsel of perfection, however, since while monetary policy can be implemented readily by an independent or quasi-independent central bank, changes in government spending and taxes as a rule go through a drawn-out legislative process; if initiated when the dilemma is first perceived, the fiscal changes desired are more than likely to be achieved only after the problem has disappeared. In consequence, the usual theoretical solution is to use monetary policy for domestic purposes, and neglect international objectives or hope that they will be taken care of by flexible exchange rates. In the latter case, however, there is another difficulty, since capital movements may respond to domestic monetary policy, offset it to a degree, and complicate matters on the international front.

Margin requirements, as already noted, might have served as an instrumental variable, but lost a great deal of their force because of the development of stock market futures and options. In the *Audacity* interview, Paul Volcker remarked:

> In 1986 someone remembered that the Federal Reserve had the authority over margin requirements and stock purchases, and complained to us: "Look, somebody's going to buy our company. It's highly leveraged, and they're planning to use the stock they're going to buy as collateral for the borrowing. That's against the law. You have to look into that."
>
> Well we did, although margin requirements were really designed to inhibit excessive market speculation, not corporate acquisitions . . . whatever we ruled, it wouldn't make much difference. If we said it violated the margin requirements, the raiders would find some other way to borrow without directly securing the loan with that stock . . . maybe we weren't as courageous as we should have been. It did not make much difference what we ruled, because the market could find a way around it.[48]

Since World War II, many countries, especially the United Kingdom, the United States, and the Scandinavian, have tried to devise measures for monetary policy beyond controlling the money supply and the rate of interest. One was limitation on the amount of total credit in the banking system. An international measure was to set a standard on bank capital at 8 percent of liabilities, agreed by central banks at the Bank of International Settlements. The familiar "moral suasion" has been attempted — warnings that the system was moving to excess in a given direction. The International Monetary Fund told U.S. bank officials, and repeated the admonition in statements at its Annual Meeting in 1976, that borrowing from banks by developing countries was building to a debt crisis. The next year Arthur Burns proposed that banks compile standardized information on developing-country debt and the part in it of bank lending. The IMF warning was ignored by both central and private banks; the latter opposed the Burns proposal when it was discussed at the BIS.[49] Defending rational expectations, Harry Johnson once suggested that if a central bank or government agency knew something the market did not know, it should publicize it.[50] Like most other economists, however, he dismissed moral suasion as a virtually complete waste of time. The classic case is Paul M. Warburg's speech in February 1929 that the New York stock market was too high, a pronouncement which interrupted the market's ascent for a few days only.

Ceilings on credit that individual banks were allowed to extend in Britain and Scandinavia were judged to be ineffective as means of monetary control. The sharp increase of asset prices in Sweden, Norway, and Finland, however, came about when these controls were removed in a wave of deregulation.

Regulation and deregulation are a hoary subject. The issue rose to prominence after World War II particularly with books on financial repression and on the need for financial deepening by Ronald McKinnon and Edward Shaw, respectively, based on the study of banking in South Korea. The South Korean government did remove a number of bank rules that favored particular borrowers, large companies, exporters, and the government itself, only to have the deregulation followed by an explosion of lending and a financial crisis.[51] McKinnon's reaction to the crisis in South Korea and to similar inflationary bursts which followed deregulation in Chile and other countries in South America was not that deregulation was a mistake, but that it was important to undertake it in a proper sequence.[52] Analogous issues arose in the shift from Socialist to market economies in Eastern Europe and the former constituent parts of the Soviet Union. Some believe in scrapping controls in one fell swoop; others incline to one or a few steps at a time to allow markets to adjust to the new conditions. A more extreme position takes the form of "free banking," in which banks are not regulated in any way, and even central banks are abolished, sometimes with the substitution of an unbreakable rule, increasing the monetary base at a fixed percentage annually.[53]

Most mainstream economists, however, are prepared to rely on monetary policy, with the general rule that that policy should be directed to stability of the "general price level," however defined, but not including asset prices.

V

Strong, Keynes, and Volcker are undoubtedly right that it is difficult to the point of impossibility to work out an additional simple rule to restrain asset inflation without running a non-negligible risk of harming output and employment. But dilemmas and trade-offs are fundamental facts of governing. A similar difficult choice in the summer of 1994 was revealed at the Jackson Hole conference of the Federal Reserve Bank of Kansas City, reported in the press, when Alan Greenspan, the chairman of the Federal Reserve Board, advocated tighter monetary policy to fend off prospective inflation, while Alan Blinder, the vice chairman, worried that higher interest rates might direct effort away from fuller employment. The sometime dilemma between domestic and international goals has been mentioned more than once. There are dozens more: between central bank service as a lender of last resort and moral hazard, as in insurance, that protection against loss from disaster increases its likelihood as those protected act with less caution; between full disclosure called for in a democracy to avoid the government or central bank favoring "insiders," and secrecy so as not to alarm the public about the safety of the system;[54] between government regulation and market discipline;[55] for an individual bank whether to write off problem loans or work them out, etc.

Outside banking, many more policy dilemmas and analytical questions exist: whether it is more efficient for a country, market, or firm to be pluralistic with initiative and creativity diffused through many parts of the whole, or more centralized and disciplined. The fundamental difficulty here is that on stable trend a decentralized system is more efficient, assuming no economies of scale at the center, whereas in crisis, central direction is needed to organize rescue efforts coherently. Unhappily, shifts back and forth between the two systems as conditions change are almost impossible because of the inflexibility of institutions, the Coase theorem to the contrary notwithstanding. On shipboard, the captain may stay below in his cabin in smooth sailing, but must come back on deck or to the bridge to assume responsibility in storm or in navigating tricky passages. Any rule that consigned him to one place or the other would be wrong.

Many, perhaps most, economists believe in rules, and especially in rules to be laid down in macroeconomic policy. Ignore asset markets is one such. Design policy exclusively for domestic goals is another. When asset and output prices are stable or move in the same direction, or domestic and international goals call for the same policy response, both of which happen much of the time, such rules are supportable. When speculation threatens substantial rises in asset prices, with a possible collapse in asset markets later, and harm to the financial system, or if domestic conditions call for one sort of policy, and international goals another, monetary authorities confront a dilemma calling for judgment, not cookbook rules of the game. Such a conclusion may be uncomfortable. It is, I believe, realistic.

NOTES

1. Friedman and Schwartz 1963, pp. 261–62.
2. *New York Times,* 29 May 1994, p. 33.
3. *New York Times,* 29 May 1994, p. 36.
4. Ibid.
5. Smoler 1994, p. 9.
6. *NBER Reporter* 1993 (spring), p. 1.
7. *NBER Reporter* 1994 (winter), p. 21; ibid. 1994 (spring), p. 32.
8. *NBER Reporter* 1994 (fall), pp. 8ff.
9. Summers 1985, p. 633.
10. Chandler 1956, p. 312.
11. Ibid., p. 423.
12. Ibid., pp. 329–30.
13. Keynes 1930, 2:241.
14. Ibid., pp. 423, 428, 445, 458, 460–61.
15. Ibid., pp. 433–35. In *Manias, Panics and Crashes* (Kindleberger 1989, pp. 155–58), I assembled expressions of contemporary belief that in some of the nineteenth-century crashes in Europe and the United States it was impossible to borrow money at any price.
16. Keynes 1930, 1:243.
17. Ibid., pp. 254–55.
18. Ibid., p. 255.
19. Ibid., p. 249.
20. Ibid., p. 257.
21. Ibid., p. 254.
22. Keynes 1936, pp. 147–64.
23. Keynes 1930, 2:190–98.
24. Keynes 1930, 2:254.
25. Borio et al. 1994, p. 46.

26. Ibid., pp. 45, 60, 69.

27. Ibid., p. 24 and graph 2, p. 25.

28. *New York Times,* 29 October 1994, pp. 1, 51.

29. Ibid., Table A1.2, p. 80.

30. Korty Research 1994, p. 8; see also *BIS Annual Report,* 1993, graph Mortgage Debt, p. 167.

31. Borio et al. 1994, table A1.1, p. 77.

32. *Economist,* 20 August 1994, p. 46.

33. Bank for International Settlements 1986.

34. Borio et al. 1994, p. 29.

35. Kindleberger 1986, figure 6, pp. 109–11; BIS 1991, p. 99 and 1993, p. 156.

36. Kindleberger 1991.

37. BIS study 1986 and *Annual Report* 1992, p. 169 and 1994, p. 18.

38. Akerlof and Romer 1993, pp. 30–40.

39. *BIS Economic Study* 1994, pp. 72–74.

40. *BIS Annual Report* 1993, p. 161.

41. Hoyt 1933, chap. 14.

42. "Bank rescued in Japan is sign of deeper woes," *New York Times,* 13 October 1994, p. D.2.

43. Kindleberger 1986, pp. 112–16.

44. Borio et al. 1994, pp. 60ff.

45. Volcker and Gyohten 1992, pp. 271ff. and chronology, p. 357.

46. Keizai Koho Center 1994, pp. 70 and 72.

47. Mundell and Swoboda eds. 1969, esp. paper by Egon Sohmen and comment of R. N. Cooper.

48. Smoler 1994, p. 10.

49. James 1994, p. 447.

50. Reference lost.

51. McKinnon 1973; Shaw 1973.

52. McKinnon 1994.

53. E.g., Selgin 1986.

54. For a discussion of the importance of the dissemination of financial information in the United States, see Smith and Sylla 1993. A view somewhat disturbing from an ethical point of view is that insider trading serves a useful purpose to the extent that it spreads information. On secret last-resort lending, note the Bank of England's rescue of the William Deacons Bank in January 1929, with various conditions calling for nondisclosure, and the Bank of Italy "salvaging" (to use the Italian expression) the Credito Italiano and the Banca Commerciale Italiana, along with other banks, in deep secrecy in early 1930 (Kindleberger 1986, p. 102n; and Kindleberger 1993, p. 360). A Democratic amendment to the renewal of the Reconstruction Finance Corporation legislation in July 1932, calling for publicizing the names of borrowing banks, effectively closed off that avenue of banks in trouble, as it would have advertised the parlous condition of such banks (Kindleberger 1986, p. 195).

55. In a presidential address to the American Finance Association, James van Horne admitted that some financial innovations led to excess, driven by herd instinct, but opposed regulation by the Securities and Exchange Commission (SEC) or the Financial Accounting Standards Board (FASB), stating that the ultimate discipline must come from the market. The choice between regulation and the market may depend on cultural aspects of a society. Norwegian shipowners policed themselves against risking sailors' lives in unseaworthy vessels, while British shipowners did not, and ultimately, after Parliamentary investigations, were regulated by the Board of Trade (Kindleberger 1992, pp. 34–40).

REFERENCES

Akerlof, George A. and Paul M. Romer (1993) "Looting: the economic underworld of bankruptcy for profit." *Brookings Papers on Economic Activity*, reprinted in National Bureau of Economic Research, Reprint no. 1868, pp. 1–73.
Bank for International Settlements (1986) *Recent Innovations in International Banking*, prepared by a Study Group, Sam Y. Cross, Federal Reserve Bank of New York, Chairman, established by the Central Banks of the Group of Ten Countries, Basle.
Bank for International Settlements (1991) *Annual Report*, Basle.
Bank for International Settlements (1992) *Annual Report*, Basle.
Bank for International Settlements (1993) *Annual Report*, Basle.
Bank for International Settlements (1994) *Annual Report*, Basle.
Borio, C. E. V., N. Kennedy, and S. D. Prowse (1994) "Exploring aggregate price fluctuations across countries: measurement, determinants and monetary policy implications." BIS *Economic Papers*, no. 40 (April): 1–101.
Campbell, John Y. (1994a) "Asset pricing," *NBER Reporter*, Program Report (spring): 1–4.
Campbell, John Y. (1994b) "The new Palgrave dictionary of money and finance," *Journal of Economic Literature*, 32 (2): 667–73.
Campbell, John Y. (1994c) "What moves the stock market?" *NBER Reporter*, Research Summaries (fall): 8–10.
Case, Karl E. and Robert Shiller (1986) "The behavior of home buyers in boom and post-boom markets," *New England Economic Review* (November–December): 29–46.
Chandler, Lester V. (1956) *Benjamin Strong, Central Banker*, Washington: Brookings Institution.
The Economist (1994) 332 (7877), 20 August.
Friedman, Milton and Anna Jacobson Schwartz (1963) *A Monetary History of the United States, 1867–1960*, Princeton: Princeton University Press.
Hoyt, Homer (1933) *One Hundred Years of Land Values in Chicago: The Rela-*

tionship of the Growth of Chicago to the Rise of Its Land Values, 1830–1933; Chicago: University of Chicago Press.

International Monetary Fund (1992) *International Financial Statistics,* Washington.

James, Harold (1994) "International monetary cooperation since Bretton Woods," draft manuscript, October.

Keizai Koho Center (1994) *Japan, 1994: An International Comparison,* Tokyo.

Keynes, John Maynard (1930) *A Treatise on Money,* 2 vols., New York: Harcourt, Brace.

Keynes, John Maynard (1936) *The General Theory of Employment, Interest and Money,* New York: Harcourt, Brace.

Kindleberger, Charles P. (1986) *The World in Depression, 1929–1939,* revised edition, Berkeley: University of California Press.

Kindleberger, Charles P. (1989) *Manias, Panics and Crashes: A History of Financial Crises,* 2d edition, New York: Basic Books.

Kindleberger, Charles P. (1991) "International (and interregional) aspects of financial crises," in Martin Feldstein ed., *The Risk of Economic Crisis,* Chicago: University of Chicago Press. 128–32.

Kindleberger, Charles P. (1992) *Mariners and Markets,* New York: Harvester/Wheatsheaf.

Kindleberger, Charles P. (1993) *A Financial History of Western Europe,* 2d edition, New York: Oxford University Press.

Korty Research (1994) *Investment Direction,* October.

McKinnon, Ronald I. (1973) *Money and Capital in Economic Development,* Washington: Brookings Institution.

McKinnon, Ronald I. (1994) *The Order of Economic Liberalization: Financial Control in the Transition to a Market Economy,* 2d edition, Baltimore: Johns Hopkins University Press.

Mundell, Robert A. and A. K. Swoboda eds. (1969) *Monetary Problems of the International Economy,* Chicago: University of Chicago Press.

NBER Reporter, various issues, Cambridge, Mass.

New York Times, various issues.

Reed, M. C. (1975) *Investment in Railways in Britain: A Study in the Development of the Capital Market,* London: Oxford University Press.

Selgin, George (1986) *The Theory of Free Banking,* Totowa: Rowan and Littlefield.

Shaw, Edward S. (1973) *Financial Deepening in Economic Development,* New York: Oxford University Press.

Smith, George David and Richard Sylla (1993) "The transformation of financial capitalism: an essay on the history of American capital markets," *Financial Markets, Institutions and Instruments,* 2 (2): 1–62.

Smoler, Frederic (1994) "A view from the Fed: an interview with Paul A. Volcker," *Audacity,* 3 (1), fall: 6–15.

Summers, Lawrence H. (1985) "On economics and finance," *Journal of Finance,* 11 (3), July: 633–65.

Tinbergen, Jan (1965) *On the Theory of Economic Policy,* 2d edition, Amsterdam: North Holland.

van Horne, James C. (1985) "Financial innovation and excesses," *Journal of Finance,* 11 (3), July: 621–31.

Volcker, Paul A. and Toyoo Gyohten (1992) *Changing Fortunes: The World's Money and the Threat to American Leadership,* New York: Times Books.

2

Caveat Emptor, Investor, Depositor?

I

As one who has not kept up with the subtleties of macroeconomics in which Lorie Tarshis excelled, I was relieved when the editors indicated that one could go beyond government responsibilities in stabilizing the economy, revolutionized by Keynes, with Tarshis in attendance, to other problems with government roles. Combining earlier writing on swindling schemes and their role in financial crises (Kindleberger 1989, chap. 5) with the few remarks in Lord Skidelsky's second volume on Keynes that dealt with social justice, "about which he was not passionate," (Skidelsky 1994, p. 223), I thought it might be useful to worry the problem whether "he governs best who governs least," or whether the administration of justice — one of Adam Smith's three public goods — requires some attention to ensuring that the unscrupulous in society do not take advantage of the innocent, the ignorant, and perhaps the greedy who lack judgment. The exercise is a limited one, stopping short of treatment of other ethical problems in economics — the distribution of income and wealth, free riders, entitlements of individuals, duties as well as rights, etc. It is hard not to believe that the issue is timely as one reads press accounts of Ivan Boesky, Steven Hoffenberg, Charles Keating, Michael Milken, Prudential Investors, et al. In Britain "hardly a week goes by without some unsuitable product [in life insurance] being foisted on an unsuspecting customer by an overzealous tout" (*The Economist,* January 21, 1994, p. 84). In the United States, "Revelations in the news media of deceptive sales practices and corporate misconduct involving major insurers, including Metropolitan Life, Prudential Insurance, and New York Life, have brought into question the sales practices

This essay originally appeared in B. B. Price and O. E. Hamouda, eds., *Keynesianism and the Keynesian Revolution in America* (Cheltenham, UK, and Northampton, MA: Edgar Elgar, 1998), pp. 141–54. Reprinted with permission of Edward Elgar and the editors. Thanks are due Mrs. Jane King, a psychologist, who provided guidance in a field in which my knowledge is grossly deficient, and to Peter L. Bernstein.

of the industry" (*Boston Globe,* February 17, 1994, under the headline "Exaggerated Salesmanship Hurts Consumers, Companies").

I happen not to be a student of ethics, but as I understand it, there are three broad branches — the utilitarian, natural law, and the deontological (Gustafson 1991). The utilitarian advocates morality because it pays, as implied in the headline just quoted, at least in the long run, if not the short, and for operations with an expectation of repetition. I have no idea what the ethics of natural law may be. The deontological postulates moral behavior as a duty. I assume that the Kantian Categorical Imperative, that the individual or unit should act only in ways which can be generalized, falls under this class, though it has social utility.

II

Caveat emptor (let the buyer beware) is a long-established tradition in law and practice in the Anglo-Saxon world. In rational expectations, consumers are assumed to be intelligent, informed, competent, and able to look after their own interests. An even stronger argument can be made for investors, who presumably were intelligent enough to acquire some degree of wealth, or had the luck to be genetically descended from parents who did. Maintenance of justice, apart from prevention or punishment of crime, would, in such a world, require primarily seeing to it that contracts freely entered into are faithfully carried out. It is assumed that while there may be some who cannot look after their own interests, and some who would take advantage of that inability, the results of such departures from the assumptions of well-functioning markets are readily repaired by charity or government welfare, and do not undermine optimistic conclusions as to how the capitalistic system works. In one view, Barro has held that departures from rationality and maximization are random and unpredictable so that they can be neglected (Swedberg 1990, pp. 74–75). The record suggests otherwise.

Once in his *Lectures on Justice, Police and Arms* (1759) and again in *The Theory of Moral Sentiments* (1759), Adam Smith brings out the moral chestnut, "Honesty is the best policy," in both instances slightly qualified. In the *Lectures,* the reasoning runs in terms not of moral duty, but of utility: "The trader deals so often that he finds honesty is the best policy" (Lerner 1937, p. xxxiii). This is close to the view of the political scientist Robert Axelrod, who believes that in two-person, repeat-game theory, Tit-for-Tat is the optimal strategy (1984). It finds some support in economic history. Investment in reputation paid off in medieval trade in one detailed account because the short-run benefit from cheating was lower than the long-run profit from faithful trade (Greif 1989), and a sociologist points out that deals among diamond merchants are conducted with a handshake because of a closely monitored community (Granovetter and Swedberg 1992, pp. 62–63). Both these cases, however, involved more or less equals, and even then Granovetter notes, theft and murder have occurred among diamond dealers (ibid.). An Italian economist has asserted that investment in reputation is a fragile basis on which to build rational expectations because of the limited ability of economic actors to monitor the behavior of others (Sacco 1990). This would seem especially to be true in trade between unequals: seller/buyer, borrower/lender, adult/child, employer/employee.

In *The Theory of Moral Sentiments,* Dr. Smith holds that the rule about honesty "almost always holds true" (1808, 2:142), but the exceptions are not discussed.

Lack of information may impede the efficient operation of markets. In a long list of articles, alone and with collaborators, Joseph Stieglitz has suggested that market failure comes largely from lack of information. George Akerlof, in a widely cited paper, developed the notion of asymmetric information, in which one party to a transaction had information which the other lacked, the classic instance being of "lemons" in automobiles which never functioned satisfactorily (1970). The defense under rational expectations would run in terms of private markets springing up to provide needed information if there were sufficient demand for it. Such is frequently the case as credit bureaus, manuals that rate securities, consumer periodicals that grade products for household sale testify. These are sought out by those who know what they do not know, and this does not include everyone. Adverse selection is likely to bring it about that those most in need of information are unaware of that fact.

A highly cynical argument in favor of laissez-faire, in contrast to rational expectations, is the public-choice view that governmental personnel are not to be trusted to fulfill the tasks for which they are hired, but are as self-serving and disdainful of duty as those in the private sector, or perhaps more so. The record of governmental corruption in Italy and Japan in the 1990s is especially disturbing, more in Japan where trust has been the basis of society (Dore 1992). Monitoring by the police and the media caught up slowly with the record of bribes offered for contracts, bribes taken, and contracts awarded. Corruption has been endemic in economic history, back in my knowledge to the East India Company (van Klaveren 1957, 1958, 1959, 1960), and in this country to the Credit Mobilier, the Erie Railroad, and the Teapot Dome. My interest is less in whether the government can mind its own honesty, or have it minded effectively by others, than in whether private markets need government to patrol the nature of private economic transactions in the market, as well as the fulfillment of contracts.

III

Whether theory is justified in arguing against government intervention in private exchanges, either because of rational expectations or the *tu quoque* that it has no higher moral record, economic history shows a revealed preference for such attention. At the most elementary level, government has checked the accuracy of yardsticks and scales for weighing to protect the unsuspecting consumer from the veniality of the retailer. In his chapter on metrology in *American Treasure and the Price Revolution in Spain* (1934), Earl J. Hamilton directs attention mainly to establishing uniform standards of weights and measures the better himself to make price comparisons, but is also interested in how well towns and villages in Castile adhere to royal standards, and in the attempts to combat dishonesty. Public complaint about confusing and ill-kept standards was continuous for centuries (ibid., chap. 7, esp. pp. 160ff).

Various classes of promoters and salespeople have in history and literature notoriously taken advantage of unsophisticated consumers and investors, characterized as "widows and orphans, clergymen, spinsters, retired naval and military officers, magistrates, country gentry, theologians, country misers, authors, grandmothers . . ." (Kindleberger 1989, p. 35n). Widows and orphans usually have pride of place among the innocent, and government protection of them goes back to the Code of Hammurabi in Mesopotamia in the eighteenth century B.C. This may be defended by laissez-faire economists as a normal exchange transaction in which Hammurabi traded insurance for the wives and children of soldiers against the latter's willingness to fight, which might otherwise not be forthcoming. Closer to the present day, note that there is in Britain an insurance company named Scottish Widows, and recently in France it was asserted that the country has always been protective of "the widow of Carpentras," not a real historical figure, I gather, but a generic comparable to the "little old lady in tennis shoes from Dubuque" (Ploix 1994, p. 338).

Beyond widows and orphans, in today's world, it is frequently stated, though more than anecdotal evidence would be hard to produce, that certain professions do well financially, but are insufficiently astute investors to safeguard their gains appropriately: doctors, dentists, movie stars, outstanding athletes. These persons, it appears, often retain financial advisers, a few among whom may, on occasion, give poor advice or behave dishonestly, as of course others in fiduciary positions may do.

One class of labor which government has felt obliged to protect was sailors against two kinds of miscreants. On the one hand were crimps, including boardinghouse keepers, publicans, brothel operators, and in some cases tailors, who extorted the pay of sailors returning from long voyages and/or sold them in a drunken state to ships requiring crews against a payment from the captain and in most cases the advance note given to the sailor to buy gear for the new voyage (Kindleberger 1992, pp. 20–21). On the other hand were shipowners who from time to time would recruit sailors in unseaworthy vessels, often overloaded but insured, with disastrous loss of life. After a series of parliamentary investigations, the British government intervened and required Board of Trade surveys of suspected vessels, loading lines for all ships to set limits to freight. Rational expectations gains some support from the fact that Norwegian shipowners had a better record on shipwreck than British, with no government regulation, and early Venetian shipping relied on mutual interest to prevent others from undermanning, overloading, using defective rigging, and the like. In Britain, however, even the interested insurance companies failed to curb adverse selection by "a few nefarious shipowners" (ibid., pp. 35–38).

Minor children, especially orphans, are everywhere deemed to require some protection of various sorts from various afflictions. It is said that a three-year-old has no clue as to the difference between right and wrong (Etzioni 1994). Most states in the United States deal with offenders under the age of 18 in special courts where they are given special consideration, although there is a claim that with drugs, drug-money, gang-related incidents, and the ease of acquiring lethal weapons a case can be made for reducing the age when they are treated as adults, to 16, or in one view to 14 when most juveniles can be held accountable for their own actions (Sexton, Graves, and Lee 1993). When in a person's life one is deemed competent to take care of property is a matter of varying opinion and legislation. Licenses to handle an automobile, a significant piece of property, are issued in most states at age 16. The voting threshold, based presumably on some measure of judgment, is 18. A person is typically competent to buy alcoholic drinks at 21. Some people of wealth, as I understand it, turn over full control of a bequest left to an heir only at still higher ages, 25, 30, or even 40. Probate courts in Massachusetts do not allow the distributions of funds of a trust being dissolved to minors under 21 without the approval of the court to ensure that the terms of the trust have not been violated. How and when property of wards in chancery in Britain, or controlled by Orphans

Courts in Germany, are released I do not know. The significant point is that property of those deemed not to be fully competent to manage it against misappropriation or unwise allocation is given protection by government.

IV

Distinctions should of course be made among intelligence, information, and judgment on the one hand, and among their opposites, stupidity, ignorance, and credulity on the other, Measures on the Wechsler *Adult* Intelligence Scale (emphasis added), IQ (intelligence quotient) follows a normal distribution, with 50 percent of cases falling within the modal range of 90 to 109, where 100 is the mean, and 25 percent above and below, consisting of 2.2 percent above 130 and below 69, 6.7 percent between 120 and 129 and 70 to 79, and 16.1 percent between 110 and 119 and between 80 and 89. Whether the cutoff point on sufficient intelligence to handle ordinary consumer transactions is the third standard deviation below the mean (2.2 percent), or the second and third together, I have no way of knowing. I assume, however, that the intelligence needed for major purposes, for investing significant amounts of money, or for determining the quality of the assets of a bank, without deposit insurance, reaches into higher sections toward the central 82 percent.

Intelligence differs from shrewdness, which while defined as "characterized by or displaying astuteness or sagacity, sharply perceptive, clever and judicious, implying intelligence and wisdom," can, in my judgment, be intuitive. One ranked low in the IQ scale could have a shrewd sense of being conned by a second-hand automobile dealer or a boiler-room operator in penny stocks. On the other hand highly intelligent persons on the Wechsler scale seem to have shown themselves credulous.

My interest is more in the innocent and the ignorant than in the greedy. There is a French word, *gogo,* defined in *Petit Larousse* as a "credulous capitalist, easy to deceive." I have seen it used to translate the slang American word "sucker," which has also made a place in the dictionary, defined in the *Shorter Oxford* as one who is gullible or easily deceived, although the definition did not indicate whether such a person was a capitalist. Capitalists presumably should take care of themselves, do more than kick the tires, including asking questions, even reading the small print in the advertisement and the prospectus.

Some decry "blaming the victim" but when the victim is credulous or greedy, or covetous of wealth being acquired around him, there may well be merit in blaming him or her. Before she expressed French sympathy for the widow of Carpentras, Mme Ploix noted that the *Economist* had opposed the British government making good the losses of the depositors in the B.C.C.I. default since they chose that bank deliberately, risking their money for higher returns than those in the market. "Whether they were irrational (*fou* in the French), greedy or badly informed, the decisions they took were on their own responsibility and at their own risk." She followed this and the mention of the tradition of protecting widows by deploring the Japanese banks which took care of the losses only of their wealthy clients (Ploix 1994, p. 338).

Keynes commented a number of times on ignorance, according to Skidelsky's account. In *A Treatise on Money,* dealing with the 1926 strike of the coal miners and the return of the pound sterling to par, he said that solutions to issues of this sort were above the heads of more or less illiterate voters (1994, p. 224). In the 1925 Sidney Ball lecture on "The End of Laissez-Faire," he held that objections to laissez-faire might be philosophical or merely practical, in the latter case the prevalence of ignorance over knowledge (ibid., p. 225):

> Ignorance is the chief political and social evil of the day. It fosters class suspicion, made possible the acquisition of great fortunes by insider knowledge . . . the nationalization of knowledge is the one case for nationalization that is overwhelmingly right. (ibid., p. 268)

It is not self-evident what nationalization of knowledge is. Omission of "economic" from the nature of the evil of the day might have been significant had it not been for the reference to great fortunes of the day from insider knowledge. Again in *A Treatise on Monday* in discussing the psychology of investors, Keynes wrote "They do not possess even the rudiments of what is required for a valid judgment and are the prey of hopes and fears aroused by transient events and as easily dispelled" (ibid., p. 336). Some of the ignorance which disturbed the conclusions of classical economic theory was uncertainty, or ignorance of the future (ibid., p. 539). Despite his genius, sophistication, and wide knowledge in many fields, Keynes shared this last brand of ignorance with the rest of the human race as he lost three fortunes, though he made four for himself and one for his college. It is hard to imagine that he would have been taken in by a swindler.

As economist, I am not competent to judge the work of psychiatrists, psychologists, and sociologists on character, both honest and criminal. I am impressed, however, by Eric Fromm's discussion of character as molded by genetics on the one hand and environment in early childhood on the other. Fromm's discussion is limited to the latter. At birth, a child naturally acquires faith in goodness, love, and justice, as it is fed, sheltered, and comforted when sick or hurt. In many cases, this faith in goodness (or God) is ruined at an early age — four, five, or six — sometimes even earlier — by becoming aware of parents lying, fighting, betraying the child's trust in them and in their unceasing benevolence. Some respond by growing independent, others by retreating from self-reliance, frequently moving into worldly aims — money, power, prestige (Fromm 1964, pp. 28–30). In an earlier study, Fromm distinguished four types of "unproductive" personality orientations: the receptive, exploitive, hoarding, and marketing (1947, pp. 61, 111). The receptive person is trusting and wants to be loved; the exploitive takes what he or she wants by force or cunning, ready to grab and steal, or in intellectual endeavor to plagiarize. He or she is also ridden by envy of others who have more (ibid., pp. 62–63). The hoarding and marketing patterns interest me less in the present connection of possible government protection of the innocent from the unscrupulous. Nonetheless Fromm has some interesting observations. While the exploitive person wants power and wealth, the hoarding orientation is to preserve it, and is risk averse. Property in this case is a symbol of self. The marketing orientation calls for education and intelligence, but not reason, and the salesman or shopkeeper who characterizes it is said not to be himself interested in honesty, but, echoing Adam Smith and the Maghrib traders cited earlier, interested in what honesty will get him in the market (ibid., p. 77). This is belief in ethics for its utilitarian value.

As a psychoanalyst who sees patients with a variety of personality disorders — a skewed sample of humanity — Fromm is presumably not in a position to offer opinions on the proportions of an ordinary population who are receptive, exploitive, hoarding, or marketing among the unproductive class, or their size relative to productive persons. Nor does he seem to have an interest in the transition in a family from a buccaneering entrepreneur in one generation to a hoarding descendant interested in trustee-type securities in later generations. Criminologists may have some notions of the relative sizes of the exploitive orientation on the one hand, and their possible victims, the receptive, but I have not had an opportunity to open up that foreign field.

V

It would be helpful if there were measurements of the distribution of honesty, greed, readiness to violate the law, the last separately for violent and for white-collar crime, but psychologists of my acquaintance tell me that they are unaware of any such. One argument against the popular notion of locking up for life those who commit three felonies — "three strikes and you are out" — is that the propensity for such crime diminishes sharply after age 50. The same may not be true of white-collar crime. In the chapter on swindles in *Manias, Panics and Crashes* (1989), I observed that swindles rose with business booms, as the number of sheep to be fleeced multiplied, and rose again after the bubble burst after asset prices had declined a considerable distance, as speculators who had lost a great deal of money tried to dig their way out of trouble by any and all means including peculation. The caution of consumers and investors seems likely to move with the business cycle, especially with booms and busts in asset markets, securities to a major degree, but also in real estate and ordinary business ventures, including those starting up in boom. In an occasional talk on financial crisis, I elicit a nervous laugh in saying that nothing disturbs a person's judgment so much as to see a friend get rich.

Keynes was preoccupied with "animal spirits," those of investors both in markets for titles to assets and debt, and in markets for productive facilities. These spirits presumably varied within the lifetime of an investor or entrepreneur, with more risk-taking in youth, less in old age. They also varied from generation to generation, as already noted. In the 1920s, Keynes several times observed that Britain was dominated by third-generation men (Skidelsky 1994, pp. 232, 261).

More is needed than animal spirits. In a *Manchester Guardian Supplement* in 1923, Keynes called for

> clear-eyed public spirit, a substantial amount of which was needed to preserve the balanced and complicated organization by which the British lived. . . . unless men are united by a common aim or moved by objective principles, each one's hand will be raised against the rest and the unregulated pursuits of individual advantage may soon destroy the whole. There has been no common purpose lately between nations or between classes except war. (ibid., p. 121)

The terms "clear-sighted public spirit," "common aim (or common purpose)," "objective principles," are not self-evident, especially in terms of nations and classes with no mention of individuals. One can infer from the passage, however, that what modern capitalism requires is trust, as has been said by many, notably Kenneth Arrow (1974) and Paolo Sylos Labini (qtd. in Kindleberger 1993, p. 87). Trust, based on ethical principles, is again an attribute difficult to measure.

One form of knowledge which Keynes does not discuss is that needed by depositors adequately to judge the solvency of banks. Advocates of "free banking" suggest that any rogue bank that lends too recklessly will be tamed by other banks that demand payment of its bank notes in specie, stop accepting its paper, or stop lending it federal funds (Selgin 1988; for an illustration of the last, see Spero 1980). If such a bank fails under free banking — the absence of bank regulation and of deposit insurance — its ignorant depositors suffer as most people are unable to judge the worth of a bank's assets and will fail to withdraw their funds in time. Charles Goodhart observes that bank notes were originally of high denominations, and the poor were left to deal only in coin because of their inability to judge the risk element in bank portfolios. As a prudential matter the ill-informed and the poor had to be protected (1989, p. 58). As knowledge of banking spread and the utility of paper instead of specie, the denominations of bank notes were progressively reduced and the ordinary person began to use bank checking accounts. Even so deposit insurance was added in the United States after the rash of bank failures in the 1930s. Advocates of free banking argue that the system is self-regulating and that central banks can be abandoned. Goodhart rejects this notion on the ground that banks differ from mutual funds. The assets of mutual funds are securities quoted in markets, making their value transparent. Loans of banks, on the other hand, are of uncertain value (ibid., passim).

VI

In a laissez-faire world it would be adequate if the consumer, the investor, and the depositor were wary in protecting their interests, or if sellers and bankers were uniformly competitive and honest in providing full disclosure. Not all consumers, investors, and depositors are, or can be made, rational, competent, and informed. Those under some age cannot guard their own interests, nor can those at the lower end of the distribution of intelligence, or who halted education at a low level. Information is perhaps more readily tackled. Its major source in youth is the family. Where that is unable to provide it to the requisite degree, there is schooling. As noted earlier, it is not clear what Keynes meant by the "nationalization of knowledge," beyond universal education. Some wariness at an early age is being taught in Boston elementary schools after a series of alleged attempts at kidnapping young children. In adolescence and in secondary school, one presumably loses innocence at a rapid rate by exposure to the media on the one hand, and, if lucky, to good literature on the other. High school courses in civics, and college and university teaching of history, political science, economics, and philosophy may be of use in shopping, investing, and dealing with credit.

One who was wary in youth and middle age may become less so, and overly trusting, in advanced years. The evidence is primarily anecdotal. Newspapers report cases of a young second wife of a wealthy older man, a housekeeper, a chauffeur in the case of older women, a casual friend, or even an acquaintance persuading an old person to write a new will, disinheriting relatives, and leaving an estate to the newcomer. Suits by the disinherited often seek to prove "undue influence" and the falsity of the statement of the testator that she or he was "of sound mind." There is little that education or government can do in such cases, beyond adjudication of the matter in court.

If wariness in the face of exploitive conduct cannot be caught, what of honesty and fair dealing? The view that a three-year-old cannot tell the difference between right and wrong has been noted, and the psychiatrist's opinion that personality is strongly influenced by experience in the few years immediately following. Ethics and its teaching in the United States has been called a growth industry, with a new profession of ethicist having developed in the past thirty years (Gustafson 1991). An experiment exploring personality traits is afforded by the "ultimate game" in game theory, in which one person (A) is given a sum of money to divide with another (B), under a rule of the game that if B accepts what A awards, both keep the sums they have, whereas if B rejects the award, neither gets any money. In a rational world, A awards B the smallest finite amount, because B either accepts it or gets nothing. In practice, however, in repeated experiments with small amounts of money such as $10, A awards nearly half the sum to B, on the basis of some notion of "fairness." (Other outcomes may occur, the experimenters hypothesize, if sums as large as $100, or $1,000 or $10,000 were involved.)

Fairness probably differs from honesty if there is truth in the cliché concerning honor among thieves. Presumably principles of fairness and honesty are expounded, if not in the family at an early age, in kindergarten and the early elementary grades, as well as in more advanced years. A former commissioner of the Securities and Exchange Commission gave $10 million to the Harvard Business School for research and teaching of ethics, but the courses are elective, the professors do not include the stars of the faculty, and registration for the classes is reported to be low as students are preoccupied with learning technical business courses. James Gustafson reports "one would be hard put to it to provide solid evidence that an undergraduate course in ethics makes student behavior more moral," and that "the limited success of the growth industry of ethics to date, or in the future, may be rooted in the deeper tendency of individuals, communities and institutions to pursue their own desired and immediate self interest — a tendency not readily reformed by ethics teaching alone" (1991).

Without a solid understanding of the matter, I gather that the teaching required must come in the early formative years and in the family. If, as seems evident in the United States today, well-functioning families are not universal in a time of divorce, desertion, units where both parents work and children are warehoused in day-care establishments, little can be done by government policy, at least in the short run, in shoring up support for spreading trust in economic life. I am afraid I have no view whether Head Start can help.

There is always the possibility of postgraduate education when the person enters the real world of work. Professions typically set standards for the conduct of their membership, sometimes enforced by license, after passage of examination and attestation to the individual's good character. To some degree, such standards are a cartel device to limit numbers and raise income levels. If one ignores the latter possibility, one may call attention to a new code for lawyers, laid down by the Committee on Ethics and Professional Responsibility, which expounds "elementary ethical notions," presumably acquired in childhood, such as that a lawyer should not charge two clients for the same time, if for example, she or he worked on one case while traveling by airplane to deal with another. The Committee Report urged a high level of conduct because violations hurt the public opinion of lawyers and may inhibit laymen from using the legal system. Amitai Etzioni decries this utilitarian or consequentialist notion of ethics, as contrasted with moral behavior that would obtain in a world of trust (1994). Other professions: medicine, accountants, financial advisers, even real-estate dealers and the like produce codes. Monitoring behavior to see that it conforms to the standards of the code, however, seems difficult to carry out through peer surveillance, and is generally left to the police and/or courts.

One device to protect investors against the abuse of insider information is the appointment of outsider directors, who are not executives of the company. In one view, while insider trading in securities markets troubles most people, "it probably contributes to the efficient dissemination of information" (Hochman 1994, p. 18). There should be legal, efficient, and fair ways to this end. A difficulty with the device is that outsiders are typically insiders in other companies, with insiders' points of view, are appointed by insiders of the company in question and beholden to them. Such boards can lose their "contestability" as the watcher and the watched share the goals of company profits and higher share prices (*Economist,* January 29, 1994, Survey). German practice is to have two boards, one for management which includes a company's executives, and a supervisory board which does not, though it typically includes the company's bankers. The supervisory board of *Metallgesellschaft,* which went bankrupt after losing more than $1 billion trading oil futures in New York, claimed that the management board never informed it of its trading in oil futures. One wonders whether the supervisory board would have been equally disturbed if the speculation had gained substantial profits instead of losses. As I write, the *New York Times* records large profits from trading in options on the stock of the Grumann (airplane) company beginning March 1, 1994, when the announcement of its takeover by the Martin Marietta company was not made until March 7. A profit of $218,700 was made by an unknown player on an investment of $12,500 to buy options on 25,000 shares on the Chicago Board Options Exchange (March 8, 1994, p. D-1).

The New York Stock Exchange monitors insider trading within its precincts by computer study of activity in shares which rise or fall precipitously before the announcement of news affecting the company's profitability. At a meeting at the Exchange some years ago I was told that in some cases, people with insider information would place orders abroad in an effort to escape this surveillance, using public telephones. Small orders to buy or sell which could be handled on the foreign bourse would not attract attention. When an order was large, however, the Zurich market, let us say, might find it necessary to lay off part or all of an order in another foreign market. Brokers in London, it was said, had become wary of large orders in American shares coming from other European markets, and found it useful to "mislay" the order for a few days, to see if there was breaking news.

Those hurt by misleading sales pitches may recover their losses in whole or more usually in part, through bringing suit in courts, in some instances in concert with others in class-action suits. Independent suits are expensive, unless a lawyer is employed on a contingent-fee basis, paid nothing unless he wins the case, in which instance he may earn as much as a third or half of the award. As trust leaks out of American capitalism, lawyers multiply, advertise their readiness to help people who have been injured in any way by suing in the courts, sit on both sides of business deals—ordinary contracts but especially mergers and acquisitions, takeovers both hostile and friendly, bankruptcies, incorporations, initial public offerings (of previously privately owned stock), etc., etc. Legal advertising speaks primarily to people's rights, rather than duties, and ascribes any injury to the wrong-doing of another, rather than to the randomness of events. Lawyers abhor limits to mal-practice suits and no-fault accident insurance. Asians, especially the Japanese, are more stoical in these matters, have and use fewer lawyers in relation to population size. Ronald Dore writes that the Japanese especially dislike low-trust relations, and dislike poker in which bluffing plays a large role (1992, p. 170).

Use of the courts can be overdone. "Strict liability" frequently penalizes the producer of a product when the injury occurs through the carelessness of the user. A philosopher, Albert Borgmann, is reported as stating that rampant individualism in the United States has led to a movement to dismiss personal responsibility and take on the role of the victim (Staples 1994). On the other hand, the other party understand-ably seeks to blame the victim, even in cases of those inexperienced because of youth, old age, or low intelligence where it may not be warranted. Often it is appropriate, to be sure, as in the B.C.C.I. case referred to above quoting Mme Ploix. There is no general rule, and as in much of life, circumstances alter cases.

VII

If a society contains unscrupulous members ready to exploit the incompe-tent, and maintenance of high standards cannot be handled privately by professional and industrial groups, the maintenance of justice falls to government. The control of monopolies and suppression and punish-ment of outright fraud I leave to the antitrust division of the Department of Justice, and the Attorney General at the national level and public prosecutors at the state and local. More is called for, however, as the existence of the Bureau of Standards, Pure Food and Drug Administra-tion, Federal Trade Commission, Securities and Exchange Commission, Federal Deposit Insurance Corporation, Comptroller of the Currency, Federal Reserve System, state insurance commissions, etc., etc., demon-strate. A problem with these agencies is that they are sometimes cap-tured by the industry they are supposed to regulate, although this can be nothing more than an attempt of regulator and regulated to work out a means of operating. That such is usually the case seems unduly optimis-tic. One issue on the current agenda in Washington is whether the four agencies that supervise banking should be consolidated into one, so that the responsibility is unambiguously fixed. The proposal to this end, resisted by the Federal Reserve System, may be a response to the view that competition among the regulating agencies evolved into a competi-tion in deregulation (Kane 1987).

In addition, regulation may be porous rather than watertight. Deposit insurance initially covered deposits of $5,000, a number gradually raised with inflation to $10,000, $20,000, then to $40,000. I am told (hearsay, but from a reputable source) that the joint committee of the Congress to reconcile bills calling for a further increase, one house specifying $50,000, the other $60,000, compromised on $100,000. The market then developed "deposit brokers" who would take deposits in the millions, and divide them among many banks, $99,000 or some such number in each, weak banks that offered high rates of interest to gain deposits, many of them later failing. Meanwhile wealthy, competent depositors earned high rates of interest, fully insured from banks which, without insurance or much lower limits, they would have avoided.

I conclude somewhat pessimistically that there is no easy general rule, whether leaving the individual to guard his or her interests in purchasing, investing, and banking, wary of the danger of malfeasance, or closely regulating industry, finance, and banking. Business-to-business dealings between firms of broadly comparable size can doubtless be left to the market, and in many (most?) cases this is true of business dealings between firms and individuals. But some business-to-individual exchanges and some individual-to-individual ones may involve the unscrupulous and the naive. Improving the family, schools, policing markets, improving the efficiency of courts of law, all are needed but the likelihood of substantial and rapid improvement is slight. In a bromide which includes the word "price" but is not economic, the price of liberty is eternal vigilance.

REFERENCES

Akerlof, George A. (1970) "The Market for 'Lemons': Quality Uncertainty and the Market Mechanism." *Quarterly Journal of Economics* 84, no. 3 (August): 488–500.
Axelrod, Robert (1984) *The Evolution of Cooperation.* New York: Basic Books.
Dore, Ronald (1992) "Goodwill and the Spirit of Market Capitalism." In Mark Granovetter and Richard Swedberg, eds., *The Sociology of Economic Life.* Boulder, Colo.: Westview Press. 159–79.
Etzioni, Amitai (1994) "What's Wrong?" *New York Times,* February 14, p. A17.
Fromm, Eric (1947) *Man for Himself.* New York: Holt, Rinehart and Winston.
Fromm, Eric (1964) *The Heart of Man.* New York: Harper and Row.
Goodhart, Charles (1989) *The Evolution of Central Banks.* Cambridge, Mass.: MIT Press.
Granovetter, Mark, and Richard Swedberg, eds. (1992) *The Sociology of Economic Life.* Boulder, Colo.: Westview Press.
Greif, Avner (1989) "Reputations and Coalitions in Medieval Trade: Evidence

on the Magribi Traders." *Journal of Economic History* 49, no. 4 (December): 857–82.

Gustafson, James M. (1991) "Ethics: An American Growth Industry." *The Key Reporter* 56, no. 3:1–5.

Hamilton, Earl J. (1934) *American Treasure and the Price Revolution in Spain, 1501–1650.* Cambridge, Mass.: Harvard University Press.

Hochman, Harold M. (1994) "Economics and Distributive Ethics." Inaugural Lecture, Lafayette College, Easton, Pa. (February 3), unpublished.

Kane, Edward J. (1987) "Comparative Financial Reregulation: An International Perspective." In R. Portes and A. Swoboda, eds., *Threats to International Financial Stability.* Cambridge: Cambridge University Press. 111–45.

Keynes, John Maynard (1930) *A Treatise on Money.* 2 vols. New York: Harcourt Brace.

Kindleberger, Charles P. (1989) *Manias, Panics and Crashes.* Rev. ed. New York: Basic.

Kindleberger, Charles P. (1992) *Mariners and Markets.* New York: Harvester/ Wheatsheaf.

Kindleberger, Charles P. (1993) "Social Intangibles Relevant to Economic Processes." In S. Biasco et al., eds., *Markets and Institutions in Economic Development.* New York: St. Martin's Press. 87–101.

Lerner, Max (1937) "Introduction," to Adam Smith, *The Wealth of Nations.* New York: Modern Library. xxiii–lvi.

Ploix, Hélène (1994) "*Postface*" to *Histoire mondiale de la spéculation financière*, French translation of C. P. Kindleberger, *Manias, Panics and Crashes.* Paris: Editions P.A.U. 337–41.

Sacco, Pier Luigi (1990) "On the Fragility of Reputational Equilibria under Systematic Uncertainty: What Is Wrong with Rational Expectations." *Banca Nazionale del Lavoro Quarterly Review,* no. 175 (December): 459–74.

Selgin, George (1988) *The Theory of Free Banking.* Totowa, N.J.: Rowan and Littlefield.

Sexton, Robert L., Philip R. Graves, and Dwight R. Lee. (1993). "Lowering the Age Requirement for Adult Courts: An Analytical Framework." *Atlantic Economic Journal* 21, no. 4 (December): 67–70.

Skidelsky (Lord) Robert (1994) *John Maynard Keynes.* Vol. 2. New York: Penguin/Viking.

Smith, Adam (1808) *The Theory of Moral Sentiments.* 11th ed., 2 vols. Edinburgh: Bell and Bradfute.

Spero, Joan Edelman (1980) *The Failure of the Franklin National Bank.* New York: Columbia University Press.

Swedberg, Richard (1990) (Interview with) "George A. Akerlof," *Economics and Sociology.* Princeton, N.J.: Princeton University Press.

3

Is the Dollar Going the Way of Sterling, the Guilder, the Ducat, and the Bezant?

The dollar declined an additional 20 percent in April against the yen, less against the Deutschemark (and, to be sure, rose against the Canadian dollar and the Mexican peso). The meeting of the G-7 finance ministers at the end of the month insisted that the depreciation was not justified by fundamentals, that the yen was overvalued, the dollar undervalued, but offered no program for correcting the position. U.S. authorities, under the leadership of Robert Rubin, former foreign-exchange trader, as Secretary of the Treasury, appear to feel that market forces are too massive to mess with, as demonstrated by the inchoate attempts of leading central banks to support currencies, including the dollar, in the last few years. They reject the recommendation of Michael Camdesuss, managing director of the International Monetary Fund, that the Federal Reserve raise interest rates to hold foreign balances here and attract more, thus bidding the currency up. A *New York Times* story on May 1 said that the Group of Seven was in eclipse.

There is a suspicion in Wall Street that U.S. authorities have reverted to "benign neglect" of the dollar, explicit under President Reagan, with Donald Regan in the Treasury. Depreciation of the dollar stimulates exports, restrains imports, and pumps up the income statements of U.S. multinational corporations bringing back profits from abroad. First things first. Foreign economic relations are not that large a part of the American economy, and don't matter on the scale of domestic price stability which dollar depreciation has not disrupted so far. The country has fairly full employment, positive growth, a soft landing in prospect. In 1925 the British made a bad mistake when they restored the pound to par and experienced swingeing deflation. They gained when the pound left gold in September 1931, and if the world outside was hurt

---

This essay was reprinted with permission from *The International Economy* 9, no. 3 (May–June 1995): 609–11.

by still falling world prices as nonsterling currencies appreciated, that was its problem.

Benign neglect went into the discard in the 1980s as the dollar appreciated until the Plaza accord of September 1985, but seems now to have been revived because of a feeling of helplessness. With trillions of dollars traded around the clock by private holders — nonfinancial corporations, mutual funds, pension funds, hedge funds, banks, and individual speculators — one may not like it, but the wisest tactic is to relax and take what comes. If the world has an exchange problem, let Japan and Germany take care of it.

Not much attention is paid in this country to the world interest, as attention was not paid in London in 1931. Some welcome flexible exchange rates, especially banks. In the first quarter of 1995, Citicorp's profit of $829 million included $324 million from dealing in exchange. As noted, multinationals enjoy a depreciating dollar, however much they resent an appreciating one with the need to mark profits down because of accounting standards. Trading banks win either way.

In the 1920s, the eastern United States, especially the banking community and within it, Benjamin Strong, governor of the Federal Reserve Bank of New York, and J. P. Morgan & Co., took a strong interest in the currency troubles of Europe, and helped out on frequent occasions. Their concerns were not shared throughout the country. President Hoover thought eastern bankers were under the thumbs of Europeans; and the Federal Reserve Board in Washington, along with governors of some of the other regional Federal Reserve Banks, resisted the leadership of New York. Today, the rest of the country may have more interest in the stability of the dollar, and New York less.

After Hitler's invasion of Poland and the Japanese attack at Pearl Harbor, the country was united in winning the war and then building a stable world economy, even at considerable cost. Now U.S. interest dominates, first and foremost, leaving little concern for the public good of a stable vehicle currency that is used as a medium of exchange, unit of account, and store of value throughout the world. Such a multiple role was played by sterling from about 1850 to 1913, and by the dollar from 1940 to 1973. The transition between the two was awkward. The world depression of the 1930s was so wide, so long, and so deep, in my judgment, because no country took charge, with its currency as a symbol of that role. Britain could not, and the United States would not. Now the position looms up that the United States can or will no longer anchor the world economy. President Bush said the country had the will but not the wallet. Joseph Nye, Harvard political scientist and Clinton bureaucrat, having in mind that the country is undertaxed compared with most of the industrialized world, reversed the remark: the country has the wallet but not the will to correct its twin deficits in the federal budget and the balance of payments.

So far so good, but the omens are frightening. If the United States continues to falter, there is no currency, backed by a strong country willing to allow its international use, as there was not during the interwar period. Germany and Japan for a long time resisted substantial use of their monies internationally. Despite its wobbly behavior, the dollar is still the unit for pricing oil, many other commodities, and for the majority of international bond issues. It is surprising to one with a long memory that foreign lenders who supported the dollar over the last decades by buying and holding dollars did not insist on exchange guarantees, Roosa bonds, instruments denominated in the lender's currency, or even two- or three-pay obligations popular in the 1920s. It is clear that the gold clause cannot be revived in international lending after the debacle of the 1930s when private contracts were abrogated by governments on grounds of *force majeur*. The Japanese switch partway out of bonds to real estate (Rockefeller Center) and business corporations (movie companies) proved less than adequate as a safeguard. Central banks worldwide, not to mention leading insurance companies like Nippon Life of Tokyo, have huge losses on their books, or losses that would be on their books if their dollars and dollar instruments were carried at market instead of cost. Some ingenuity has gone into the development of options and futures to hedge against risk, but to a considerable degree these seem to have shifted risks from banks to nonbanks such as Proctor and Gamble, Metallgesellschaft, and Orange County.

James Tobin, Yale Nobel laureate in economic science, has proposed putting sand in the works by taxing international movements of funds, especially liquid funds, or regulating speculators by making them put up margin. There is doubt whether such devices could be made to work. Instant world communication by telephone, facsimile, and computer, and the spread of banking facilities worldwide, including to island tax havens, make the task of designing such inhibitors look like a labor of Sisyphus.

One episode in financial history attracts me, the squeeze engineered by Lazard Frères for the French Ministry of Finance in the spring of 1924 when the franc was under attack by speculators in Holland, Germany, and Austria. With a $100 million loan from J. P. Morgan, the franc was driven up, the speculators routed, and, perhaps a fateful result for the 1930s, several Austrian banks that had financed the action were forced into bankruptcy. $100 million is of course a derisory amount today when a trillion dollars changes hands around the world in 24 hours, but the thought occurs to me that a more concerted effort to resist the speculators, aggressively, and to inflict painful losses on them might help, at least in the short run.

In the longer run, the respite for the franc gained in March and April 1924 was lost because there was no change in the fundamentals. The Chamber of Deputies was unwilling to pass new taxes to bring the budget to balance. The Finance Ministry was unable to fund the heavy weight of short-term debt which fed cash into the market each week. In the theory of rational expectations, market prices are always determined by fundamentals. In a more historical view, the short and the long run differ. Punishing speculators would help in the short run by discouraging them from piling on rate movements. Over the longer period, the dollar can be stabilized, and perhaps regain its world money role, only by more thorough-going therapy, correcting the deficits, raising savings rates. Many economists believe that the latter task can be accomplished by diddling with the tax system, this despite the abject failure of the experiment in 1983. Lower taxes then meant conspicuous consumption, not saving. Major forces — called by Mancur Olson "distributional coalitions" but more popularly known as vested interests — block the way to taxation, reducing social security, holding down the deductibility of mortgage interest, etc., etc., etc. It is easy to blame the country's leadership, the Administration, the Congress, lobbies, the other fellow. To quote Pogo, the enemy is us.

What is the likelihood of correcting the undervaluation of the dollar, the overvaluation of the yen and DM by monetary policy; raising interest rates here, lowering them there? In my view not much. What's needed is a revolution, not the political one of last November's election, with its phony promises to balance the budget and lower taxes, but one which addresses deeper problems: the budget, to be sure, the balance of payments, industrial productivity, and a shift away from preoccupation with instant wealth to matters of ethics, poverty, health, fraying infrastructure. Such changes need a defining moment like the beheading of Charles I, the storming of the Bastille, the Great Depression of the 1930s (not a moment admittedly), the attack on Pearl Harbor. Such moments are infrequent. Without one, the outlook for a world stable money is dark, as the dollar follows sterling, the guilder, the ducat, and the bezant.

4

Currency Debasement in the Early Seventeenth Century and the Establishment of Deposit Banks in Central Europe

Bank histories, Charles Jones has said (1982), can be divided into the orthodox, the heroic, the Populist, and the statist. In the orthodox, which cover especially central banks, interest attaches to evolving bank functions and policies, as the central bank acquires a monopoly of the note issue, works out policies for rediscounting and open-market operations, learns how to respond to the need for a lender of last resort in financial crisis. Heroic histories detail the rise and sometimes fall of banks that change history on a wider level, e.g., the de Medici, the Fuggers, the Pereire brothers. To Populist historians, banks exploit the mass of men and women, at home and on occasion abroad. Statist histories note that some banks are created to serve the interest of a state. The Bank of England and the Bank of France, for example, were both established to help finance the state in time of war.

Early banks are covered only partly by these categories. The more usual classifications relate to deposit banks, lending banks, exchange banks, banks of issue, and state banks. The functions are often combined in a single institution, or a bank may be started for one purpose, add others, or change directions. This essay is concerned primarily with public banks of the seventeenth century and their intended and realized functions. In particular it deals with the state function not of acquiring resources for state use, but of providing the public good of money. Money is a medium of exchange and a unit of account. The medium-of-exchange function can be discharged publicly, privately, or both. As a unit of account, however, money is a standard of measurement, like weights and measures generally, used to measure prices. Discharge of the function requires at a minimum some surveillance, if not operation,

This essay was reprinted with permission from Societá Ligure di Storia Patria, *Banchi pubblici, banchi privati e monti di pietá nell' Europa preindustriale* (Genoa, 1991), 1:37–46.

of mints, and in the seventeenth century called for the establishment of public banks of deposit to replace or complement debased money with good.

Early deposit banks developed in the fifteenth century in Spain, notably in Barcelona and Valencia. In addition to handling various classes of deposits, storing valuables, holding assets in escrow, they served as fiscal agent for the state, ending as a rule bankrupted by emergency loans to the state which could not be repaid (Usher 1943). The Bank of Barcelona had a responsibility for the coinage in the requirement that it retire worn coins from circulation. It was closely associated with a mint, presumably by advancing moneys with which to buy precious metals (ibid., p. 15). Usher also notes that the public bank of Barcelona required bills of exchange to be paid there from its founding in 1401.

Exchange banking was originally handled privately by dealers at semiannual or quarterly fairs. Venice was considered a permanent fair from the beginning of the thirteenth century (Luzzatto 1934, p. 40). Dealers, including private banks, cleared domestic and international payments, settling unmatched balances either by specie payments or by bills drawn for payment elsewhere or at a later date. This was exchange banking, as opposed to money-changing, which dealt solely in coin. A recent book on fifteenth-century money and banking in the Europe of "Latin Christianity" (France, Italy, and Spain) makes a distinction between private moneys (bills of exchange) and money issued by the power of princes, i.e., coin minted directly by the prince or under his authorization (Boyer-Xambeu, Deleplace, and Gillard 1986). The two, of course, are laced with interconnections. Many mints are run privately, and much debasement of coinage is undertaken by princes to gain seignorage. As early as the twelfth century, princes would be offered moneys to persuade them not to debase the local coinage (Bisson 1979).

Bank lending in early modern times was, on the whole, less for the mobilization of capital for investment than for the provision of funds to government to make war, or loans for consumption at the level of the pawnshop.

The first note-issuing bank in Sweden in 1656 was established to overcome the difficulties posed by copper money, when the basic unit, a ten-daler piece, weighed forty-three pounds (Heckscher 1954, p. 89). When the bank was transformed in 1668 into the Bank of Sweden, the first national bank, it was divided into two sections, one to issue banknotes, the other to make loans. The division anticipated the British Bank Act of 1844, which divided the Bank of England into an Issue Department and a Banking Department.

Though it was called an exchange (*Wissel*) bank from the beginning, the principal purpose of the Bank of Amsterdam, founded in 1609, was to improve rather chaotic monetary conditions. Standards are a public good, and the standard of money should be unchanging just as the length of the yardstick and the weight of the pound. In primitive money conditions in the Eastern Mediterranean without banks, coins were weighed and assayed and sewn up in bags or purses with the amount stated on the bag by the money-changers and attested by government, with strong penalties for misspecification (Udovitch 1979, p. 267). Early banks in Spain stored money (and valuables) sealed in bags, although it is not stated whether the contents were attested by government (Usher 1943, p. 16). As late as the nineteenth century in Egypt, one unit of money was the "purse" (Marlowe 1974, p. 153). The public-good character of a stable and recognizable money lies in lowering transaction costs for trade by providing a means of avoiding the onerous burden of individuals weighing and assaying large numbers of coins.

The production of public goods is handicapped in the absence of a monopoly government by the "free rider," the unit that anticipates that it will get the benefit of the good, without contributing to it, and looks after its own interest. In minting, this can take the form of monetary debasement to extract more seignorage. With many mints, there is the fallacy of composition, each mint debasing a little, with the total adding up to progressive deterioration of the money. The States-General of the United Provinces or the Holy Roman Emperor will try to limit the number of mints and establish standards for coins in terms of denomination, weight, and finesses. With many mints control is difficult of enforcement.

In 1585 the States-General of the United Provinces tried to limit each of the seven provinces to one mint each, but Holland already had two, and six towns in the east, which long had had mints, were unwilling to give them up (van Dillen 1934, p. 81). In the loose federal system, the higher level could not impose its will on the lower. A similar experience is recorded in the Holy Roman Empire two decades later when the Electoral Chancellor at Mainz proposed that mints in the Empire be limited to no more than three or four to a *Kreis* (a circle), except for those with silver mines, only to be opposed by six towns in the Lower Saxony Circle which already had mints: Lübeck, Hamburg, Rostock, Bremen, Brunswick, and Magdeburg. The defeat of the initiative led these and other towns with the privilege to establish additional mints, and even some towns without the privilege (Gaettens 1982, p. 75).

Uncontrolled or inadequately controlled minting in the United Provinces gradually led to depreciation of the coinage in circulation from twenty stuivers to the (imaginary, that is, uncoined) unit of account, the florin, to thirty to thirty-five stuivers, as gold coins disappeared from circulation and new good coins were raised in denomination. Attempts to reform the currency were unsuccessful. In 1606 the Amsterdam council embarked on a plan to establish a bank, "the chief motive of which was the improvement of monetary conditions." It was to be patterned after the Bank of Venice and that of Seville, about the latter of which little is known (van Dillen 1934, pp. 80–84). It is curious that the example of Venice is so frequently cited, but not that of Genoa. This was doubtless because of the close connections of Venice with South Germany.

It is not clear from the standard accounts how much of the trouble in the United Provinces arose from foreign coin, largely that of the Holy Roman Empire. Small states are porous in matters of coin circulation, as Adam Smith explained a century and a half later in his digression on the Bank of Amsterdam. *The Wealth of Nations* ascribes the establishment of the Bank of Amsterdam as an attempt to remedy the "great quantity of clipt and worn foreign coin which the extensive trade of Amsterdam brought from all parts of Europe" (1776 [1937], pp. 446–55). But debased coin crossed state borders not only in payments for trade, but also through a Gresham's-law process. Debased money in a single territorial unit is taken abroad and exchanged at its nominal value for good coin which is brought back to be minted into more base money. In the early seventeenth century the process started slowly and picked up speed as first professional money-changers and then amateurs took up the activity. The neighboring province losing its good coin and acquiring bad would try various measures: forbidding the export of good coin and the import of bad, forbidding all exchanges of money for money, all to no avail in a world of carts loaded with produce on market days. A final defense was to raise the denomination of its good coin, or lower that of the bad in a game-theoretic tactic of Tit-for-Tat which accelerated the depreciation in general.

The process had begun in Italy, according to a Schwabian historian, and spread northward through Switzerland to the Holy Roman Empire (Schöttle 1922–24, pp. 78–80). A table representing average depreciation records that the silver thaler (the unit of account) went from 1 florin in 1582 to 1 fl 4 kreuzer (one-fifteenth of a florin) in 1606, 1 fl 8 krz in 1607, and 1 fl 14 krz in 1609 (Shaw 1895, p. 209). The depreciation continued to creep until it accelerated in hyperinflation, starting in 1619 as more and more people participated in minting debased and even counterfeited coins, and fewer and fewer persons were ready to accept them at their nominal value. The hyperinflation was called the *Kipper-und Wipperzeit*, the time of tilting and wagging, the expression coming from rhyming slang. *Kippen* means to tilt or tip, and *Wippen* is to wag, or to rise up and down as in a seesaw. The designation, which was intended to be highly derogatory, came from the action of money-changers in wagging their hand-held scales before the eyes of dupes, as they pretended to weigh the highly debased coins, worn, adulterated with copper, sometimes entirely copper painted white (but not clipped, Redlich asserts), in hoodwinking unsophisticated common folk (Redlich 1972, pp. 18ff.).

If the purpose of establishing the Bank of Amsterdam was to stabilize the money by converting it to a deposit on the bank's books at its actual weight and fineness, it quickly extended from domestic transactions to bills of exchange. The City decreed that all bills of exchange of six hundred florins or more must be paid at the Bank in bank money, rather than current coin. Van Dillen states that this was a provision adopted from the Bank of Venice (1934, p. 84), without specifically identifying the Banco della Piazza di Rialto, established in 1587, and known as the Banco di Rialto. This bank dealt in bills of exchange, but I have not seen that the Venetian government imposed a requirement that bills of exchange be paid there. Such a requirement was laid down for ·Venice's Banco del Giro, established in 1619, ten years after the Bank of Amsterdam. That Bank had originally been founded to assist the government in buying silver for the mint (Lane 1973, p. 300). It is possible that the Banco del Giro regulation was patterned after that of the Bank of Amsterdam, which became known as the *Wisselbank* or Bank of Exchange. One historian finds it "significant" that the *Wisselbank* was established in the same year as the Dutch truce with Spain (Schama 1988, p. 345), a truce that ushered in a tremendous expansion of Dutch foreign trade (Israel 1989, chap. 4). Since the discussions leading to the establishment of the *Wisselbank* went back well before the truce could have been in sight, however, it is hard to ascribe its foundation to a prospective expansion of trade.

The other Dutch banks of the early seventeenth century—those of Middelburg set up in 1616, of Delft in 1621, and of Rotterdam in 1635—were founded well after the Bank of Amsterdam, "chiefly at the request of the English cloth importers"—a clear connection with assisting payment in foreign trade (van Dillen 1934, p. 84). There may have been an indirect tie to the monetary disorders on the Continent, since depreciation of the German currency (appreciation of sterling) made it hard for British cloth exporters. This would have been the case especially of Delft in 1621 at the height of the *Kipper- und Wipperzeit.* It is tempting to connect the establishment of the bank at Middelburg before the peak of the debasement with the abortive scheme of Alderman Cockayne of 1614 to halt the export of undyed and unfinished cloth to Holland for processing and sale to Germany. The Bank of Rotterdam, moreover, was likely a response of the rapidly growing British colony in that city — 22,000 in 1622 and 50,000 at the end of the century (Klein 1984, pp. 117–18), well after the peak of the currency disorders that were stabilized in 1622–23. But the timing for the bank of Delft, 1621, is at the height of what was called in Britain "currency manipulation" (Supple 1959, chap. 4). The monetary disorders of the Hapsburg Empire were not the sole reason for the troubles of British cloth importers (Thirsk and Cooper 1972, chap. 1) to be sure, but the timing of the lesser Dutch banks is suggestive.

The Bank of Amsterdam was forbidden to allow its depositors to overdraw their accounts, and presumably this extended to a ban on all extensions of credit. It did, however, make advances to the Bank for Lending. This was established in 1614 largely for consumption loans supported by collateral, akin to pawn-broking, but also for limited extensions of business credit. The Bank of Amsterdam did advance funds to the Dutch East India Company in periods of stress, as a sort of lender of last resort. These loans were on a limited scale until the eighteenth century when the City of Amsterdam made substantial advances to the East India Company which had suffered losses in the Fourth Anglo-Dutch war, and the Bank came to the City's rescue with disastrous consequences. Before that time, the difference between the Bank's deposits and its stock of precious metals had been small. It was able to survive the crisis of 1672 when the French invasion of Holland created a series of runs, runs that brought the banks of Middelburg and Rotterdam to bankruptcy. Until the Fourth Anglo-Dutch war, the Bank of Amsterdam functioned much like the 100 percent reserve model of bank advocated in some quarters today.

The Bank of Hamburg was founded in 1619 as the *Kipper- und Wipperzeit* approached a climax, and was patterned after the Bank of Amsterdam (Sieveking 1934, p. 125). Some traders who dealt with Holland and Friesland had objected to the founding of such a bank as early as 1614, but its establishment in 1619 enlisted the support of the English mercantile colony, some Dutchmen (ibid.), and Portuguese Jews (Kellenbenz 1958, pp. 253–54). It was connected with a Lending Bank, again mainly for small loans and pledged personal articles (Sieveking 1934, pp. 128–30). The main pressure, one would judge, came from the accelerating debasement of the German currency. The silver thaler went from 1 fl 22 krz in May 1618 to 1 fl 36 krz in October 1619 and 1 fl 45 krz in December of that year. The wild burst of debasement and inflation began later in the summer of 1621, with the rate going to 2 fl 62 krz at the end of July 1621 to 4 fl in September and 8 fl 30 krz in February and

March 1622 before the stabilization movement took hold (Shaw 1895, p. 209). These are average figures, not necessarily representative of any particular locality. The debasement varied widely from state to state, and was on the whole much greater in the South than in the North. A nineteenth-century historian who Redlich says is "surprisingly reliable" (1972, p. 10) said that the debasement at the peak reached only one and a half or two florins in the North, and as much as 15 in Nuremberg with its thirteen mints. The destruction of trade from depreciation was particularly painful in the great Hanseatic cities, however, so that Hamburg and Lübeck took the lead in working toward stabilization, as early as 1619, followed in the next years by Bremen and the prince of Mecklenbürg (Opel 1866, pp. 229–30). Hamburg, it has been said, led the way to a fixed exchange rate in 1619 "against the fluctuating money of the other states" (Kellenbenz 1958, p. 254).

Proposals for a deposit bank had been advanced in Ulm in Schwabia, but in October 1619 quite a different bank was established, one to provide loans to the mint to buy gold and silver in Genoa (Schöttle 1922–24, p. 85). This was a function of the Venetian Banco del Giro established also in 1619 — Lane calls it "the purpose" (1973, p. 330). Along with Augsburg and Nuremberg, Ulm was closely connected with Venice (Lane 1944, p. 70), but it is not evident that Ulm drew the idea from there. In any event, Schöttle states that the bank in Ulm halted operations in the first quarter of 1620, and that the mint took over and coined the silver available in the local pawnshop.

The Bank of Nuremberg was founded in 1621 for the same reason as the Bank of Hamburg two years earlier — to stabilize the currency. It failed in this, however, possibly as a result of having to contend with much more in the way of bad moneys, from its thirteen mints as well as from the city's boundaries. As a result, the benefits of a good money had to wait two more years, to 1623, when the return to the Augsburg Imperial Ordinance of 1559 was finally achieved, restoring the weight and fineness of the coinage, oaths for mintmasters, visits of imperial assayers, coin-testing days, and the like, as stabilization spread from North to South. Lane claimed that "the type of giro-bank that Venice developed was widely imitated in the seventeenth century as in Amsterdam, Hamburg and Nuremberg" (1973, p. 330). This must refer to the Banca della Piazza di Rialto of 1587 rather than to the Banco del Giro of 1619, which was anterior to the Bank of Amsterdam and simultaneous with the Bank of Hamburg. The Banco di Rialto, it may be noted, however, was not designed to correct the circulation of debased coinage so much as to replace private banks that overissued deposits and drove bank money to a discount against coin. The Banks of Amsterdam and

Hamburg on the contrary produced a premium of bank money over coinage. The Bank of Nuremberg, as it happened, met the same fate as most of the primitive banks of deposit in Spain, being pressured to lend money to the state (or city) and ultimately being unable to make good its deposits in coin. This was at the height of the Thirty Years' War in the 1630s (Sieveking 1934, p. 133). The Bank of Amsterdam barely escaped this fate at the time of the French invasion of Holland in 1672, when the Bank of Hamburg was forced to close its doors temporarily. As already related, bankruptcy befell the Bank of Amsterdam a century later. Note that public banks were obliged to attempt to come to the rescue of the state in lender-of-last-resort operations. These proved fatal at a time when bank money was convertible into coin that could become exhausted. As similar operations developed in the nineteenth and twentieth centuries, however, they failed to harm the bank undertaking them either because the requirement of conversion was suspended, as in 1847, 1857, and 1866 in England, or because the central banks undertaking such lending had an infinite capacity to print banknotes.

A sharp contrast runs between the deposit and exchange banks of Italy, the United Provinces, and the Holy Roman Empire on the one hand, and the Bank of England established late in the century, on the other. Many migrants to Britain in the second half of the seventeenth century had recommended the establishment of deposit and exchange banks like those in Venice, Amsterdam, and Hamburg. The Bank of England differed, however. It did not accept deposits in debased coin, or take over the transfer of bills of exchange. Rather it made loans, largely to the state, and issued bank notes (Richards 1965, pp. 136–46).

The coinage of Great Britain had deteriorated in the period, despite the more complex passage of debased foreign coin across its borders because of the island location. In contrast to the *Kipper- und Wipperzeit,* as described by Macauley in a famous passage on 1660 at the start of the reign of James II, clipping was widespread (1906, 4:181ff.). Milled edges of coins were devised at the time to combat clipping, and the threat of hanging as a penalty. Feavearyear states that all classes clipped, filed, washed, and sweated good money, exported good, and imported base, albeit at greater cost than on the continent (1963, p. 5). By 1694 the coinage had become so bad that the public refused to accept it — as in the Holy Roman Empire in 1622. There followed a debate on whether to cry up the national value of the debased coin, or to call it in and recoin. The alternative of establishing a bank of deposit seems not to have arisen at that late date. In the debate with Lowndes for depreciation and Locke for recoinage, Locke won. A tax was levied on houses to cover the costs of minting. L. 5.5 million in clipped money was turned in and

L. 2.7 million of new coin produced from it (Li 1963). The loss was borne by the holders.

In sum, the Banks of Venice, Amsterdam, and Hamburg, said to be alike, were created for essentially different purposes: the Bank of Venice (Banco della Piazza di Rialto) to prevent credit expansion by private banks from debasing bank money relative to coin; the Bank of Amsterdam to correct excessive issue of coin by domestic mints (plus some importation of base coin); the Bank of Hamburg to halt the export of good coin and the intrusion of bad. To improve the domestic payment mechanism, and stabilize the unit of account, the Banks of Amsterdam and Hamburg added a requirement for clearing of bills of exchange, which assisted foreign payments and led to an agio of bank money over current coin. The banks of Middelburg, Delft, and Rotterdam were created entirely to assist in foreign-trade payments. Usher is restrictive in insisting that the essential function of a bank is in creating credit (1953, p. 3). In the seventeenth century banks sought to stabilize the unit of account and clearing payments. It was when they expanded credit that they found themselves in difficulty.

REFERENCES

Bisson, T. N. *Conservation of Coinage, Monetary Exploitation and Restraint in France, Catalonia and Aragon, c. 1000–1125 AD.* Oxford, 1979.
Boyer-Xambeu, M. T., G. Deleplace, and L. Gillard. *Monnaie privée et pouvoir des princes. L'économie des relations monétaires à la Renaissance.* Paris, 1986.
Feavearyear, A. *The Pound Sterling: A History of English Money.* 2d ed., revised by E. Victor Morgan. Oxford, 1965.
Gaettens, R. *Geschichte des Inflationen.* Minden, 1982.
Haley, K. H. D. *The Dutch in the Seventeenth Century.* New York, 1972.
Hamilton, E. J. *American Revolution and the Price Revolution in Spain, 1501–1650.* New York, 1934; reprint, 1965.
Heckscher, E. F. *An Economic History of Sweden.* Cambridge, Mass., 1954.
Israel, J. I. *Dutch Primacy in World Trade, 1585–1740.* New York, 1989.
Jones, C. Paper given at the 44th International Congress of Americanists, Manchester, England, 8 September 1982.
Kellenbenz, H. *Sephardim an der unteren Elbe: Ihre wirtschaftliche und politische Bedeutung von Ende des 16. his zum Beginn des 18. Jahrhunderts.* Wiesbaden, 1958.
Klein, P. W. "Little London: British Merchants in Rotterdam during the 17th and 18th Centuries." In D. C. Coleman and P. Mathias, eds., *Enterprise and History: Essays in Honour of Charles Wilson.* Cambridge, 1984. 116–34.
Lane, F. C. *Venice: A Maritime Republic.* Baltimore, 1973.

Li, M.-H. *The Great Recoinage of 1696–1699.* London, 1963.
Luzzatto, G. "Les Banques publiques de Venise (siècles XVI–XVIII)." In J. G. van Dillen, ed., *History of the Principal Public Banks.* London, 1934; reprint, 1964. 39–78.
Macauley, T. B. *History of England from the Accession of James II.* London, 1906–48.
Marlow, J. (pseudonym). *Spoiling the Egyptians.* London, 1974.
Opel, J. D. "Deutsche Finanznoth beim Beginn des dreissigjahrigen Krieges." *Historische Zeitschrift* 16 (1866): 213–68.
Redlich, F. *Die deutsche Inflation des frühen 17. Jahrhundert in Zeitgenössichen Literatur: Die Kipper und Wipper.* Cologne, 1972.
Richards, R. D. *The Early History of Banking in England.* London, 1965.
Sanches Sarto, M. "Les Banques Publiques en Espagne jusqu'à 1815." In J. G. van Dillen, ed., *History of the Principal Public Banks.* London, 1934; reprint, 1964. 1–14.
Sieveking, H. "Studio sulle finanze genovesi nel Medioevo e in particolare sulla Casa di San Giorgio." In *Atti della Società Ligure di Storia Patria.* Vol. 35. 1905–6.
Udovitch, Abraham L. "Bankers without Banks: Commerce, Banking and Society in the Islamic World of the Middle Ages." In Center for Medieval and Renaissance Studies, *The Dawn of Modern Banking.* New Haven, Conn., 1979. 255–74.

5

Free Minting

It is tempting as we honor the memory of Egon Sohmen to speculate on how he would have reacted to the current interest in "free banking." He was, of course, Austrian by birth, and the advocates of free banking are sometimes lumped together as the "Austrian School." He was, moreover, a fierce proponent of flexible exchange rates, and an opponent of fixed rates, strongly believing that exchange rates unaffected by intervention of monetary authorities would work smoothly — a view he might have modified had he lived to observe the rise of the dollar in the free market from 1982 to February 1985, its decline in the two subsequent years, and the gyrations since. If one had any faith in revealed preference, there would seem to have developed a revealed preference in governments for intervention after the disenchantment with free floating — not successful intervention perhaps, but some modest stability preferred to chaotic over- and undershooting.

It is possible to advocate flexible exchange rates but hold back from free banking, as does Milton Friedman. Egon Sohmen was in that camp, rather than an adherent of the Austrian school, which advocates both flexible exchange rates and free banking. Like Friedman, he may have wanted to abolish central banks, to be sure, while insisting on strict control of the money supply that requires some sort of government intervention or regulation. Friedman differed, as it happened, from Henry Simons, a Chicago monetarist, who would enforce 100 percent reserve money by making all capital apart from money take the form of equity in an effort to restrict the issue of private debt that could be used as money substitutes (1967). To go as far as Simons in restricting the money supply would go too far in Friedman's view in government intervention in private behavior. Sadly we do not know Egon Sohmen's view on this further point.

This essay originally appeared in Herbert Giersch, ed., *Money, Trade and Competition: Essays in Memory of Egon Sohmen* (Berlin et aliis: Springer-Verlag, 1992), pp. 11–22. Reprinted with permission of Springer-Verlag.

Free banking in developed countries is difficult to judge by contemporary experience, since there is none. Its advocates resort either to theory, as Friedrich A. Hayek (1976) and Roland Vaubel (1984) do, to economic history in the cases of Lawrence White (1984) and Eugene White (1990), or both (especially Selgin 1988). The theory rests on the belief that banks will work to gain acceptance for the (note or) deposit liabilities they issue, and will themselves restrict their amount. Banks that overissue will find their deposits discounted in the market. In this view, good money drives out bad, the opposite of the widely believed version of Gresham's law. Vaubel defends his position by claiming that Gresham's law in the ordinary view depends on fixed rates of conversion between different forms of money, whereas his model allows for the money of one bank to vary in price against the monies of others. But money is the one asset with a fixed price in terms of itself, and when the deposits of Bank A vary in price with those of Bank B, there is a problem whether one can call either of them money in a true sense, as opposed to non-interest- or interest-bearing securities. Under the 1860 National Bank Act in the United States, with no central bank, and on those occasions when the Treasury did not take over the role of lender of last resort, panics gave rise to the issuance of certificates by local clearinghouses — a system that Friedman has defended. Selgin, moreover, makes the clearinghouse a central institution for restraining banks from overissue (1988, pp. 28–29, 136, 137, etc.). During monetary troubles under the National Bank Act, the notes issued by the separate clearinghouses went to premia and discounts as wide as $10, $15, and $20 per $1,000 against New York, and of course possibly wider premia and discounts against one another (Sprague 1910, pp. 203ff, 291ff). In these circumstances it can be said that there was local money, but no national money. A system of free banking in a single country would appear to represent a flexible exchange network rather than a currency area.

It may happen theoretically that good money drives out bad, and as noted below this has occurred on occasion when the debasement of an existing money has gone so far that no one is willing to accept it and some new medium of exchange is required. I have hypothesized that normally bad money drives out good because the buyer chooses what money he or she will spend; in ordinary times buyers' markets prevail and buyers choose the currency in which the purchase is made. In this view, in sellers' markets, when goods are scarce, the seller could claim and gain the right to determine the currency of the bargain. But this is theory, with no historical agreement on when buyers' markets become sellers' markets and vice versa. A book on minting in parts of France and Spain in medieval times notes that many contracts specified the kind of currency to be used in fairly general terms: "best coin," "good coin," "money of legitimate weight," or mancuses (a coin) "of the best gold," "alternative payment in fine silver." In one area at a given time, it was exceptional "to designate payment in unspecified deniers or sous" (Bisson 1979, pp. 63–64, 67, 73–74, 79, 83). The history in which these phrases appear is largely devoted to minting as a service to the public, when debasement was rife and money was "conserved" or "confirmed" as good coin mainly by public payments to the King, prince, lord, or other minter to dissuade him from debasing his coinage, as was the general practice.

I offer a few paragraphs on modern history before turning to an episode in the currency disorders of early modern times in the German states, an episode that I find illuminating.

The history of so-called free banking in the United States is not relevant to the present discussion, since while there was free entry into banking, banking itself was regulated. From the Free Banking law of New York State of 1838 until the National Bank Act of 1860, many states adopted laws providing for "free banking." In all of them, however, the group starting a bank had to deposit specified securities with the state treasury up to the amount of the notes issued, dollar for dollar (Ng 1988). Wildcat banking occurred in Indiana and New Jersey under their laws because of mistakes made in the lists of securities eligible for deposit (Rockoff 1975, pp. 141–68). Ng claims on the basis of a great deal of evidence that this free-banking era failed to lower bank profits significantly, so that the freedom did not greatly increase entry.

I disregard this U.S. experience and turn to other historical episodes involving Scottish banking between 1772 and 1845 (L. White 1984), and the *caisses patriotiques* of the French revolution (E. N. White 1990).

The L. White book on free banking in Scotland between 1772 and 1845 has evoked a considerable literature. The basic question is whether it was in fact entirely free, or whether there were some limitations on banks in issuing notes. For one thing, three major banks exercised an informal control akin to central-bank surveillance in collecting the notes of each other and of smaller banks, and presenting them for conversion into coin or Bank of England notes when it was suspected that a particular bank was leaning toward overissue (Checkland 1975). The Second Bank of the United States behaved in the same fashion from its establishment until 1836, when President Andrew Jackson vetoed the renewal of its charter (Hammond 1957), ushering in the brief period of wildcat banking in Michigan before the "free-banking" period from 1838 to 1860. Secondly, with respect to the Scottish experience, the success of free banking is disputed on the ground that unlimited liability of the owners of banks exercised a restraining influence on overissue. Lawrence White's study starts after the failure of the Ayr bank in 1772, which ruined its stockholders, many of them Glaswegian "tobacco lords" (merchants who had become rich from the Maryland tobacco trade) who were obliged to sell their vast estates to make good the liabilities to depositors for which they were jointly and severally liable (Carr, Glied, and Mathewson 1989). The three leading banks that acted informally as a central bank in checking note issue, among themselves and by others — the Bank of Scotland, Royal Bank of Scotland, and the British Linen Company (all chartered by the Scottish Parliament) — did have limited liability. Others did not. White is aware of the limited-liability question but dismisses it as unimportant on the ground that when limited liability became available in 1862, the other banks did not adopt it immediately. Ng argues the contrary. The issue need not delay us, since both the note conversion practices of the three leading banks and unlimited liability make the case different from current proposals for free banking with no government regulation and only the general laws of limited liability.

Public acceptance of the notes issued in the 1790s by the *caisses patriotiques* of France fits my analysis of good money driving out bad when the bad money — in this case the *assignats* — becomes completely worthless. This is really not good money driving out bad, but some kind of money being sucked into the vacuum created by the collapse of existing money. It is not currency competition so much as the tendency of any system without money to create one, for example, the cigarette money of Allied prisoner-of-war camps in World War II. Another example is furnished by the rentenmark issued by the Rentenbank, which was created in Germany in the fall of 1923 when the mark became worthless. This has been cited as evidence that good money can drive out bad, by Vaubel (in a private letter), and by Bernholz (1989). The currency troubles of the early seventeenth century furnish more examples of new monies being created to fill the void left by collapse of the bad, but I have difficulty in regarding these cases as upsetting the ordinary interpretation of Gresham's law.

In this paper, I propose to examine another case, the so-called *Kipper- und Wipperzeit* in Germany which spilled over into parts of Europe more widely, mainly in 1619–23 at the outset of the Thirty Years' War. Minting in the Holy Roman Empire was not legally free. A series of sixteenth-century ordinances laid down the numbers of mints allowed to each "Circle," the weight and fineness of various coins, provisions for coin testing, oaths for mint masters, and the like. They were widely disregarded. One of the more authoritative historians of the period blames the depreciation and inflation on the weakness of the Imperial organization and control (Opel 1866). I shall start by sketching the institutional background.

The Holy Roman Empire was a "holding company" for a congeries of political units varying in size from the substantial, like Austria, Brandenberg, and Bavaria, through principalities, duchies, states ruled by counts, bishoprics, imperial cities, and Hanseatic cities, down to small cities. They were joined for monetary purposes with neighboring units into "Circles," often following ancient tribal boundaries like those of Swabia, Franconia, Westphalia, or such kingdoms as Burgundy. The Holy Roman Empire laid down the rules for minting, and for testing to see that the rules were obeyed. With the Reformation accomplished and the Counter-Reformation that culminated in the Thirty Years' War (from 1618 to 1648) looming on the horizon, the reigning authorities — nobility, church officials, city authorities, and even the Emperor — saw the need for more revenue to raise and equip their armies, largely of mercenaries, and to strengthen fortifications. Tax systems were rudimentary. It was difficult to increase domain rents in periods of bad harvest. One relatively easy means of acquiring revenue was to debase the currency, extracting greater seignorage.

There are several interesting aspects to the debasement. First, it was confined to subsidiary coins. Gold coins and the silver thaler (reichsthaler) were not debased, although they disappeared into hoards. The reichsthaler functioned in effect as a unit of account, against which to measure the depreciation of the lesser coins, most of which were originally silver. Merchants who used thalers and higher coins, and the mint owners or leasers, ended up with great fortunes in hoards, while the lower classes, using subsidiary coin, except for peasants living largely in the "natural" economy, were ruined, along with those on fixed incomes, like government officials, clerics, teachers, creditors repaid in debased coins, and political units without mints that collected taxes in depreciated money. Second, debasement in one political unit spread across state boundaries in "mosaic Germany," and over German borders into Poland and Denmark, indeed creating what was called a "commercial," as opposed to a monetary, crisis in Britain (Supple 1959). The degree of debasement differed from Circle to Circle, although it was generally greater in the upper (southern) Circles, and less in the lower ones, including the Hanseatic cities (Opel 1866, p. 231). Third, the crisis built up slowly long before the outbreak of the Thirty Years' War — from at least 1600 — and rose to panic proportions in Upper Saxony before the war had reached its territory. Moreover, stabilization was worked out with some difficulty in 1622 and achieved in 1623, decades before the end of the war, differing in this respect from the German inflations after World Wars I and II (Gaettens 1982, p. 91).

The mechanism for the spread of debasement was Gresham's law, bad money driving out good, and involved the activities of princes, mints, exchangers, and the common people. Adam Smith has described how small states are porous in monetary terms, with foreign coins circulating widely. He may have exaggerated the ability of Britain and France to control their own money (certainly if the remarks were meant to apply to the first half of the sixteenth century), but he understood exactly that juridical units with limited territory traded with their neighbors on an extensive scale and used foreign as well as domestic coins, without being exposed to the transactions costs of exchanging foreign for domestic money, or the converse, on every transaction. One nineteenth-century writer referred to the "monetary pathology of border regions" (*münzkranke Grenzlande*) (Opel 1866, p. 216). As late as 1816 at least seventy coins—from Holland, France, Belgium, and various German states—circulated in the Rhineland, while Prussian coins were rarely seen (Tilly 1966, p. 20). "The shortage of small coin suitable for paying wages was perhaps the most serious problem of all. Through the 1840s, at least, manufacturing areas in the Rhineland were supplying themselves with a motley collection of small silver and copper coins from all over Western Europe" (ibid., p. 22). Conversions were made from the coins of one country to another under these circumstances by means of a unit of account—often an "imaginary money" in that it was not actually coined, but a unit that required some sophistication in handling (Einaudi 1936, pp. 242–43). Even today, it is suspected that $180 billion in U.S. currency issued in excess of estimated normal needs in the United States circulates largely abroad, in the drug trade, other illegal traffic, and as parallel currency in countries with currency troubles (*New York Times,* 1990).

It is difficult in the literature on the *Kipper- und Wipperzeit* to determine exactly where the debasement of the wide variety of subsidiary coins originated. On one showing, the bad money started pouring into southern Germany from Italy and Switzerland with the entry point at Lindau on Lake Constance (Schöttle 1922–24, pp. 70–80). The same account, however, mentioned that the counterfeiting of the Upper Rhine Circle that included Strassburg was particularly aggravating to the southern circles of Bavaria, Swabia, and Franconia. The important point, however, is that wherever it started it spread from one state or city to the adjoining territories.

The mechanism ran as follows: a prince, elector, duke, count, abbot, bishop, or whoever needed more funds, would seek to increase his seignorage by a slight debasement. The numbers of mints grew, some officially owned by the state, some leased to private individuals against payment to the state authority or authorities. With rentals, the mint operator added his profit to that of the seigneur. After a time, counterfeiting added to the debasement. Light coins would be taken abroad and exchanged for heavier coins, either at fairs or in exchange booths set up in cities and towns. The good coins would be brought back to the original mint for recoinage into a greater nominal value of debased coins. In due course, the neighboring territory found it necessary to take steps to stop the loss of its circulating medium. One such defense was to debase its own coins. Thus the debasement and counterfeiting spread from one state to another, crossing into Poland (Bogucka 1975) and elsewhere. The debasement in Bohemia accelerated in 1622 after the Emperor leased minting rights for Bohemia, Moravia, and Lower Austria to a consortium for 6 million gulden a year. In the first two months before a great decline in confidence in the coins occurred, the consortium minted 30 million gulden of new coin, and in the next ten months twelve million gulden (Klima 1978). Klima insists that the Bohemian inflation of 1621–23 was *unconnected* (his emphasis) with the general European economic situation of the time, calling attention to the particular features of the Czech situation, such as the uprising of the Protestant estates and their defeat and confiscation by the Catholic forces. It is difficult, however, to accept such a conclusion when everywhere else on the Continent debasement was spreading, and, as Klima himself says (ibid., p. 376), light foreign coins were penetrating Bohemia.

Most of the literature on the *Kipper- und Wipperzeit* is restricted to given states and Circles, with the richest detail available for Upper and Lower Saxony (Redlich 1972; Wuttke 1916; Opel 1866). An attempt had been made by the Emperor in 1603 and 1604 to limit the number of mints to four to a Circle (except for states with silver mines), but the effort was opposed by the Lower Saxon Circle, in which there were six existing mints in Bremen, Hamburg, Lubeck, Rostock, Brunswick, and Magdeburg. This allowed other towns with minting privileges to establish further ones, and even encourage those without privileges to follow suit (Gaettens 1982, p. 75). In Brunswick, where 17 mints had existed in 1620, there were 40 in all by 1623, including a converted convent with 300 to 400 workers (Langer 1978, p. 80). The Duke of Weimar leased out 10 mints at 600–800 gulden weekly (Opel 1866, p. 224).

The imperial ordinance providing for mint assayers in each Circle, and Coin Testing Days, fell by the wayside. One General Assayer, Rentzsch, observed that the debasement was particularly acute in the

Upper Saxon Circle and that some mints kept supplies of good groschen on hand to show the Assayer on his periodic visits (Wuttke 1916, p. 136).

Numerous measures were undertaken to halt the cross-border traffic in good and bad coin—good out and bad in—but to little effect. Especially on market days, it was impossible to halt the carts and examine packages. Some towns and principalities tried jawboning, warning the lower classes against the exchangers, who often included lawyers, doctors, Jews, and even women; forbidding transactions of money against money, as opposed to money against goods (Opel 1866, p. 224); and threatening the exchangers with punishment ranging from confiscation of the coins and all the exchangers' goods to mutilation (cutting off a hand), death, and burning at the stake. At the height of the inflation set in motion by the debasement and the ultimate refusal of producers to sell for the debased money, riots broke out in various cities, involving several hundred participants and ending in deaths of some rioters. The populace blamed the mint masters and the exchangers, especially the Jews, but most historians writing on the subject denounce the princes, dukes, counts, abbots, city authorities, and the like that sought to increase their incomes by further seignorage. One account suggests, however, that the traffic of the period lacked sufficient means of exchange in the light of a protracted monetary famine and inadequate development of credit and banks (Opel 1866, p. 222).

One defense against debased currency was the establishment of deposit banks. These received deposits of coin that was assayed and weighed, and a receipt was issued for a specific amount. The system had developed slowly in Spain and Italy (Usher 1943), but made its way north when the Bank of Amsterdam was established in the early stages of the *Kipper- und Wipperzeit*. The proposal was put forward in 1606 and the Bank opened its doors in 1609. A second Dutch bank was established along the same lines at Middleburg in Holland in 1616, two more at Hamburg and Venice in 1619, and two further ones at Delft and Nuremberg in 1621, at the height of the debasement. The Swabian Circle proposed the establishment of a bank of deposit in the fall of 1619, but the project was altered to make it a fund to buy silver in Genoa to induce the local mint to overcome the shortage in southern Germany (Schöttle 1922–24, p. 85). The Bank of Amsterdam started as a 100 percent reserve bank, with the costs defrayed by a small charge on transactions, later took on the role of an exchange bank (*wisselbank*) to monopolize the discharge of bills of exchange in international trade over a certain sum, and ultimately, a century and a half later, made loans to the city of Amsterdam, which was making good the losses of the Dutch East India Company, and was bankrupted. Its start, and that of those that followed up to 1621, was to provide an acceptable means of payment during the monetary disorders.

On other than a local level, effective stabilization for distant trade, however, had to wait for acute inflation and a virtually complete breakdown of trade and payments. The working classes and others who had been exploited in the early stages of debasement, giving up their good coins for progressively worse ones, finally proved unwilling to accept them where they had any choice. Goods stopped coming to the market, as in the spring of 1947 in the western zones of Germany. Government accounts could no longer be kept (Friedrichs 1979). Children played with "tinsel money" in the street (Langer 1978, p. 30). The reichsthaler, which had risen in price from 1 fl 12 kreuzer (out of 60 to a florin or gulden) in 1596 (on average, with considerable variance among regions, and thus far inadequately studied) to 1 fl 32 krz in 1618, reached 2 fl 20 krz at the end of 1620, 6 fl 30 krz in December 1621, and 10 fl in March 1622 (Shaw 1895, p. 103). The variance was wide: In Leipzig, for example, the reichsthaler was worth 9 to 12 gulden in September 1623, in Gotha, 15 gulden in June 1622. In Nurnberg it went from 13 gulden 30 krz in January 1622 to 16 gulden 30 krz in February of the same year (Opel 1866, p. 233).

The stabilization process, during the early stages of the Thirty Years' War, as already noted, took place slowly and piecemeal. It started in 1619, as the northern cities, which centuries before had been linked in a Wendish monetary union, tried to organize to halt the debasement and restore the currency to its old basis. Similar efforts were pursued in the South among the Swabian, Franconian, and Bavarian Circles. A number of mints stopped producing debased coins in 1622 when it proved impossible to get the populace to accept them. Gradually stabilization was achieved piecemeal, and spread. When the process was well along, in June 1623, the Elector of Saxony appointed a commission to make recommendations on currency policy. This commission furnished him a 26-page memorandum the next day, outlining a return to the Imperial Ordinance of 1559, a step taken shortly thereafter, including the reinstitution of the Mint Testing Days, which had been allowed to lapse for five years (Gaettens 1978, pp. 92–93). Shaw states that a great imperial deputation was convened in 1623 to establish the final return to the Augsburg Ordinance of 1559, but this is not treated in the German histories that I have seen. Opel lists the various ordinances bringing back the standards of the Augsburg Ordinance, one in September 1621, 10 in 1622, 10 in 1623, and the last, the first action of the Emperor Ferdinand II, in February 1624 (Opel 1866, pp. 261–62).

All accounts of the process emphasize that while there were safe-guards that sought to prevent currency debasement — limitations of mints, oaths of mint masters, Coin Testing Days, prohibitions against coin traffic, official assayers, and the like — they were essentially unen-forced and in the case of traffic unenforceable. While most histories, moreover, lay the blame on the rules of the states and cities, Opel (1866), whose account is said to be "surprisingly reliable" (Redlich 1972, p. 10 n), is virtually alone in observing that growing trade created a shortage of coins — comparable to the bullion famine of the fifteenth century (Day 1978) — and especially in the "limitless domination of Terri-torialismus in trade" (*schrankenlose Herrschaft des Territorialismus im Verkehrsleben*) (1866, p. 266). In a long passage he excoriates the battle of all against all, cities trying to increase their profits at the expense of their neighbors, the lack of territorial organization and of strong central authority. There was, he claimed, too much interest in short-run gains, and the old feudal territorial organization lacked strong ties of authority (ibid., pp. 264–68). The same theme is echoed in 1990 in a discussion of the unification in Europe:

> Centralism has never been a German strong point; it was never more than a Prussian forte. Federalism is the German tradition, from the Hanseatic League via German Confederation to the Federal Republic of Germany. (Buschmann 1990)

The Austrian School of free banking believes that banks will restrict deposit growth in their long-run interest, seeking to build a strong money to gain acceptance, to cultivate reputations for prudence and care. The school, and especially Vaubel, deny that money as a unit of account is a public good that can be underproduced by free riders con-cerned primarily with short-run profits. They ignore the record of eco-nomic innocence, especially of the laboring classes, which were taken advantage of by the unscrupulous, and the widely agreed necessity for government to establish standards in measuring goods sold at retail to protect the naive from venal traders. Like many in the field of public choice, they believe that private choices are made with intelligence and after consideration of long-run benefits, while public choices are venal, in the interests of the officials themselves.

One could perhaps argue that the disaster of the *Kipper- und Wipperzeit,* which I have treated more generally in another paper (Kin-dleberger 1995), was the result of bad public choices by the authorities in the various states. But the central authority was so weak that it was unable to look after the public good, and the large number of territories with minting privileges ensured that no one else but the Emperor was in charge. The abundant free riders infected one another, like a security market in a bubble. The inflation and debasement were halted when the stronger northern and southern states organized themselves to enforce established standards.

Good money driving out bad did occur, but only as in 1792 and 1923 when the old good money had become so depreciated as to be worthless. What works in crisis cannot be elevated into an algorithm for adoption on trend. I conclude that free minting in a world of small states with no one in charge was — and by analogy, free banking unrestrained by regulation would be — a disaster. One could cite the experience of the Savings and Loan Associations in the United States following the deregulation of 1986.

I would hope that this seventeenth-century experience with free minting would persuade Peter Bernholz and Roland Vaubel to join Egon Sohmen in recognizing the need to have some sort of public control of the money supply, as opposed to free banking. I have explained elsewhere that there may still be inflationary bubbles under such a system, as the market monetizes credit beyond that decreed by government, but short-run profit making will go much further to destabilize the system under free minting or unregulated free banking.

REFERENCES

Bernholz, Peter. 1989. "Currency Competition, Inflation, Gresham's Law and Exchange Rate." *Journal of Institutional and Theoretical Economics* 145 (3): 465–88.
Bogucka, Maria. 1975. "The Monetary Crisis of the XVIIth Century and Its Social and Psychological Consequences in Poland." *Journal of European History* 4/1 (spring): 137–52.
Buschmann, Günter, 1990. "All Lights Are Green at the Gateway to Europe." *The German Tribune,* no. 1405, 28 January, 6. A summary translation from the German in *Deutsche Allgemeine Sonntagsblatt,* Hamburg, 19 January 1990.
Carr, Jack, Sherry Glied, and Frank Mathewson. 1989. "Unlimited Liability and Free Banking in Scotland: A Note." *Journal of Economic History* 49 (4): 974–78.
Checkland, S. G. 1975. *Scottish Banking: A History, 1695–1973.* Glasgow: Collins.
Day, John. 1978. "The Great Bullion Famine of the Fifteenth Century." *Past and Present* 79:3–54.
Einaudi, Luigi. 1936. "The Theory of Imaginary Money from Charlemagne to the French Revolution." Reprinted in translation in F. C. Lane and J. C.

Riersma, eds., *Enterprise and Secular Change,* Homewood, Ill.: R. D. Irwin, 1953. 229–61.

Friedman, Milton. 1967. "The Monetary Theory and Policy of Henry Simons." *Journal of Law and Economics* 10 (October): 1–13.

Friedrichs, Christopher R. 1979. *Urban Society in an Age of War: Nördlingen, 1580–1720.* Princeton, N.J.: Princeton University Press.

Gaettens, Richard. 1982. *Geschichte der Inflationen.* 2d ed. Minden.

Hammond, Bray. 1957. *Banks and Politics in America.* Princeton, N.J.: Princeton University Press.

Hayek, Friedrich A. 1976. *Choice in Currency: A Way to Stop Inflation.* London: Institute of Economic Affairs.

Kindleberger, Charles P. 1995. "The Economic Crisis of 1619 to 1623." In Charles P. Kindleberger, *World Economy and National Finance in Historical Perspective.* Ann Arbor: University of Michigan Press. 201–29.

Klima, A. 1978. "Inflation in Bohemia in the Early Stages of the Seventeenth Century." In Michael Flinn, ed., collection of papers, *Seventh International Economic History Congress,* Edinburgh.

Langer, Herbert. 1978. *Kulturgeschichte des 30 Jährigen Krieges.* Leipzig.

The New York Times. 1990. "$180 Billion in U.S. Currency Eludes Tally; Is It Abroad?" 20 February, pp. D.1, D.4.

Ng, Kenneth. 1988. "Free Banking Laws and Barriers to Entry, 1838–1860." *Journal of Economic History* 48/4 (December): 877–90.

Opel, J. O. 1866. "Deutsche Finanznoth beim Beginn dreissigjährigen *Krieges.*" *Historische Zeitschrift* 16:213–68.

Redlich, Fritz. 1972. *Die deutsche Inflation des frühen 17. Jahrhundert in der zeitgenössischen Literatur: Die Kipper und Wipper.* Cologne: Böhlau Verlag.

Rockoff, Hugh. 1975. *The Free Banking Era: A Re-examination.* Salem, N.H.: Ayer.

Schöttle, Gustav. 1922–24. "Münz- und Geldgeschichte von Ulm im ihren Zusammenhang mit derjenigen Schwabens." *Würtembergische Viertelsjahreshefte für Landesgeschichte,* Neue Folge, no. 31:54–128.

Selgin, George A. 1988. *The Theory of Free Banking: Money Supply under Competitive Note Issue.* Totowas, N.J.: Roman and Littlefield.

Shaw, William A. 1895. *The Monetary Movements of 1600–1621 in Holland and Germany,* Transactions of the Royal Historical Society, new series, vol. 9. London: Longmans, Green. 189–213.

Smith, Adam. 1776. *An Inquiry into the Nature and Causes of the Wealth of Nations.* Cannan ed. New York: Modern Library, 1937.

Sprague, O. M. W. 1910. *History of Crises under the National Banking System.* New York: Kelley, 1968.

Supple, Barry E. 1959. *Commercial Crisis and Change in England, 1600–1642.* Cambridge: Cambridge University Press.

Tilly, Richard. 1966. *Financial Institutions and Industrialization in the Rhineland, 1815–1870.* Madison, Wisc.: University of Wisconsin Press.

Usher, A. P. 1943. *The Early History of Deposit Banking in Mediterranean Europe.* Cambridge, Mass.: Harvard University Press.

Vaubel, Roland. 1984. "The Government's Money Monopoly: Externalities or Natural Monopoly." *Kyklos* 37 (fasc. 1): 27–58.

White, Eugene N. 1990. "Free Banking during the French Revolution." *Explorations in Economic History* 27:251–76.

White, Lawrence H. 1984. *Free Banking in Britain: Theory, Experience and Debate, 1800–1845.* Cambridge: Cambridge University Press.

Wuttke, Robert. 1916. "Zur Kipper- und Wipperzeit in Kursachsen." *Neues Archiv für Sächsische Geschichte und Altertumskunde* 15:119–56.

6

Economic and Financial Crises and Transformation in Sixteenth-Century Europe

I

Financial revolutions in Europe have been ascribed to the Italian innovation of the bill of exchange in the thirteenth and fourteenth centuries, and to the British ordering of government debt at the end of the seventeenth and beginning of the eighteenth. Some attention, but less, has been paid to the series of crises and transformations of the sixteenth century focused especially on the 1550s, with at least five broad and parallel changes in national and international finance:

1. in money, from gold to silver, and in the seventeenth century to copper;
2. in fairs, from merchants dealing mainly in goods to fairs of merchant bankers, specializing in finance;
3. in trade, a shift of primacy from the Mediterranean to the Atlantic and the North Sea;
4. in banking, from the Age of the Fuggers to the Age of the Genoese; and
5. in finance more generally, the increasing sophistication of capital markets and credit instruments.

The century was one of discoveries, wars, and financial crises which acted as catalysts to financial change. The changes were wider than financial, to be sure. One prominent historian observes that in the fifteenth century, innovation was an unfamiliar and suspect idea, but that with the spread of printing and the vernacular to accompany the shrinking Latin, innovation and change abounded in the sixteenth century. The age teemed with innovators in cultural, religious, and scientific life including such figures as Calvin, Copernicus, Galileo, Luther, Mercator, Montaigne, Rabelais, and Shakespeare. This essay is restricted, however, to economics and finance in which change and innovation were copious enough.

II

The fifteenth century was characterized by a scarcity of precious metals in Europe called a bullion famine (Day 1978 [1987]), especially acute in small coins used by working people in daily life. Some shopkeepers extended credit to customers in the form of "tallies," notched sticks, split between tradesman and customer. Jacquet Coeur, the renowned French merchant, is reported (twice) to have been unable to sell goods from his fully laden galley in Valencia in 1451 because its inhabitants had no acceptable money (North 1994, pp. 41, 66).

Gold came to Europe from the Sudan, first across the desert mostly to Alexandria where it was traded with Venice, later, after the Age of Discovery, up the Atlantic Coast of West Africa in Portuguese ships. In one estimate, the gold arriving annually amounted to 700 kg at the beginning of the sixteenth century (ibid., p. 74). In an age of pestilence, war, and quarrels, hoarding was rational, whether as merchants' capital, ecclesiastical treasure, or Gresham-law hoards. In addition, the melting pot, losses at sea, and ordinary wear and tear in hand-to-hand circulation reduced the supply of money in precious metals by 2 or 3 percent a year for gold coins, 4 to 5 percent for silver and copper (ibid., pp. 109–10). North records a sharp decline in the monetary use of gold between the middle of the fifteenth century and the second half of the sixteenth, though the numbers, all moving in the same direction, show varying degrees of decline from region to region, in tax collections, bequests, and gold hoards discovered later (ibid., pp. 85–86).

The European money supply rose at the beginning of the sixteenth century as the Fuggers obtained control of gold mines in Hungary, silver mines in Tyrol and the Erzgebirge. Gross additions exceeded net, as the Fuggers early in the century sent silver to Venice, whence it was shipped to the Levant to purchase luxury goods — pepper, spices, silk — and in part to exchange for gold which was cheaper in the eastern Mediterranean than in Europe. As production rose, however, more and more was sent to the Spanish Netherlands, along with copper and brass to pay for woolens and to exchange for Portuguese spices brought from the Far East and Spanish gold. Silver production in central Europe reached its peak in the 1530s and declined thereafter. As it declined, German miners emigrated to England, Ireland, France, Spain, and the New World (Vilar 1969 [1976], p. 169; Spooner 1972, p. 25; Brandi 1939, p. 337).

Spooner records the number of these skilled miners going to Ireland as 400; Brandi and Vilar (loc. cit., p. 107) note that the miners going to the Americas included 24 for San Domingo, financed by the Welsers, bankers from Nuremberg.

North estimates that Central European silver output doubled between 1470 and 1520 and rose further with the new mine at Joachimstal in the 1520s, before declining sharply in the following decade (1994, text and table, p. 71). Then came a mass of gold from the New World — 60 tons from 1492 to 1550, funneled by the Spanish and Portuguese to Bruges, Antwerp, and Florence, where mints switched over from silver to gold (ibid., p. 74). This was booty, not new production; production, when it started, was in silver. The silver mountain at Potosí in Peru (modern Bolivia) was discovered in 1545. Originally worked with mercury (needed for the amalgam process) from Almadén in Spain, controlled by the Fuggers from a concession granted as collateral for loans to Charles V, its production rose sharply in the 1560s when mercury deposits were discovered in Huancavelica in the Andes in 1563. Imports into Seville reached peaks in 1580 to 1585 and 1590–1600 (Vilar 1965 [1976], chaps. 14 and 15). Tables of silver imports into Europe are given in Hamilton (1934, p. 34), Attman (1986), and Morineau (1985). It is generally recognized that Hamilton's estimates understate imports for the early years of the seventeenth century, as he counted only those imports recorded by the official Casa de la Contratación in Seville, and missed out on smuggling, landings at Lisbon, and specie loaded by Dutch and English East India ships directly in Cadiz, without letting it get upstream to Seville. In addition considerable silver went from Peru to Acapulco in Mexico between 1573 and 1815, and thence to the Philippines in the "Manila Galleon" — between two and three million pesos a year by 1590, reaching 12 million in 1597 (Borah 1954, p. 123). In Manila it was used to buy silk brought there by Chinese merchants.

How much specie remained in Spain, how much in other Europe, and how much was carried to the east are questions for which definitive answers have not been provided. Attman estimates silver imports into Europe of about 260 tons a year, and exports of 114 tons, about 1600, leaving a surplus of about 150 tons. North retains the second figure, lowers the first to 220 tons, and estimates a net accretion to European silver stocks of about 100 million annually at the end of the sixteenth century (North 1994, p. 79 and n. 23, p. 217). Royal edicts required imports to be registered at the Casa de la Contratación, where the royal tax of one-fifth was collected. When the Spanish silver fleet arrived, Seville had liquid funds in prodigious abundance, followed shortly by a scarcity as the specie spread over Spain, Europe as a whole, and was shipped eastward (Braudel and Spooner 1953, p. 288). While Seville was perhaps more volatile monetarily than other European cities,[1] the latter also alternated between easy and tight money (ibid.).[2]

Loans to Charles V and Philip II earned not only interest but also permission to export silver, as did especially *asientos*, bills drawn on Lyons and especially Antwerp to pay troops, Spanish and German mercenaries fighting in the Spanish Netherlands against the French, or to put down revolt. The "Dover Road" went by ship to the English channel and Antwerp, cut off, however, when England was at war with Spain. The "Spanish Road" consisted in shipping silver in galleys from Barcelona to Genoa, converting it to gold, taken by mule pack train through Piedmont, Savoy, and Franche-Comté, and Lorraine to the Spanish Netherlands (Parker 1972, p. 59). Other routes led from Spain to Nantes through France to the Spanish Netherlands, a safe conduct given on the proviso that one-third of the specie remain in France (Lapeyre 1953, p. 25). Lapeyre also notes some shipments to Rouen by Simon Ruiz where one could obtain better rates, especially after 1586 (ibid., p. 455).

In his classic study of monetary movements in France from the voyage of Columbus to the setting of the price of the livre in gold in 1726 after the Mississippi bubble, Frank Spooner holds that France was not unified monetarily. Silver circulated in the west after the middle of the sixteenth century — gold coin before — and copper in the east, infiltrating from Germany. With monetary troubles in 1540 to 1550, silver testons, the nominal equivalent of the English shilling, were converted to copper money (1972, pp. 4–43). At one stage in the transition, the merchants of Lyons insisted that two-thirds of every payment, especially of bills of exchange at fairs, be made in gold (ibid., p. 98), echoing a similar order of Charles V in Spain in the 1530s. This latter lasted only a month as it crippled Spanish trade with the Brabant and Flanders (ibid., p. 133).

Maria-Therèse Boyer-Xambeu, Ghislain Delaplace, and Lucien Gillard make a sharp distinction between bills of exchange, private money traded at fairs, and coins which were royal money (1986).[3] They recognize, however that while, in principle, only the king has the right to coin precious metals, in practice he farmed out this privilege, as was also the case in the exploitation of the royal domain and tax collection, because kings, apart from Prussia, had only limited bureaucratic staff.[4] Achieving a central monopoly of the coinage took two centuries. Moreover national borders were porous, and foreign coins circulated freely. A French edict of 1557 counted 190 coins of different sovereigns in use in the country (ibid., p. 70).

From time to time, kings would debase the coinage to gain seignorage, especially in time of war. Henry VIII of England started to debase the currency on a small scale as war broke out in 1542 between England and Scotland — along with confiscating goods, church property, and imposing forced loans. When the fighting extended to France in 1544 the debasement was extended, and after his death in 1547 went still further under his successor, Edward VI. From 1544 to 1551, the resulting seignorage amounted to £1,270,000, as the price of silver at the mints was raised from £2/8/8 per ounce to £4/8/0, and that of gold from £27/16/5 to £37/1/10. The seignorage gained was £1,270,000. On May 15, 1550, seignorage had covered more than one-third of the war's total cost of £3,500,000 (Challis 1878, pp. 253–54). Revaluation was undertaken in October 1551 to £3/5/2 for silver and £36 for gold, and once again, back to the 1543 levels in 1559 under Elizabeth I (Gould 1970, p. 11). The economic literature offers something of a debate, whether the debasement of the English coinage, resulting in depreciation of the exchange rates against the Low Countries, had a major impact on English exports, but this need not detain us. Of interest is that the Holy Roman Empire, in an ordinance of Charles V at Augsburg, devalued the gold taler in 1551. A further adjustment took place in 1559 and served as the standard to which the Empire returned in 1623, following the progressive debasement since 1600 in anticipation of the Thirty Years' War (Kindleberger 1991 [1995], p. 262). "Many princes in the sixteenth and seventeenth centuries did a roaring business in currency depreciation and sale of offices to raise money" (Ehrenberg 1896 [1928], p. 31).

The weight of the groat of the Spanish Netherlands had been reduced in 1520 from 0.49 grams of silver to 0.42 grams. In 1548 as supplies of silver from the New World began to increase, the value of gold against silver rose. In 1551 another adjustment of the groat took place, to 0.40 grams of silver. By the time of the Treaty of Westphalia in 1648, it was down to 0.25 grams (van Houtte 1977, p. 422). Similar adjustments took place all over Europe. Earl Hamilton claims that Charles V and Philip II of Spain resisted debasement, but the succession of financial crises affecting that country — 1557, 1575, 1598, 1607, 1627, and 1657 — and shortages of silver, led Castile to blacken its coinage with copper in a compound called *vellon* (*billon* in France) (1934, chaps. 3, 4). Hamilton observes that many economists at the time thought that debasement was unobjectionable for gold and vellon, but could be the ruin of commerce if undertaken for silver (ibid., p. 67).

There were difficult problems of getting the relative prices of gold, silver, and copper coins right as relative supplies kept changing and various mints adapted to them with longer and shorter lags. Gresham's law was kept busy. Undervalued coins would be hoarded, melted down, exported. Overvalued coins would be spent, and exchanged for gold coin where sophisticated dealers could take advantage of naive people. In addition to the problems with full-weight coins, there were counterfeiting, clipping (until milled edges in the second half of the seventeenth century), rubbing, and sweating (shaking good coins in a bag to collect the dust) (Challis 1978, p. 275). Adjustments in the gold/silver ratio were continuous. In Castile, the bimetallic ratio, decreed legally at the mint, stood at 10.11 to one between 1496 and 1536, 10.61 to one from 1537 to 1565, followed by one major step to 12.12 to one in 1566, and another in 1609 to 13.3 to one (Hamilton 1934, p. 71). The pioneering quantity theorist, Jean Bodin, favored 12 to one because he believed in the harmony of numbers (Vilar 1969 [1976], p. 173; and Spooner 1972, p. 94). Six, divisible by 1, 2, and 3, was the perfect number; double it and one gets 12. But as sometimes happens, theory was overtaken by events. Boyer-Xambeau, Deleplace, and Gillard provide a table of bimetallic ratios in Europe, and the differences between the highest and the lowest. Most countries show changed ratios between 1550 and 1560 — but not Spain, Portugal, or Milan; and England with Elizabeth's revaluation in 1559 went from 11.1 to 13.3, the highest number in the table except for Venice at 14 in 1600 (1986, p. 230).

The shift from gold money in the first half of the century to silver in the second was less important than the inflation, or so-called price revolution. Debate over its causes started with the controversy between Malestroit and Jean Bodin, and continues to the present day (Fischer 1996, pp. 70–91). Like Bodin, Hamilton ascribed the rise in prices in the sixteenth century to the rise in the money stock coming from silver from the New World. Later historians lay the beginnings, at least, to demographic factors, especially the fact that population growth recovered after the Black Death of 1348 more rapidly than agricultural production (Outhwaite 1989; North 1990, chaps. 6, 7). The case against the quantity theory is that prices started to rise well before the massive imports of silver from Peru and Mexico in the 1550s and 1560s, and rose higher in basic foodstuffs than in industrial goods and wages. North offers a telling comparison of the decades 1561–70 and 1511–20 for prices on the Baltic South Coast: grain up 274 percent, other foodstuffs 161 percent, industrial goods 119 percent, and wages 81 percent, with commercial and other property between these last two numbers (1990, p. 225). His estimate of the rise in the money supply from 1510 to 1570 is 22 percent, leaving out, of course, unknown amounts of bills of exchange and other forms of credit (ibid., p. 226). The turning point when prices started to rise differed from market to market, but occurred mostly in the first half of the century, and frequently in 1515, 1520, or 1525, well before the massive flow of silver from the New World to the Continent (ibid., chap. 6).[5]

While the second half of the sixteenth century saw a major shift of money from gold to silver, there is another view that the role of specie has been exaggerated as compared with that of credit. Specie was required for certain payments, notably the wages of mercenary soldiers, for settlement of a portion of balances at fairs within Europe, and for net imports from the eastern Baltic, the Mediterranean, and the Far East. Vilar quotes a Spanish sixteenth-century source stating that the fair at Medina del Campo was a factory for contracts, but with never a coin traded there (1969 [1976], p. 146). This brings us to the transformation of European fairs from dealers in goods to those mainly involved in finance.

III

Fairs started out to accommodate foreign merchants who were granted special legal protection during the period of a fair which they were not otherwise entitled to. They were held for days or a few weeks at specific times, some twice, some three, some four times a year. The earliest were those in the Champagne country of France in the twelfth and thirteenth centuries, dealing largely in British wool and Flemish woolen cloth. Regular procedures were developed, starting with a set number of days for cloth, then leather, later goods of weight (*avoirs du poids*), such as metals, followed by days for settlement. In settlements, each merchant would cast up a balance of what he had bought from and sold to whom, and receive or pay the balance, first as a rule in coin, increasingly in bills of exchange drawn on another place and/or the next fair. In due course, especially in the sixteenth century, trade in bills of exchange, usually for three months "usance," took over from dealing in goods. Borrowers and lenders, including agents of rulers among the former, would attend fairs to deal in credit instruments.

The fairs of Spain were dominated by that at Medina del Campo, although bills were traded in significant amounts at Burgos. The fair at Bruges in the fifteenth century lost out to Antwerp in the sixteenth. The latter started with two fairs a year for goods, and took over two from Bergen-op-Zoom, the Antwerp foreport, which specialized in finance. In the middle of the century, Antwerp followed Bruges in building a bourse, named after the house of one Burs in Bruges where financial trading had concentrated. The Antwerp Bourse was entirely devoted to finance, the English Merchant Adventurers selling their cloth in an open-air market near the docks. Sir Thomas Gresham built the Royal Exchange in London in 1566 on the pattern of the Antwerp Bourse.

Stapling, the concentrated selling of commodities, took place in other countries separate from fairs. The British Merchants of the Staple (wool) located at Calais moved in 1559 to Le Havre, as has been mentioned. In Spain, wool was traded by Spanish merchants at Burgos, accessible to the export port of Bilbao on the Bay of Biscay. British merchants sold goods for export to the New World at San Lucar, a foreport of Seville, which even had an English church (Kellenbenz 1970, p. 336).

The role of foreign merchants in Spain has been studied in a symposium in Cologne, edited and with a long overview by Herman Kellenbenz (1970). There was movement. Trade in Alicante and Valencia had been dominated by Germans, Florentines, and Venetians in the fifteenth century, but they were eclipsed and overtaken by the Genoese in the sixteenth century (Lapeyre 1970, p. 112). There were three northern groups in Seville before 1566: British and Dutch, lumped together, Bretons, and Hanseatics; about 1570 as silver from the New World arrived in great quantities, the Genoese merchant-bankers took over, financing trade to America, asientos for the Spanish Netherlands, and acquiring licenses to export silver (Berthe 1970, p. 241). The Spanish in Seville found themselves reduced to commission agents, without risk. Kellenbenz raises, but fails to answer, the question whether foreign merchants limited Spanish growth in the second half of the sixteenth century (1970, p. 349).

Some foreign merchants were settled in Spain; some like the Flemish came only for the fairs. While there was an English house in Antwerp, some 600 Merchant Adventurers came for at least one fair a year (van Houtte 1977, p. 178). As trade changed, so did the numbers of merchants: there were only 12 Portuguese merchants in Antwerp in 1526, 97 in 1570, when Portuguese exports of spices, olive oil, southern fruit, and especially salt from Setubal, that displaced Biscay salt from Bourgneuf in France, were flourishing (ibid., pp. 176–77). In 1551, there were 38 firms found in the Genoese nation in Antwerp, 23 "Lombard" [*sic*], 20 Luccan, and 13 Florentines (ibid., p. 181).[6] While the Spanish were outdone at home by foreign merchants, Spanish merchants in Antwerp rose from 200 in 1553–54 to 300 by 1560 (Lynch 1964, p. 272). Late in the century, a significant contrast ran between Antwerp with mostly foreign merchants, distributing luxury goods and English woolens, and Amsterdam dealing in bulk goods — herring, grain, and salt — with native-born dealers (van Houtte 1977, p. 186).

Fairs did not stay put. Francis I of France first attracted the Genoese nation from Geneva to Lyons, then pushed it out to Besançon in the Franche-Compté, from which it moved by stages to Piacenza outside

Genoa, though it kept the Italianized version of the Bensançon name as Bisenzone. The Merchant Adventurers persuaded the English government to drive the rival Hanseatic merchants trading in woolens from the Steelyard in London. They were first ejected in 1552, allowed to return in 1553, but finally driven away in 1556 (deRoover 1949, p. 221). When England found itself in a trade war with Margaret of Parma, the Regent of the Spanish Netherlands, it first threatened to move the Merchant Adventurers, selling woolen cloth, to Emden in Germany, and finally in 1564, when the Regent was unable to obtain the release of some merchants and seamen imprisoned in Spain and guarantee that English trade with Spain would be open and free, did so (Ramsay 1975, p. 208). G. D. Ramsay states somewhat guardedly that if there was a turning point in English commercial history, this was it.

By the end of the sixteenth century, fairs in Spain had lost their raison d'être and gone into decline, along with the banks supporting them, this despite attempts at modernization. In 1569, some dealers thought the five months between the October and the May fairs too long, and 50 days for each fair also overextended. The two existing fairs were shortened to 30 days, and a third of 40 days added. In 1601 a fourth was introduced. In addition, payment of taxes and interest on royal debt were removed from the fair to make room for more merchandise transactions. These actions failed to arrest the decline. For one thing, the king prolonged the fair of 1574 for a year. With the revolt in Flanders exports of wool declined. Dutch entry into the East Indies trade hurt Portuguese business. And a tax on exchanges, the *alcabalas,* pushed numbers of merchants out of dealing in merchandise to money or investing in *juros,* perpetual 5 percent bonds (Fernandez de Pinedo 1990, pp. 1042–47).

IV

The century was characterized by the shift of Italian and Spanish trade in particular, and European trade in general, from the Mediterranean to the Atlantic and the north — especially the English Channel and the North Sea (Lynch 1964, chap. 9). Spanish armies and navies had been held down on the two fronts. With success in 1571 in the battle of Lepanto against Turkey (and the euphoria generated by rising silver imports), Spain turned its military attention from the east to the west and north. In particular, it sought to strengthen its ground armies in the Eighty Years' War (from 1568 to 1648) against revolt in the Spanish Netherlands, partly in the Counter-Reformation, but primarily to hold on to the territory (ibid., chap. 7). One episode in the course of the war was the Spanish Armada, sent to clear the Channel to Antwerp for Spanish shipping. Its defeat in 1588, following by three years the sack of Antwerp by Spanish mercenaries, proved not to be decisive. The loss of sailors was not enormous and the efficient Spanish bureaucracy repaired 48 of the 56 ships that made it back to Spain, and built new to fill Spanish needs in the Atlantic and the North (Lynch 1964, pp. 326–27).

In the sixteenth century Venice with a rising population was having a hard time feeding itself. Attempts were made from time to time to add to normal supplies from the Terra Ferma (Po Valley), Sicily, and Turkey, by road from Bavaria, and even from Poland by way of the Black Sea. In 1590 the worst harvest in Italy in 20 years required more strenuous measures. First Venetian ships proceeded to the Baltic, then English, Dutch, and Danish ships penetrated the Mediterranean with grain from Danzig. Within a few years Venetian buyers were acquiring grain in Antwerp and Amsterdam, paying for it with exchange on Nuremberg, Antwerp, and occasionally Besançon (Aymard 1956, chap. 4, esp. pp. 154–64).

Leghorn on the Tyrennean Sea, built by the Medici in the fifteenth century as a Tuscan rival to Pisa, was made a free port by the Grand Duke of Tuscany in 1590. It served especially English shipping: Thomas Mun served part of his apprenticeship there from perhaps 1597 to 1607 before becoming a director of the East India Company (deRoover 1957). Until Dutch and English ships penetrated the Mediterranean, its trade with the North had been conducted largely by Venetian and Genoese vessels. Hanseatic shipping ventured into the Bay of Biscay for salt and wine, ultimately being overtaken by Dutch ships in the wine trade with Bordeaux, which in turn in the eighteenth century were displaced by French vessels (Crouzet 1968). But Spanish sailors played an important part in the shift of merchandise traffic from south to north, especially those from Viscaya on the Bay of Biscay, where Bilbao was the leading shipbuilding city.

It is remarkable in retrospect that the Flemish and Brabanters, with so much in the way of exports and imports, were not more distinguished in shipping, having been dominated initially by the Hanseatics and the Italians, and then by the English, Dutch, and Zeelanders.

V

The Italians were the leading bankers in the fifteenth century, especially the Florentines in Bruges, though they began to transfer their activities to Antwerp (and Lyons) at the end of the period. The end of the century also saw the rise of South German merchant-bankers, notably the Fuggers of Augsburg, Welsers of Nuremberg, Hochstetters, Seilers, and others (Bergier 1979, pp. 108–9). South Germany had close connections with Venice from which it bought the eastern cotton needed to mix with wool in the production of fustian. In time they sent their sons to Venice to learn double-entry bookkeeping and banking. They were imitators, not innovators of credit instruments, according to Hildebrand, though they found themselves drawn into industrial investments, especially in mining, through loans to princes (1990).

The bankers of North Germany, concentrated mainly in Lübeck, which collected the revenues of the Pope from the Baltic area, were far more backward in banking, resisting Italian influences though one or two Italian bankers insinuated themselves into the city (North 1990b). For the most part, Hanseatic merchants traded in foreign ports with local money, buying the equivalent in value of what they sold. The bankers sent the papal income to Rome initially through Bruges with its Hanseatic Kontor, and later through Nuremberg.

The Fuggers of Augsburg borrowed from Cardinal Melchior von Brizen in the South Tyrol at the beginning of the sixteenth century, made loans to Maximilian, Holy Roman Emperor, for which they received the silver mines of the Tyrol, Hungary, and the Erzgebirge. In 1519, two years after Martin Luther nailed his thesis to the church door at Weimar, initiating a running war between Catholicism and Protestants, Jacob Fugger undertook to finance the campaign of Charles V as Holy Roman Emperor in succession to Maximilian. Francis I of France was also a contender for the emperorship, sought to borrow from the Fuggers, did borrow from the Genoese. The monies were needed to elicit the votes of the German princes who served as Electors. In the end, Charles V won the election, borrowing 850,000 florins for his campaign, of which 542,000 came from the Fuggers, 143,000 from the Welsers, and 165,000 (55,000 each) from three Florentine banks (Ehrenberg 1896 [1926], pp. 75–77).

In 1523, Charles V still owed the Fuggers his dues under contracts with three knightly orders in Spain which had grown with the expulsion of the Moors from Granada in 1492, those of Santiago, Calatrava, and Alcantara. The orders produced grain and other agricultural products which they marketed, with some payments of dues in kind. In addition, Calatrava contained the mercury mines at Almadén. The three orders were bound in a unit called Maestrazagos. The contract with the orders which the Fuggers had taken over ran out in 1538, and led to serious bidding for a four-year extension among the Fuggers, Welsers, and some Genoese. The Fuggers won the contract for 1538–42, despite the pressure of what Kellenbenz calls the *Staatsrat* (probably the Cortes) to favor the Genoese (Kellenbenz 1967, p. 15). Herman Kellenbenz's study is based largely on documents uncovered in the Fugger archive in Dillingen/ Donau, which seem not to go beyond 1542. The contracts are complex, specifying payments in Spain and abroad, dealing with the rights to export grain and presumably mercury. In addition to competing for these contracts in Spain, the Welsers had been engaged between 1528 and 1532 in financing Spanish exploration in the New World, including the recruitment of German miners. They maintained "factories" in Spain and in San Domingo (Brandi 1939, pp. 337–39).

In February 1525, Charles V's troops had been unpaid for three months, and he decided to attack the French to gain an indemnity. The Spanish mercenaries captured Francis I of France at the battle of Pavia. Charles V released him in exchange for his four sons as hostages. In the peace of 1529 these were in turn released on the promise of a ransom of two million escudos, plus 290,000 to pay Charles V's debt to England. One million two hundred thousand was to be paid in cash with the boat carrying the Princes to their father crossing the Bidossa River at the same time as the money crossed in the opposite direction (Vilar 1969 [1976], p. 174). Ehrenberg records that money poured into France from many sources: the king of England, the Republics of Genoa and Venice, and the Duke of Milan to pay subsidies to the Emperor (1896 [1928], p. 81).

During the 1530s and 1540s, Anton Fugger who took over the firm on the death of Jacob started lending on a vast scale. Financial trouble lay ahead as Charles V continued to borrow to conduct war against the French, and on the other side the French needed funds to resist the Emperor. In addition Charles was under strong pressure from the German Protestant princes who, allied with the Catholic king of France, in 1552 drove Charles out of Augsburg where he had been staying in Anton Fugger's house into Italy. There in a characteristic action he borrowed more money (Brandi 1939, pp. 600–611). In Antwerp, the Fuggers borrowed more money not only for Charles V but also to lend to England which was also fighting the French. The monies did not save Charles who spent 2,500,000 ducats in the battle for Metz, but failed to take it (Lynch 1964, pp. 55, 57). Ehrenberg calls 1552 the Fugger turning point. But the Spanish-French wars proceeded.

At this time, Italians were being drawn to Lyons as well as the Low Countries. The Medici bank had much earlier transferred its main branch from Geneva to Lyons. Lyons was important for French state finances, and this attracted the Florentines, who were also shifting from Bruges to Antwerp, as well as the Genoese. An innovative French financial agent, first of Francis I and then of his successor Henry II (1547 to

1557), Cardinal Toulon, organized in Lyons the Grand Parti. As earlier noted, the French kings had been borrowing heavily from the start of the English wars in 1543. The loans were described as "short-term, but permanent," that is, they ran from fair to fair, three months apart, at 3, 3.3, or 4 percent making for annual rates of 12, 14, and 16 percent, but were rolled over automatically. Banks accepted deposits from "widows and orphans" at 5 to 8 percent per annum, and lent to the king at 10 (Doucet 1937, part 1, p. 475). The Grand Parti was organized in 1555 to sort out this chaotic situation. This was a royal loan, raised from the public, not banks, a 10-year term, a sinking fund, and compound interest. Ehrenberg claims that it was the first royal loan open to all. Doucet insists that it was nothing new, having been patterned after a French loan of 1552 (ibid., pp. 494–95). Subscriptions were received quarterly, and the interest rate came down to 12 percent a year. There was a continuous rush to buy, from locals, foreigners, among the latter even a Turkish pasha. Women sold ornaments to raise cash, servants contributed, and amounts were sent in from Toulouse, Montpellier, and Riom, to add to the amounts raised in Lyons. Every man ran to it as to a fire (Hauser 1929–30, p. 249, quoting Jean Bodin; Doucet 1937, part 1, pp. 490–503; Ehrenberg 1896 [1928], pp. 302–6).

The enthusiasm did not keep up. The sinking fund was not kept up; interest was not paid but was added to principal. Starting as a floating debt of 1,500,000 ecus (4,500,000 livres), the loan finally reached 9,700,000 livres. This proved not enough to pursue the war and Henry II turned to borrowing from bankers again. He pledged the yield on the salt tax in Brittany and various regions in southern France, as well as the customs of Lyons, although this was already committed as collateral for a loan from Florentine bankers. At the beginning of 1558, the Grand Parti plus loans amounted to 13,200,000 livres, with interest payments at 2,600,000 (Doucet 1937, part 1, pp. 505–6). With armies in Italy and in the north at the battle of St. Quentin, plus a resumption of war with the revolting Spanish Netherlands, financial ruin arrived for France.

The Spanish armies under the Duke of Alba did no better than the French. Charles V had abdicated the Spanish throne in 1555 in favor of his son, Philip II, and that of the Holy Roman Empire in 1556, to be succeeded by his brother, Maximilian I. Spanish armies had done well in Italy, defeating papal forces at Milan and Naples, but this encouraged Philip to renew attack on the French at St. Quentin in 1557. Despite the failure of the treasure fleet to arrive from America, he hired German mercenaries, using monies borrowed from the Fuggers in Antwerp. The Fuggers originally lent their own funds. They started borrowing in order to lend in the 1540s, a practice which Ehrenberg states was safe originally, dangerous later. In financing St. Quentin, the house borrowed at 9 percent and charged 12 or 13 (1898 [1928], p. 1130).

Philip II and Henry II at St. Quentin exhausted both their finances and their armies, which they were forced to disband. Peace came at Chateau-Cambrésis in 1559. In the meantime, however, both monarchs had stopped servicing their debts. In Lyons, the French suspended the sinking fund, added current interest due to principal. Philip II paid off maturing debts with juros, and confiscated the silver fleets of July 1 and September 20, 1557 (van der Wee 1977, p. 371). The flooding of Spanish markets with juros converted many Spaniards into rentiers, deserting commerce for the noble life (North 1994, p. 92).

Both Genoese bankers and Germans negotiated with Castile to settle Philip's debts. The clever Genoese had loaned less and settled earlier and on more generous terms than the Tuscans and Germans who held out for two years, earning the Genoese bankers—Grimaldi, Centuroni, Espinosas, et al.—a preferred position in Spanish finance in the future (Ehrenberg 1896 [1928], p. 118; van der Wee 1977, p. 371). While the final eclipse of the Fuggers waited until the Spanish financial crises of 1575 and 1596, 1557 marked the start of the Age of Genoa which lasted 70 years until two more Spanish royal bankruptcies in 1607 and 1627 brought them down. The Habsburgs squeezed all they could from South German bankers and then turned to Genoa — or welcomed the invading Genoese bankers (Arrighi 1994, pp. 124–25). Giovanni Arrighi's Marxian analysis holds the Age of Genoa — a Braudelian designation — to have been the first of four cycles of systemic capital accumulation — Genoan, Dutch, English, and U.S.

In addition to the Spanish and Anglo-French hostilities, France was harassed by religious wars. Persecution by Catholics of the Lutherans and Anabaptists of Germany and Holland did not have much impact on business or finance. The rise of the peculiarly French form of Protestants, Calvinism, was different (Coornaert 1961, 1:100). Some Calvinist Huguenots had been pirates in the Bay of Biscay operating on Spanish-French trade out of Nantes and St. Nazaire and, after the treaty of Cateau-Cambrésis, which the Protestants thought unfavorable to them, trade with the Indies. In the first eight wars of religion in France, in 1562 the Huguenots occupied Rouen and Lyons, the premier French cities in trade and finance, respectively. Successive peace treaties were followed by new outbreaks of hostilities with the third war ended in 1570 in the Treaty of St. Germain, only to be followed two years later by the massacre of St. Bartholomew in which Catholics attacked Protestants throughout France. Huguenots' piracy in the Atlantic continued uninterrupted. Peace treaties and new outbreaks followed one another until the Edict of

Nantes of 1598 granting the Huguenots freedom of worship, finally re-voked almost a century later by Louis XIV in 1685 leading to a massive emigration of Huguenots to Geneva, Amsterdam, Hamburg, London, and the American colonies (Lapeyre 1955, pp. 413ff).

The religious wars in France were paralleled in the Spanish Nether-lands by the War of the Counter-Reformation, applying the Inquisition to the Low Countries. Cardinal Granvelle, Philip II's agent under the rule of the regent Margaret, was expelled in 1562 in a victory for the Calvinist princes. This led to the dispatch of the Duke of Alba to Brus-sels, his ruthless suppression of resistance, the sack of Antwerp in 1568, and the outbreak of the Dutch revolt in 1572. Lynch states that the Counter-Reformation was more a war to secure Spanish territory than motivated by religious zeal (1964, chap. 8, esp. pp. 236, 257, 263). The Huguenot attack on Lyons in 1562 and the Dutch blockade of the Scheldt in 1585 each led to emigrations of merchants, Protestants, Jews, and foreigners, in the latter case stimulating the economic and financial growth and ultimate primacy of the Dutch republic and the beginnings of commercial and financial growth in Hamburg.

The Grand Parti of 1555–57 furnishes an early example of the dis-tinction between bank-based and market-based capital markets (Sar-cinelli 1996). As noted, it was not the first. After Henry II stopped paying sinking fund and deferred interest, the price of the bonds sold to the public and traded in markets fell to 70 (Doucet 1933, part 2, p. 3).

The French crown also borrowed on *rentes* beginning in the four-teenth and fifteenth centuries, but on a larger scale in the sixteenth, and especially after 1560. The rente was a loan with payment of service as-signed to a tax, or increasingly to a town or city which sometimes raised the tax, but in any event stood behind the service of the debt. In the sixteenth century French rentes were largely assigned to the country un-til 1566, when they were guaranteed by the Hotel de Ville of Paris (Schnapper 1957, p. 80, and part 2, chap. 2). After the 1559 bankruptcy, the king and Paris entered into the Contract of Poissy with the church, in which the Pope promised that the French clergy would pay over six years the accumulated arrears of the Hotel de Ville of Paris (ibid., pp. 155–58). Similar development of rentes with smaller cities than Paris took place between 1515 and 1560 in the Spanish Netherlands and is called by James Tracy a "financial revolution" (1985). Rentiers would not accept the guarantee of every town, and those marketing rentes from Amster-dam hesitated to sell them in port cities, such as Bruges, where Dutch goods and ships might be confiscated if interest fell into arrears (ibid., pp. 112, 129).

Schnapper writes that the history of the rente has been neglected because of historians' fascination with the bill of exchange (1957, p. 9). Both evolved during the sixteenth century. The evolution of the bill of exchange in Antwerp at the hands of Italians and Flemish — but not the South Germans who clung to medieval techniques — has been recited in great detail, especially by de Roover (1949); van der Wee (1963, 1977, 1991a, and 1991b, chap. 3); Boyer-Xambeu, Deleplace, and Gillard (1986, chap. 5). Begun early in the thirteenth century, its functions expanded in the sixteenth century as it became successively assignable, transferable, negotiable, and from the 1540s discountable, bridging time and space, serving as private money as distinct from specie which was the money of the prince. Boyer-Xambeu and her colleagues term the *asiento*, the special bill of exchange by which the Spanish transferred money from Spain to the Spanish Netherlands to pay their troops, a perversion of the monetary role of letters of exchange. This is because it specifies payment in specie, the only form of payment the mercenaries would accept. Nor did it have the flexibility given the Italian bill used by Italians and Flemish in Antwerp (ibid., pp. 295–96).

The rente in France evolved over the century in similar fashion from something like a mortgage, perpetual in term, given when acquiring property, some rentes in kind for wine and grain. Originally rentes did not circulate but were held for purchase of property, given as dowry, or bequeathed in an estate. Amounts started small in the sixteenth century, issued even by laborers to acquire small bits of land, and rose sharply as they came into use by the nobility and then the middle class (Schnapper 1957, part 1). Tracy sketches the growing market for Dutch rentes, initially in the Spanish Netherlands, but gradually finding buyers at home in Holland and especially Amsterdam. With the growth of Amsterdam after the sack of Antwerp, and the shift of capital out of trade and industry, into finance, a rentier class grew up. Brewers in Delft and grain dealers were large purchasers (1985, chap. 5). Tracy concludes that towns started selling rentes on the open market because they were unable any longer to force their citizens to lend to them (ibid., p. 219).

The sixteenth century was a revolutionary time in European finance. Commerce moved from sporadic fairs to continuous trading. Financial transformations include shifts from gold to silver, from dominance by Italians in the Mediterranean to the South Germans and then the Flemish, ultimately the Dutch. The Age of the Fuggers gave way to that of the Genoese. Silver from the New World produced or, as more generally agreed, accelerated a price revolution. Religious and other wars created enormous demands for money to hire mercenary soldiers. Financial crises abounded.

The high pressure of events produced at least two financial transformations so far-reaching as to be called "revolutions." Herman van der Wee (1991b, p. 1173), the doyen of the financial history of the Spanish Netherlands, called the transformation of short-term credit through the development of the bill of exchange a financial revolution situated between that of the Italians in the thirteenth century, initially producing the bill of exchange, and that of Britain in the seventeenth, which substituted a rational for a chaotic system of government debt (Dickson 1967). James Tracy calls the Dutch development of a market in rentes a financial revolution not so much because of the large sums of money raised in the 1550s, but because the wealth of the provinces was mobilized for the first time.

France participated in these changes perhaps more slowly than Britain and the rest of Continental Europe.[7] Boyer-Xambeu and her colleagues write that farming of princely and royal domains and taxes was given up in the middle of the sixteenth century, except in France which caught up only in the eighteenth century, a lag that held back the development of French banking (1986, pp. 82–83). Coornaert recognizes that the French failed to keep up with the financial techniques of its competitors, perhaps connected, he suggests, with a cultural trait, the traditional French spirit of moderation (*mesure*) (1961, pp. ii, 126).

Henri Hauser concluded that the bankruptcies from 1557 to 1559 probably interrupted the march toward modern finance and economic growth (1929–30, pp. 241, 255). van der Wee modifies this conclusion and states that the innovation in finance led the royal houses of Europe to follow grandiose schemes, were disruptive in the short run, positive in the long (1977, p. 391). This is a supply-side viewpoint. It is possible to conclude the reverse, that the grandiose schemes of royal houses put pressure on financial markets and led to innovation, not perhaps in short-term commercial credit, but in the shift from bank-led to market-led capital markets.

APPENDIX

A game for nonprofessional historians is to note in the literature "turning points" or "decisive limits," usually in terms of a given year, decade, event. Comparison among them is impossible, to be sure, since the various authors have different outcomes in mind. Nonetheless, a selection may hold interest.

Arrighi 1994, p. 125	1557 as start of the Age of the Genoea.
Braudel 1966 [1975], 2:941	1556 peace between the Pope and the Duke of Alba an important turning point for western civilization.

Ibid., p. 1055	"The War of Granada, A Turning Point," arrival of Alba in the Netherlands in 1567.
Ehrenberg 1896 [1928], p. 106	1552 a turning point for Charles V and the last time the Fuggers held the Emperor's fate in their hands.
Ibid., p. 328	"From about 1552 a real madness or mania for the Bourse loans of Antwerp and Lyons seized on the masses all over Europe."
Friis 1953	General thesis: believes that the financial crisis of 1557 was largely the result of the disastrous grain harvest in Europe in 1556. Van der Wee is doubtful (1963, 2:214n).
Gascon 1971, p. 250	Grand Parti turned finance from commerce to speculation.
Ibid., p. 671	Records the disagreement on the date of the collapse of Lyons as a dominant financial center among Ehrenberg, paying more attention to public than to commercial credit, 1562; Doucet, focusing on public credit alone, 1575; and Lapeyre, based on the papers of Bonvisi of Lucca, 1590. Gascon claims that the documents studied by Ehrenberg, Doucet, and Lapeyre were not as full as the papers of four Lyons notaries that he used.
Hauser 1929–30, p. 254	The period which was opening [after 1559] was a period of economic retardation, at least for the countries which played leading parts.
Israel 1995, chaps 7, 8, and 9	The Dutch revolt begins 1572 after the arrival of the Spanish of Alva in 1567, who arrested 9,000, executed 1,000, including the Counts of Egmont and Horn.
Lapeyre 1955, p. 413	Second phase of the religious wars in France, the massacre of St. Bartholomew, 1572.
Ibid., p. 44	1585 a critical date in western European history with battle of Atlantic (with England) that lasted to the end of the century.
Lynch 1964, p. 164	Treaty of Cateau-Cambrésis between Spain and France in 1559 confirmed Spain's prestige in southern Europe, weakness in the north.
Ramsay 1975, p. 211	If there was a turning point in English commercial history, it was reached (1564) when the Merchants Adventurers transferred from Antwerp to Emden. Long-standing supremacy of Netherlands market for British trade never restored.
Ibid., p. 137	1550 usually taken as the turning point in the movement from gold as the dominant currency in France to silver.

Spooner 1972, p. 57	Loans of Charles V in Antwerp and the Grand Parti in Lyons led to breaking point in 1550s. Spanish bankruptcy in 1557 soon entailed bankruptcies of the Low Countries, Naples, Milan, and then of the French monarchy.
Vilar 1969 [1976], p. 161	1557 the greatest crisis of the century.
van der Wee 1963, vol. 2	Chapter 6 is entitled "The Decisive Years, 1520–c.1550."
Ibid., p. 215	Peak of south German expansion reached in 1520s, final decay in 1550s.
Ibid., p. 221	"The feverish credit boom of the fifties had also caused a fatal crisis and a state bankruptcy in Lyons' money market . . . the *financial impulse* was completely broken."[8]
Ibid., p. 432	The political crisis of the 1550s caused Antwerp's foundation to disintegrate, killed its supremacy of the financial market. Commerce flourished after 1559, and Antwerp revived. But it was no use. The crisis of the mid-1560s was a definite turning point.

NOTES

1. In writing on bankruptcy in preindustrial Europe, Mark Steele states that Seville had a well-known reputation for banking instability, and that insolvency in Seville often led bankers to flight or to seeking holy sanctuary to avoid imprisonment for debt (1990, pp. 192, 199). An article on private banks and municipal power in Seville, unhappily in Spanish which I do not read, has a long series of appendices, the second of which, with eight tables, provides lists of banks and exchange dealers, including in sections E and H lists of bankruptcies with brief notations. Table E deals with the crisis of the 1550s, H with that of the 1590s (Tinoco Rubiales 1991, pp. 1067–1133). Appendix 11, in prose not tables, covers the exhaustion of the municipal treasury and bankruptcy of banks in 1600–1601 (ibid., pp. 1124–31).

2. Braudel and Spooner use the French expressions for ease and tightness, "*largesse*" and "*etroitesse.*" The English translation of van der Wee's study of the Antwerp money market uses the Italian terms, "*larghessa*" and "*strettezza,*" Lapeyre, a Frenchman, writing on Spain the Spanish, "*larqueza*" and "*estrecheza.*"

3. I have used the French rather than the 1994 English translation because the latter is rather drastically abridged.

4. Henry II reigned in France in the 1550s with a relatively small bureaucracy — 10,000 *officiers* — Le Roy Ladurie 1995 [1997], p. 164.

5. Le Roy Ladurie observed that Charles IV of France in 1564 quadrupled

the salaries of the four regents of the medical school in Montpellier. These had been frozen since the end of the fifteenth century, despite the fact that inflation had raised prices two to three times (1995 [1997], p. 191).

6. Italians also dominated Lyons. In 1571, the origins of foreigners in Lyons banking were: Florence 42, Milan 36, Lucca 28, Genoa 27, Germans (including Swiss) 22, other Italians 15, Portuguese 4, English 1, Flemish 1, Spanish 1, or a total of 154 Italians and 29 of other national origin. Most of the big foreign merchant-bankers—e.g., the Centuroni and Capponi of Florence, Ruiz of Spain, became naturalized, but true settlement was rare. Jean (Hans) Kleberg, the "good German," whose family originated in Nuremberg, became a Swiss citizen. He stood out from others of the German "nation," because of his many charities, though the designation may say something about the avarice of other Germans, numerous Welsers, Tucher, George Obrecht of Strassburg, and Israel Minkel, a Swiss (Gascon 1971, p. 359 passim; Ehrenberg 1896 [1928], pp. 184–85). Lapeyre writes that one would think Lyons an Italian republic, with the French a "nation" like the Milanese, Genoese, Florentines, Luccans, and Germans. Decisions about trading were made by the Italians (1955, p. 124).

7. In the conclusion of his book on the Spanish merchant-banker, Simon Ruiz, Lapeyre observes that the financial techniques of Catholic Europe remained medieval, dealing primarily in foreign bills. His remark was applied to the Fuggers who were Catholic, despite their direct loans (1955, p. 599).

8. Ehrenberg and Braudel believe Lyons was over only in 1575, Lapeyre in 1589: "In our view the crisis of 1557 *broke the expansion* for good."

REFERENCES

Arrighi, Giovanni (1994) *The Long Twentieth Century: Money, Power and the Origin of Our Times*. London and New York: Verso.
Attman, Artur (1986) *American Bullion in the European World Trade, 1600–1800*. Göteberg: Kungl. Vetenskap-och Viterhets-Samhället.
Aymard, Maurice (1956) *Venise, Raguse et le commerce du blé pendant le seconde moitié du XVIᵉ siècle*. Paris: S.E.V.P.E.N.
Bergier, Jean-François (1979) "From the 15th Century in Italy to the 16th Century in Germany: A New Banking Concept." In Center for Medieval and Renaissance Studies, *The Dawn of Modern Banking*. New Haven: Yale University Press. 106–29.
Berthe, Jean-Pierre (1970) "Les Flamands à Seville au 16ᵉ siècle." In Hermann Kellenbenz, ed., *Fremden Kaufleute auf der Iberischen Halfinseli*. Cologne and Vienna: Bühlau Verlag. 239–51.
Boorstin, Daniel J. (1985) *The Discoverers: A History of Man's Search to Know His World and Himself*. New York: Vintage Books.
Borah, Woodrow W. (1954) *Early Colonial Trade and Navigation between Mexico and Peru*. Berkeley and Los Angeles: University of California Press.
Boyer-Xambeu, Marie-Thérèse, Ghislain Deleplace, and Lucien Gillard (1986)

Monnaie privée et pouvoir des princes. Paris: Presses de la Fondation Nationale des Sciences Politiques and Editions of CNRS.

Brandi, Karl (1939) *The Emperor Charles V: The Growth and Destiny of a Man and a World-Empire* (translated from the German). London: Jonathan Cape.

Braudel, Fernand (1949 [1972]) *The Mediterranean and the Mediterranean World in the Age of Philip II.* Vol. 1. New York: Harper and Row.

Braudel, Fernand (1966 [1975]) *The Mediterranean and the Mediterranean World in the Age of Philip II.* Vol. 2. New York: Harper and Row.

Braudel, Fernand, and Frank C. Spooner (1955) "Les métaux monétaires de l'économie du XVIeme siècle." *Extract of Relazioni del Congresso Internazionale de Science Storiche.* Storia moderna, Vol. 4. Florence: G. C. Sansoni. 23–64.

Challis, C. E. (1978) *The Tudor Coinage.* Manchester: Manchester University Press.

Coornaert, Emile (1961) *Les Français et le commerce international à Anvers.* 2 vols. Paris: Marcel Rivière.

Crouzet, François (1968) "Economie et société (1715–1789)." In François-Georges Pariset, ed., *Bordeaux au XVIIIème siècle.* Bordeaux: Fedération historique du Sud-ouest. 193–286.

Day, John (1978 [1987]) "The Great Bullion Famine of the Fifteenth Century," in John Day, *The Medieval Market Economy.* Oxford: Blackwell.

Dickson, P. G. M. (1967) *The Financial Revolution in England: A Study in the Development of Public Credit,* 1699–1756, New York: St. Martin's Press.

Doucet, Roger (1933) "Le Grand Parti de Lyon au XVI siècle." Parts 1 and 2. *Revue Historique* 171, no. 3 (May–June), pp. 472–513; no. 4 (July–August): 1–41.

Ehrenberg, Richard (1896 [1928]) *Capital and Finance in the Age of the Renaissance: A Study of the Fuggers and Their Connections* (translated from the German). New York: Harcourt, Brace.

Fernandez de Pinedo, Emiliano (1991) "Crédit et banque en Castille aux XVIe siècles." In Giuseppe Felloni ed., *Banchi pubblici, banchi privati e monti di pietà nell' Europa preindustriale.* Genoa. 2:1037–50.

Fischer, David Hackett (1996) *The Great Wave: Price Revolutions and the Rhythm of History.* Oxford and New York: Oxford University Press.

Friis, Astrid (1953) "An Inquiry into the Relations between Economic and Financial Factors in the Sixteenth and Seventeenth Centuries: I, Two Crises in the Netherlands in 1557." *Scandinavian Economic History Review* 1, no. 2:191–241.

Gascon, Richard (1971) *Grand commerce et vie urbaine au XVIe siècle: Lyon et ses marchands.* 2 vols. Paris: S.E.V.P.N. (Mouton).

Gould, J. D. (1970) *The Great Debasement: Currency and the Economy in Mid-Tudor England.* Oxford: Clarendon Press.

Gould, J. D. (1979) "How It All Began: Origins of the Modern Economy." Review of *The Tudor Coinage,* by C. E. Challis. *Economic History Review* 32, no. 2 (May): 271ff.

Israel, Jonathan I. (1995) *The Dutch Republic: Its Rise, Greatness, and Fall, 1477–1806*. Oxford: Clarendon Press.

Kindleberger, Charles P. (1995) "The Economic Crisis of 1619 to 1623." In Charles P. Kindleberger, ed., *The World Economy and National Finance in Historical Perspective*. Ann Arbor: University of Michigan Press.

Lapeyre, Henri (1953) *Simon Ruiz et les "asientos" de Phillippe II*. Paris: Colin.

Lapeyre, Henri (1955) *Une famille des marchands, Les Ruiz: Contribution à l'etude du commerce entre la France et l'Espagne au temps de Phillippe II*. Paris: Colin.

Lapeyre, Henri (1970) "Les marchands étrangers au royaume de Valence aux XVᵉ et XVIᵉ siècles." In H. Kellenbenz, ed., *Fremden Kaufleute auf der Iberischen Halbinsel*. Cologne and Vienna: Bühlau Verlag. 100–17.

Le Roy Ladurie, Emmanuel (1995 [1997]) *The Beggar and the Professor: A Sixteenth-Century Family Saga* (translated from the French). Chicago: University of Chicago Press.

Lynch, John (1964) *Spain under the Hapsburgs*. Vol. 1, *Empire and Absolutism, 1516–1598*. New York: Oxford University Press.

Morineau, Michel (1985) *Incroyable gazettes et fabuleux métaux: Les retours americaines d'après les gazettes hollandaises XVIᵉ–XVIIIᵉ siècles*. Paris: Cambridge University Press/Editions de la Maison des Sciences de l'Homme.

North, Michael (1990a) *Geldumlauf und Wirtschaftskonjunktur in südlichen Ostseeraum an der Wende zur Neuzeit (1440–1570)*. Siegmaringen: Jan Thorbecke Verlag.

North, Michael (1990b) "Banking and Credit in Northern Germany in the Fifteen and Sixteenth Centuries." In *Banchi pubblici, banchi privati e monti di pietà nell' Europa preindustrial*. Genoa. 2:811–26.

North, Michael (1994) *Das Geld und seine Geschichte, Vom Mittelalter bis zum Gegenwart*. Munich: C. H. Beck.

Outhwaite, R. B. (1969) *Inflation in Tudor and Early Stuart England*. London: Macmillan.

Parker, Geoffrey (1972) *The Army of Flanders and the Spanish Road, 1567–1659: The Logistics of Victory and Defeat in the Low Countries' Wars*. Cambridge: Cambridge University Press.

Ramsay, G. D. (1975) *The City of London in International Politics at the Accession of Elizabeth Tudor*. Manchester: Manchester University Press.

Roover, Raymond de (1949) *Gresham on Foreign Exchange: An Essay on Early English Mercantilism*. Cambridge, Mass.: Harvard University Press.

Roover, Raymond de (1957) "Thomas Mun in Italy." *Bulletin of the Institute of Historical Research* 30, no. 81 (May): 80–85.

Sarcinelli, M. (1996) "The Italian Financial System in the Mid-1990s: A Difficult Transition." *Banca Nazionale del Lavoro Quarterly Review* 49, no. 196 (March): 3–35.

Schnapper, Bernard (1957) *Les rentes au XVIᵉ siècle: Histoire d'un instrument de crédit*. Parts 1 and 2. Paris: S.E.V.P.E.N.

Spooner, Frank C. (1972) *The International Economy and Monetary Movements in France, 1493–1725.* Cambridge, Mass.: Harvard University Press.

Steele, Mark (1991) "Bankruptcy and Insolvency: Bank Failure and its Control in Pre-Industrial Europe." In Giuseppe Felloni, ed., *Banchi pubblici, banchi privati e monti de pietá nell' Europa preindustriale.* Genoa: Societá ligure di storia patria. 1:183–204.

Tinoco Rubiales, Santiago (1991) "Banca privada y poder municipal en ciudad se Seville (Siglo XVI)." In *Banchi pubblici, banchi privati e monti di pietà nell' Europa preindustriale.* Genoa. 2:1053–113.

Tracy, James D. (1985) *A Financial Revolution in the Habsburg Netherlands: Renten and Renteniers in the Country of Holland, 1515–1565.* Berkeley: University of California Press.

Vilar, Pierre (1976) *A History of Gold and Money, 1450–1920.* London: New Left Books.

Wee, Herman van der (1963) *The Growth of the Antwerp Market and the European Economy (Fourteenth–Sixteenth Centuries).* Vol. 2. The Hague: Martinus Nijhoff.

Wee, Herman van der (1977) "Money, Credit and Banking Systems." In E. E. Rich and C. H. Wilson, eds., *Cambridge Economic History of Europe.* Vol. 5, *The Economic Organization of Early Modern Europe.* Cambridge: Cambridge University Press. 290–392, 651–59.

Wee, Herman van der (1991a) "Les banques européennes au moyen âge et pendant les temps modernes (476–1789)." In Herman van der Wee, H. Bogaert, and G. Kurgan-van Hentenryk, *La banque en Occident.* Antwerp: Fonds Mercator. 71–264.

Wee, Herman van der (1991b) "The Medieval and Early Modern Origins of European Banking." In *Banchi pubblici, banchi privati e monti di pietà nell' Europa preindustriale.* Genoa. 2:159–73.

Should Emerging Markets Climb Back Down?

August 1982 was the month of truth for Third World syndicated bank loans, when Mexico announced that it could not meet its debt service. A question arises whether February 1994 was the equivalent for mutual and pension fund investments in emerging markets.

Moments before, the entire outlook was rosy. Noting the swelling flow of private capital into these markets, the World Bank was toying with the notion that it could cut down on official lending. In a story in the *New York Times* on February 28, Saul Hanson extolled the genius of Nicholas Rohatyn, son of Felix and an official of J. P. Morgan, for his forecast of exploding investor interest in emerging markets.

One day later, on March 1, the *Times* carried another story by Hanson. This one carried the headline: "Big Losses as Emerging Markets Fall." Hanson noted that, although Morgan had earned $200 million from trading in emerging markets during the fourth quarter of 1993, many of the major dealers — with Morgan listed first among five others — had lost $30 to $100 million each in recent weeks. Fidelity's New Markets Fund fell 9.5 percent in that week. A Dutch trader at ING securities gave the view from Europe, observing that "I'm sure that every one lost money. People went into the downturn fairly long."

Floyd Norris, the *New York Times's* consummate financial reporter, continued the saga in his contribution of April 1, titled "After Flying High Emerging Markets Fall Back to Earth." Norris noted that most of the money in the T. Rowe Price New Asia Fund came in as the fund was reaching its peak price at the end of the year. He proceeded to regale readers with an account of Fidelity's New Markets Fund, which opened for business on May 4, 1993. The fund scored a return of 38.8 percent for the period ending December 31, by which time its assets had reached $283 million. The assets peaked out at $380 million on January 19. On March 31, the fund was down to $149 million, with 70 percent of the

This essay was first published as a guest appearance in Peter L. Bernstein's newsletter, *Economics and Portfolio Strategy,* October 1, 1994. Reprinted with permission.

shrinkage accounted for by shareholder redemptions — rats leaving a sinking ship. In the end, the rat strategy was better than that of the innocents who remained aboard and suffered even larger losses than the rats had incurred. "Few funds have had so meteoric a rise," Norris observed, "or so quick a fall."

In such circumstances, one is tempted to find something or someone to blame: Mother Leary's cow in the Chicago fire of 1871; the Congressional subcommittee working on a chemical duty for the Smoot-Hawley tariff in Jude Wanniski's account of the Great Crash; the tart riposte of Secretary of the Treasury James Baker to a German monetary official just before Black Monday, October 19, 1987.

In February 1994, the black spot was slapped on the hand of Alan Greenspan, who started interest rates on their upward move on the fourth of that month. This decision killed David J. Askin's Granite Partners, a $600 million hedge fund based upon a seemingly foolproof technique for trading mortgage-backed bonds. George Soros's bull position in yen cost the Quantum Fund $600 million, an event rapidly followed by sharp downturns in all the high-flying markets of 1993, both equities and bonds.

A *Boston Globe* reporter, Stephen Bailey, displayed unquenchable optimism. On February 27, he credited the boom in emerging markets to the passage of NAFTA but had to admit that emerging markets were "turbulent." He went on to say, however, that "Despite some setbacks so far this year, emerging markets are no investment fad." He is entitled to his opinion.

Bailey's is only one of many voices in the babble of mixed results. Archibald Cox, Jr., resigned in May of this year from Tiger Management Corporation after he failed to raise a billion dollars for direct investments in China and Southeast Asia. A week later, American International Group announced that they had raised a billion dollars for an Asian Infrastructure Fund for investments in energy, transportation, electric power, and petrochemicals in China and India, to be managed by two former World Bank executives.

In early May, the *Economist* magazine's Economic Intelligence Unit, under the heading "How do you minimize your risk in emerging markets?" advertised a Country Risk Service at $495 per country per year — with a menu of 87 countries to choose from. The Unit's Global Business Research ran a two-day conference in June on investing in emerging markets at a cost of $1,195, justifying the occasion with the observation that "With interest rates profoundly [sic] low, and U.S. stock valuations at record highs, funds must search further — and assume extra risk — to try to maintain the double-digit gains they have grown accustomed to." I was reminded of the nineteenth-century British tag, used by John Stuart Mill and several times by Walter Bagehot in *Lombard Street:* "John Bull can stand many things, but he cannot stand two percent." Even the International Finance Corporation, a subsidiary of the World Bank formed to promote private enterprise, was advertising the 1994 edition of its *Emerging Stock Markets Handbook* ($75) in the *Economist* magazine in July under the heading "Don't let the world's most exciting markets emerge without you!"

Funds are being formed for a growing list of more exotic countries: Vietnam, Sri Lanka ("an emerging emerging market"), Africa markets like Malawi and Namibia, Trinidad and Tobago, and even — although not on the menu of the *Economist's* 87 — Myanmar. Robert Friedland recently brought a temple gong from Myanmar to Paul Stephens of the Robertson-Stephens Contrarian Fund: the fund advertises that it goes short emerging market stocks.

I do not discuss Russian security markets, an even more exotic specialty. Poland was the #1 emerging market of 1993, with a percentage gain of more than 700 percent on a limited number of stocks. Turkey was second with 210 percent and is a story in itself. The closed-end Turkish Investment Fund was recently trading at a premium of 72 percent on a net asset value that had fallen 64 percent from its peak. Collapse of the Turkish lira did not help matters. An official of Emerging Market Management at Morgan Stanley, noting that the best performing market in one year is often the worst performer in the next year, remarked that "If economic policy is not sustainable, the bottom falls out. Still," he added, "Turkey actually offers some interesting opportunities."

China makes an engaging case of how observers can oversimplify complex developments. I vividly recall when tourists and scholars in search of excitement in the 1970s and 1980s would visit Beijing, and those with a bent for the economic forecasting would each year announce that the Chinese economy had been a shambles but the new reforms guaranteed that it was about to take off. Well, in the end it happened — to an extent.

A book by Nicholas R. Lardy, titled *China in the World Economy,* recently published by the Institute for International Economics in Washington, presents estimates of Chinese income per capita at $370 a year at current exchange rates and $1,000–$1,200 on the basis of purchasing power parity. He goes on to say that total Chinese output will reach the U.S. level in 2040 and will match U.S. income per capita at the end of the twentieth century — assuming that, after the year 2000, the Chinese rate of growth settles down from four times the U.S. rate to twice the U.S. rate.

Don't hold your breath. Growth follows an S-curve, not a logarithmic progression. The trees never reach the sky.

If one wants excitement and a risky shot at double-digit returns, how diversified or specialized should an investor be by area, country, industry, and time horizon? I am an economic historian, not a security analyst, so I offer primarily the conventional wisdom in answer to this question.

I think it would be useful if there were a fund, like an S&P 500 index fund, that owned shares of all ostensibly honest companies in developing countries. By and large, the rest of the world is going to grow faster than the United States over the long run. Catch-up is a game that the world has been playing for the last millennium, or, more conservatively and leaving out Mandarin China and the Ottoman Empire, since 1400 A.D.

Parenthetically, my inclusion of the word "honest" is problematic. The late Fred Hirsch believed that the world was consuming its moral capital. Ethicists may question whether it ever had much. Jacob Van Klaveren, a German economic historian, considered the British East India Company the most corrupt private enterprise the world has ever known. Immorality may, like many other phenomena, move in cycles, with two peaks: one at the top when the suckers swarm in to be swindled and another at the bottom when the high fliers find themselves in trouble and cook the books to get out.

If we can finesse the issue of investing in crooks, most pundits would diversify first, then specialize after you have learned your way around. The pundits too often forget that diversification has costs.

I am reminded of an occasion in the 1930s when I was listening to a brilliant young economist pontificate that "I think a truly rational investor would calculate at what prices he would buy and sell every security in the world." Rational indeed, except that George Stigler won the Nobel Prize in economics for reminding us that information is costly to obtain. As the advertising of Global Business Research and the International Finance Corporation remind us, information does run into money. It seems to me that the emerging market fund industry has too many specialized flavors, as Howard Johnson offers 28 kinds of ice cream.

That is in the long run. In the short run, you get turbulence and this year's high flyer = next year's dog. Noise players can get excitement in emerging markets or in Las Vegas, Atlantic City, Ledyard, and up and down the Mississippi River. Not quite. A wide diversified list will produce gains and losses over time, but unlike gambling, where the aggregate is sure to lose, the likelihood that one wins on balance is high. Growth is not a fad.

Finally as to industries. I am impressed with Tiger Management's aborted plan, and the AIG Asia Infrastructure Fund's notion of long-term investments in energy, transport, electric power, and petrochemicals, but they should also include communications. Sensible infrastructure over time produces growth, if perhaps less than spectacular profits. The objective is to avoid the temptation to embark on "big-dam foolishness," as at Aswan and in India—not to mention the U.S. Army Corps of Engineers. One can also produce too much steel, as the experience of the Soviet Union has so brilliantly demonstrated. But sensible infrastructure over time produces growth, if perhaps not spectacular profits.

The World Bank was originally supposed to take on major projects in developing economies, leaving labor-intensive consumer and durable goods to the private market. If private markets move into power, Chinese toll roads, and the like, will the World Bank move toward the public goods of water, education, health, and the environment, or will the Bank move in the opposite direction to industries that sell to the private markets? I am enough of a believer in the efficiency of markets to leave the last to companies like those whose A shares are traded on in Shanghai and Shenzen.

Twenty-five years ago, Raymond W. Goldsmith, distinguished economist, statistician, and worldwide financial analyst, said that financial crises belong to the childhood of capitalism, not the maturity. Childhood, yes. But as we now contemplate emerging markets being added to the excesses that developed over time in conglomerates, REITs, mergers and acquisitions, leveraged buyouts, initial public offerings, mutual funds in general after the hospitalization of money funds, investment in shopping malls, office buildings, hotels, condos, luxury housing, collectibles (especially Van Goghs), and derivatives—looking back at all that, one wonders whether Goldsmith was not premature on maturity.

8

Retirement Reading for Bankers

At a recent conference I met an old acquaintance, a banker with European antecedents. After I had given a paper on the history of capital flight, he asked for a list of 100 books on economic and financial history to read in his forthcoming retirement.

What a beguiling task. It proved, however, that 100 was the wrong number. I easily picked 35 to 40 favorites, but the circle widened after that to such an extent that choices became too close. With difficulty I stretched the list to 50.

Is the list only for the retired or about-to-be? Not at all—although it may take a still-active person considerably longer to work his or her way through the list.

One can make one's own rules in a task of this sort. Novels are permitted, since nineteenth-century novelists are long on realism, and Defoe was a forerunner. There are one or two books in the history of thought on money and finance that cannot be excluded, and for good measure I have thrown in some general and social history and analysis with a financial flavor.

The list is long on Europe, short on the United States, blank elsewhere, the consequences of professional deformation. No attention is paid to whether a book is still in print or out of print, since interlibrary loans, especially in the United States, are more and more possible. My own four works in the field are omitted, out of (misplaced?) modesty, though I secretly believe that one or two might make the grade if it were possible to be objective.[1]

Some writers—Braudel, Dickens, and de Roover—make the list with two books. Where there is a close call I offer an alternative selection, as book clubs do. Annotations vary in length, depending less on the merit of the work than on how lively is my memory—and how full are my notes.

No simple organizing principle leaps to mind, by country or period. It should be simple for the adventurous to find a good place to start. I do

---

This essay originally appeared in *Forbes,* July 13, 1987, pp. 262ff. Reprinted by permission of FORBES Magazine © Forbes, Inc., 1987.

not intend that anyone should start with number 1 and work his or her way down to 50 in disciplined order.

Novels

1. Honoré de Balzac, *César Biroteau* [1837] (Paris: Le Livre de Poche, 1972). This is one of a series of cautionary tales of the nineteenth century about the dangers of speculation, written after the boom of 1828 in Paris building sites. The hero, César Biroteau, is a perfumer who strays from the path of the business he knows to buy building lots around the Madeleine, despite the strong warnings of his shrewd but shrewish wife. Some readers with a propensity to gamble, however mild, may find the story too uncomfortable.

2. Daniel Defoe, *Roxana, the Fortunate Mistress* (1724) (London: Oxford University Press, 1964). Defoe's best-known work of economics is *Robinson Crusoe.* It is economics because it illustrates the choices Crusoe had to make when he was alone, and the distribution of income as well as specialization in production when he was joined by Friday. But in financial history the novels about the rascals — *Roxana, Captain Jack,* and *Moll Flanders* — are more edifying. Defoe was a journalist, a merchant, and a traveler. He was constantly in debt and had strong ideas on the stock market, commerce, morality. A favorite was the moral danger of poverty, with the prayer "Give me not poverty, oh Lord, lest I steal." Roxana is no better than she should have been, but the details of her financial adventures convey a rich picture of trade and finance in the seventeenth and eighteenth centuries.

3. Charles Dickens, *Dealings with the Firm of Dombey and Son, Wholesale, Retail and for Exportation* (1848) (London: Oxford University Press, 1982). Dombey, 48, was mainly a banker, his son age 8 when the book opens. The son dies before fulfilling the father's ambition to become a partner. The novel is sentimental in the extreme but has many isolated passages mocking banks and bankers.

4. Charles Dickens, *Little Dorrit* (1857) (Boston: Houghton Mifflin, 1894), *Little Dorrit* deals with debtor's prison, bureaucracy, and swindling, the last inspired by the railway mania of 1847 that collapsed in 1848, rather than the boom of the early 1850s that imploded in 1857. Merdle, the swindler — Dickens's distaste for him will be understood by those who know French — is said to be enormously rich, making killings here and there, a member of Parliament, trustee of this, president of that. But Dickens is irritatingly vague on exactly what Merdle's technique of swindling is. Bureaucracy is caricatured by the Circumlocution

Office where the work of "form-filling, corresponding, minuting, memorandum making, signing, countersigning backwards and forwards, and referring sideways, crosswise and zigzag" goes on.

5. Friedrich Spielhagen, *Storm Flood* (in original German *Sturmflut*) (1877) (New York: German Classics, volume 11, n.d.), is a novel that compares an 1874 storm of the sort that occurs only once a century—it broke down coastal defenses on the Baltic Sea—with the financial storm of 1873 in Germany. It is said to be based on the career of Geheimer Oberregierungsrat H. Wagner, politician and speculator, and on a private railroad project launched by unscrupulous promoters.

6. Christina Stead, *House of All Nations* (New York: Simon & Schuster, 1938). Stead spent five years in the 1930s working in a Paris bank and wrote a brilliant novel about life in what is essentially a bucket shop. The title comes from the medieval period when merchants often congregated in a national house, as in the German house in Venice and the House of All Nations in Antwerp. The bank of the protagonist, Jules Bertillon, may remind readers of John Law, the failed banker of the 1720 Mississippi bubble in Paris, who published letters in the *Mercure de France*. The dialog is aphoristic—"Money is king, especially in a republic."

7. Anthony Trollope, *The Way We Live Now* (1874–75) (New York: Bobbs-Merrill, 1974). A taste for Trollope is usually cultivated as one approaches retirement and normally focuses on the Barchester or the Palliser series. For a banker, *The Way We Live Now* may be a little more in point. It deals with a swindler, Augustus Melmotte, and was inspired by the investment boom of 1872–73. The central investment that attracts the suckers is a railroad from Salt Lake City to Mexico City. In the end Melmotte is undone.

8. Émile Zola, *Money* (1891) (New York: Gordon Press, 1981). This is a *roman à clef* about a speculator named Saccard, patterned after the real-life Jules Mirès, a sleazy character who had a spectacular career in the 1850s and 1860s in Paris but came a cropper. Gundermann, the Germanic banker, is drawn from James de Rothschild, the French member of the Frankfurt family who never lost his strong German accent. Saccard forms a *banque universelle* that has a meteoric rise and fall. Greed abounds.

Biography and Correspondence

9. Andrew Boyle, *Montagu Norman* (London: Cassell, 1967). Montagu Norman, governor of the Bank of England from 1920 to 1944,

was an enigmatic character in many ways. Scion of an ancient banking family, he had strong views he was not always able to articulate with clarity. Moreover, in July 1931, with sterling under attack, he had a nervous breakdown and was absent when sterling went off gold in September of that year. He would rescue banks in trouble in secret, so as not to alarm financial markets, and his great but retrospectively dubious achievement was to restore the pound to gold at the old parity of 1925. Keynes's cross-examination of Norman in the testimony before the Macmillan Commission of 1931 constituted a battle of titans. Norman was partial to Hjalmar Horace Greeley Schacht, intermittently president of the German Reichsbank, and antipathetic to the French in general and to Emile Moreau, governor of the Bank of France from 1926 to 1930, in particular.

10. Lester Chandler, *Benjamin Strong, Central Banker* (reprinted New York: Arno Press, 1978). This is the authorized biography of the man who was governor of the Federal Reserve bank of New York from 1914 until his death in October 1928, and who played a key role in the development of the system and in the increasing interconnections of U.S. finance with that of Europe. President Hoover called him an "appendage of Europe," but Friedman and Schwartz in their magisterial *Monetary History of the United States* argue that the transition of financial decision-making power from New York to Washington, where the Federal Reserve Board sat, accelerated by Strong's death in 1928, played a crucial part in the deepening of the world depression in the United States.

11. Christopher Clay, *Public Finance and Private Wealth: The Career of Sir Stephen Fox, 1627–1716* (Oxford: Clarendon Press, 1978). This book is enormously helpful in tracing — through the life of one man in the household of Charles II — the need for intermediaries in lending to the crown, and the financial revolution from tax farming to bureaucratic tax collecting and government expenditure. Fox, the father of Henry Fox, the Paymaster, and grandfather of Charles Fox, the contemporary and rival of William Pitt at the end of the eighteenth century, started out with the Stuarts in exile and earned such trust of the monarch that when Charles II defaulted to the Goldsmiths and other holders of his paper (The Stop of the Exchequer of 1682), he paid Sir Stephen regularly.

12. Count Egon Caesar Corti, *The Rise of the House of Rothschild* (New York: Blue Ribbon Books, 1928). There are dozens of books on the Rothschilds. Some of the best are about the French house, based on the papers that have been made available to scholars, especially those by Jean Bouvier on the one hand and Bertrand Gille on the other. Most are journalistic rather than scholarly, as is the case in point. But the story is

worth telling and retelling, how the five sons spread from Frankfurt to London, Paris, Amsterdam, Vienna, and Naples, worked together, and, especially in London and Paris, rose to the top of the ladder in banking, horse-racing, and society. There may be better books than this about the Rothschilds — I don't know the others in English. But the Rothschilds belong on any list.

13. Joseph S. Davis, *The World between the Wars, 1919–39: An Economist's View* (Baltimore: Johns Hopkins University Press, 1975). Davis wrote this autobiography as he was approaching 90 years of age. He had been in the U.S. Shipping Mission in London during World War I, served as an economist assistant on the staff of the American delegation to the Dawes Commission on German reparations in 1924, and became a member of President Eisenhower's Council of Economic Advisers after leaving academic life. The book is only partly autobiography and to a considerable extent an account of the international economy in the inter-war period. But his comments on important figures of the times, and especially on Keynes, are of great interest.

14. Emile Moreau, *Souvenirs d'un gouverneur de la Banque de France: Histoire de la stabilization du franc (1926–28)* (Paris: Edition Génin, 1954). This autobiography, a favorite of mine, is also recommended, I understand, by Milton Friedman. It may be one of the few things on which we see eye to eye. Moreau was a canny *inspecteur des finances,* originally from Poitou, who had been 20 years the head of the Bank of Algiers and became governor of the Bank of France in June 1926 at the time of the crisis that Poincaré stabilized in July. The book is a day-by-day account of his negotiations with the French government and dealings with Montagu Norman of the Bank of England and Benjamin Strong of the Federal Reserve Bank of New York. Read especially how he copes with M. Aupetit, the secretary of the bank when he took over.

15. D. P. O'Brien, ed., *The Correspondence of Lord Overstone,* 3 vols. (Cambridge: Cambridge University Press, 1971). Samuel Jones Loyd, later Lord Overstone, was the leader of the Currency School in the middle of the nineteenth century that would be called monetarist today. A successful banker, the richest man in England of his day, and a man of strong convictions, he strikes me as the Milton Friedman of his time, powerful in debate, firm in opinion, admitting to no doubt or error. As the editor points out, Overstone slowed the adoption of the decimal system by Britain for a century. He was charitable in his private life but not toward the ideas of others. To Overstone, only gold was money, and banknotes derived their moneyness only to the extent they were redeemable in gold.

16. Fritz Stern, *Gold and Iron: Bismarck, Bleichroeder and the Building of the German Empire* (London: Allen and Unwin, 1977). Gerson Bleichroeder, Bismarck's personal banker, was Jewish, and the family managed to get his papers out of Germany at Hitler's accession to power. With these, Fritz Stern of Columbia University has produced a financial history of Prussia and Germany from the 1830s to the 1890s, detailing the role of finance in helping Bismarck make war on Austria and France, collect 5 billion francs in reparations in 1871 and 1872, and rescue some of the speculators and swindlers involved in the bubbles of railroad investment and building that collapsed in 1873. There are penetrating chapters on the role of Jews in German economic and social life and on the corruption of the press by bankers. If one is looking for parallels, compare Bismarck's lack of interest in economics and finance, except for his personal and political ends, with Henry Kissinger's.

17. John Williamson, *Karl Helfferich, 1872–1924, Economist, Financier, Politician* (Princeton, N.J.: Princeton University Press, 1971). Helfferich is a man you love to hate. He was bright, unpleasant, devastatingly wrong on such issues as unrestricted submarine warfare or how Germany should finance World War I. Williamson thinks it was unfair to call him a "financial Ludendorff" or "the most frivolous of all finance ministers." Frivolous is hardly the word for a protagonist of such venom. In polemics his tone was so harsh that he was twice sued for slander, and his personal attack on Walther Rathenau, the German finance minister, in June 1922 was said to have inspired the extremist nationalists who assassinated Rathenau.

General History

18. Luigi Barzini, *The Italians* (New York: Atheneum, 1954). One can learn much from Barzini, a brilliant journalist. He writes about general Italian characteristics like *clientismo,* the wish of everyone to have a protector and of the powerful to be surrounded by clients, and stresses the differences between North and South in a barrage of pungent aphorisms: Southerners make money in order to rule, Northerners rule in order to make money.

19. E. W. Bovill, *The Golden Trade of the Moors* (New York: Oxford University Press, 1958). The Moors crossed the Sahara Desert for centuries, carrying salt to the alluvial gold deposits of the Ashanti above the Gold Coast. In the beginning the exchanges were silent, the Moors leaving salt on the river bank and backing away, the Ashanti bringing forward what they deemed the appropriate amount of gold. Salt and

gold were added or taken back until an implicit price was settled. The Ashanti needed salt to preserve meat, and at one time the price paid was a pound of salt for a pound of gold. Some caravans of as many as 1,800 camels were lost. Guides were blinded by exposure to the sun but knew where they were by tasting the sand. When the Ashanti had been converted to Muhammadanism, one trip to Mecca bearing gold for expenses stopped in Alexandria for a few weeks and left behind an inflation that lasted years.

20. Fernand Braudel, *The Mediterranean and the Mediterranean World in the Age of Philip II,* 2 vols. (New York: Harper and Row, 1972–73). Braudel was a leading historian and a pioneer of the *Annales* school in France, which sought to change history from the recital of dynasties, wars, and high politics to penetrating the daily life of an epoch as it was shaped by mountains, sea, desert, and climate, and how people lived and communicated. Treating the inland seas as a highway, uniting its shores, the book is marvelous reading until the second half of Vol. 2, when it unaccountably reverts to a traditional history of kings and diplomacy.

21. Fernand Braudel, *Civilization and Capitalism Fifteenth–Eighteenth Century,* Vol. 2, *The Wheels of Commerce* (New York: Harper and Row, 1982–84). Long-distance runners should go through all three books of Braudel's masterly *Civilization and Capitalism* and sprinters who start with the first volume, *The Structures of Everyday Life,* or Vol. 3, *The Perspectives of the World,* may be tempted, after recovering their reading wind, to tackle the others. *Wheels,* Vol. 2, treats of local markets — fairs, shops, market towns, and the beginnings of capitalistic production in cottage industry organized by merchants — as opposed to *Structures,* dealing with traditional peasant society and *Perspectives,* on "distant trade," binding up the world (and the national) economy. All three are brilliant, erudite, even dazzling, as Braudel, the pointillist, describes life in the gap between the medieval period and the factory age.

22. Gordon A. Craig, *The Germans* (New York: New American Library, 1982). Craig is the leading American historian of Germany, focusing on the contemporary era. In this book he distills from years of research some overall conclusions about the Germans, their history, their present attitudes, and hazards a few guesses about the future. I was originally drawn to the book by the chapter on "Money," almost devoid of monetary history in the institutional sense, but penetrating on German attitudes toward money as revealed by history and quotations from Goethe's *Faust,* Wagner, Marx, et al. There is more to it, much more, with chapters on Jews, women, literature, the military, etc., and an appendix, taking off from Mark Twain, on "The Awful German Language."

23. P. G. M. Dickson, *The Financial Revolution in England: A*

Study in the Development of Public Credit (New York: St. Martin's, 1967). This may strike some as a heavy monograph, as it traces the development of British government finance after the Glorious Revolution that in 1688 replaced the Stuarts with the House of Orange. Tax farming gave way to bureaucratic handling of tax revenue and government expenditures. Chaotic debt instruments — many of them issued, in effect, by small units of the army and navy — were scrapped in favor of regular public debt. The Bank of England came into being. The period covers the South Sea bubble and Dutch investment in England. Solid, but not bedtime reading.

24. Stanley Hoffmann et al., *In Search of France* (Cambridge, Mass.: Harvard University Press, 1963). This symposium fills the need for a companion piece on France to Barzini on Italy and Craig on the Germans. Too much of it perhaps, for present purposes, deals with politics and with domestic and foreign policy, but it has two penetrating sociological analyses by Wylie and Pitts, the former on the French peasant and village, the latter on aristocratic and bourgeois values. The dominance of aristocratic values which emphasize the act of virtuosity that others cannot match — whether on the field of battle, in conversation in the salon, driving an automobile, eating splendiferously, or in the boudoir — inhibits economic growth, except insofar as it depends on scientific achievement.

25. Stephen A. Schuker, *The End of French Predominance in Europe: The Financial Crisis of 1924 and the Adoption of the Dawes Plan* (Chapel Hill, N.C.: University of North Carolina Press, 1976). This book is badly titled, and the subject matter is conveyed rather in the subtitle. Schuker, a modern historian, shows in detail how French financial weaknesses, which had their origin in the rips in French social fabric, frustrated French political aims in the post–World War I settlement. The book is meticulously researched in archives in four countries and makes compelling reading.

26. Warren C. Scoville, *The Persecution of Huguenots and French Economic Development, 1680–1720* (Los Angeles: University of California Press, 1960). My recent interest in the Huguenots was aroused by the question of whether the emigration of a tenth of their number who refused to abjure Calvinist Protestantism after the Revocation of the Edict of Nantes in 1685, with their wealth and skills (especially in glass and papermaking and in silk), hurt the economic development of France. Scoville is indecisive on the point. French economic growth was slowed, but other factors, such as the wars of Louis XIV and bad harvests, contributed. Chapter 9, on finance and agriculture, is particularly absorbing.

27. Lawrence Stone, *The Crisis of the Aristocracy, 1558–1641* (abridged edition) (London: Oxford University Press, 1967). Stone pins down the watershed between medieval and modern England to the period between 1580 and 1620, as capitalist institutions and ethics began to replace aristocratic love of gambling, conspicuous consumption, and honors. Chapter 9 on credit reminds one of today's credit card addicts who need financial restructuring, but many of these debtors were aristocrats with unpaid bills and debts to moneylenders. If the world today is a junk bond casino, as Felix Rohatyn has characterized it, the Elizabethan age saw individual indebtedness of dukes and earls as high as £60,000, when the pound sterling was a heavy currency.

28. Barry Supple, *Commercial Crisis and Change in England, 1600–1642, A Study in the Instability of a Mercantile Economy* (Cambridge: Cambridge University Press, 1959). A solid study of the disturbed monetary conditions in Britain at the opening of the modern period, with an account of the debates over bullionism, the foreign exchanges and foreign-exchange control, mercantilism, and the money supply. The debates often have an echo of present-day controversy.

29. Pierre Vilar, *A History of Gold and Money, 1450–1920* (London: New Left Books, 1976). Of the several books on the history of money, this is by far the best. There is a strong emphasis on the impact of the New World on European finances, starting with Columbus, who, over the three months that his voyage took, mentioned his interest in finding gold 65 times in his diary. The book is scholarly, but it is a page-turner.

30. Charles Wilson, *Anglo-Dutch Commerce and Finance in the Eighteenth Century* (Cambridge: Cambridge University Press, 1941). This is a scholarly account of the transitions of Holland from trade to sophisticated finance and of commercial and financial supremacy from Amsterdam to London.

Classics in the History of Financial Thought

31. Walter Bagehot, *Lombard Street* (1873) is Vol. 9 of Norman St. John-Stevas, ed., *The Collected Works of Walter Bagehot* (London: The Economist, 1978). Bagehot was for years the editor of *The Economist*, started in 1848 by James Wilson, his father-in-law, and wrote prolifically on economic and political subjects. *Lombard Street* is his most famous work, describing the operations of the London money and capital market at the end of the third quarter of the nineteenth century. There is an inconclusive debate as to whether Bagehot (pronounced BADGE-ette)

was a better writer than economist or vice versa. There is no doubt, however, that he wrote superbly.

32. Jean Bouvier, *Le Krach de l'Union Générale (1878–1885)* (Paris: Presses universitaires de France, 1960). An outsider, Eugène Bontoux, a Catholic with connections to the French nobility, left the *grandes écoles* to start a bank in Lyons at the time when France was recovering from the doldrums of the 1870s (after payment of the Franco-Prussian indemnity) and beginning to feel its oats. Bontoux challenged the Protestant-Jewish banking establishment of Paris, started off a boom in foreign and domestic investment — and fell flat. The Establishment chose not to pick him up. The details, in French, are delicious. "Krach," by the way, is French coinage for "crash."

33. Murray Teigh Bloom, *The Man Who Stole Portugal* (New York: Scribner's, 1966). This book was written following the death in 1965 of one Alves Reis, a Portuguese, who in the 1920s forged orders to the London printer Waterlow and Sons, instructing them to deliver to him the plates for printing the Portuguese 500-escudo note. He printed and spent some 200,000 of them (worth about $5 million) in that country. Roughly a fifth were used to buy foreign deposits and securities. The rest produced a Keynesian economic expansion in Portugal until Reis was caught.

34. Martin G. Buist, *At Spes non Fracta: Hope and Co. 1700–1815* (The Hague: Martinus Nijhoff, 1974). The Latin motto of the book title (But Hope Is Not Lost) may obscure what the book is about. It is, however, an account of the Dutch bank established by a Scot, John Hope, and especially the work of Peter C. Labouchere, the leading partner during the Napoleonic Wars, who had married the daughter of Sir Francis Baring of Baring Brothers, London. The merchant bank clung to commodity trade and speculation throughout the century, instead of specializing in trade or finance. Among his impressive deals were lending the United States money for the Louisiana Purchase in 1803, transmitting funds owed by Spain to France by way of Mexico, Baltimore, London, and Amsterdam to Paris, and surviving the Amsterdam financial crises of 1763 and 1772 that toppled rival banking houses.

35. John Carswell, *The South Sea Bubble* (London: Cresset Press, 1960). Two speculative bubbles were pricked in 1720, first the Mississippi and then the South Sea, whereupon the speculators departed for Amsterdam and Hamburg to conflate insurance bubbles in those centers. The financial machinations become intricate at times, and the connections among trade, the national debt, and frenzied stock exchange speculation are hard to keep clearly in mind. The Carswell book is a solid one, however.

36. Youssef Cassis, *Les banquiers de la City à l'époque Edouardienne* (Geneva-Paris: Librairie Droz, 1984). This is a study of 460 London bankers before World War I, divided among merchant bankers, deposit bankers, joint-stock bankers, etc., who are examined in sociological terms to observe their origins, education, wealth, social standing, marriage customs (in terms of who they marry), and their relations with the British aristocracy and the political elite. Unlike much sociology, however, it makes for interesting reading. The leading caste of merchant bankers is divided into Quakers, Anglicans, old foreign and new foreign groups, with a number of Jews among the last two categories. Cassis, who wrote this from Geneva but on the basis of English material, including some previously unexamined diaries, observes that the bankers were powerful and rich, largely descended from other bankers, only a few of them self-made men. He exonerates them from the charges of exercising dominant political power and of starting World War I. Their ranks, moreover, were far from solid on even such issues as free trade and the gold standard. The book will probably be translated into English. For those unwilling to wait, this original version is highly recommended.

37. Center for Medieval and Renaissance Studies, University of California, Los Angeles, *The Dawn of Modern Banking* (New Haven: Yale University Press, 1979). This is a scholarly collection of studies by leading medieval scholars in the United States and Europe that covers the rise of banking in Italy and Spain, the shift of focus to southern Germany, the rise of the bill of exchange and of credit in England, banking without banks in the Middle East under the Muhammadan ban on interest, with a particularly useful discussion of usury laws and their limited effect on the development of bank lending. It provides a running start to an understanding of the development of modern banking in the seventeenth century.

38. Paul Emden, *Money Powers of Europe in the Nineteenth and Twentieth Centuries* (New York: Appleton-Century, 1938). This is a most agreeable book of sketches, pastiches, anecdotes about banks and bankers of Britain and the Continent. Some of the stories are funny, such as the account of Labouchere's being turned down for a partnership in Hope & Co. and asking what if he married Sir Francis Baring's daughter; then, after being turned down for the hand of the daughter, on the ground that he was only a bank clerk, asking what if he were a partner in Hope. P.S., he got both the job and the girl. My copy has only one-third of the index, in a second printing from sheets, the missing two-thirds having been destroyed in the London blitz. Emden, not to be confused with Paul Erdman, whose *The Crash of 1979* almost made the novel

section, is a bright and breezy journalist of the sort whose books not only pass leisure time but fill it up.

39. Richard Ehrenberg, *Capitalism and Finance in the Age of the Renaissance, A Study of the Fuggers* (New York: Harcourt Brace, 1928). This classic study of the Fugger bank in Augsburg in the sixteenth century focuses on war and money: Money is needed to buy soldiers, but with soldiers one can acquire money. The Fuggers were involved with Venice, Austria, the Holy Roman Empire, the financial markets of Lyons, Bruges, and Antwerp, and through them with the Spanish crown, which proved their ultimate undoing. The financial center of Europe was moving northward from Lucca, Florence, and Venice. (Genoa, a rival of the Fuggers for the Spanish treasure that was overdue in payment for loans when it reached Seville, hung on longer.) The period was one of struggling capital markets. The mistake that brought down the Fuggers, and many a bank before and since, was lending too much to kings on inadequate security.

40. James S. Gibbons, *The Banks of New York, Their Dealers, the Clearing House and the Panic of 1857* (New York: D. Appleton, n.d.). If you liked Martin Mayer's *The Bankers* (New York, paperback edition: Ballantine, 1976), and thousands did, you will like *The Banks of New York* of a little more than a century earlier, which explains how banks worked in those days, setting forth the duties of the president, cashier, teller, note teller, runner, porter, etc., and including at the end a description of the brand-new clearinghouse and the recent excitement in the international panic of 1857. There is much talk of embezzlement and monitoring. "There is perhaps no record of a bank fraud extant of which the perpetrator was not honest *yesterday*" (his italics). The clearinghouse in an average market exchanges $25 million daily. A good game for the modern banker would be to decide how much of the lessons and advice is relevant today.

41. Bray Hammond, *Banks and Politics in America: from the Revolution to the Civil War* (Princeton, N.J.: Princeton University Press, 1957). I knew Bray Hammond, for many years the secretary of the board of governors of the Federal Reserve System, but did not read his books. I want to include some material on U.S. finance of general, rather than scholarly, interest. Within the last category are such blockbusters as Milton Friedman and Anna Schwartz's *Monetary History of the United States* (Princeton: Princeton University Press, 1963); Margaret Meyers, Benjamin Beckhart, and James G. Smith's four-volume *New York Money Market* (New York: Columbia University Press, 1931, 1932; Vol. 1 [at least] reprinted in 1971); W. Randolph Burgess, *The Federal Reserve Banks & the Money Market,* revised edition (New York: Garland

Publishing, 1983). A later Hammond volume is *Sovereignty and the Empty Purse: Banks and Politics in the Civil War* (Princeton: Princeton University Press, 1970). Choose your tipple.

42. John Maynard Keynes, *Economic Consequences of the Peace* (New York: Harcourt Brace, 1919), *Collected Writings,* Vol. 2. This is a curious item, difficult to classify, perhaps even belonging under "fiction." It is a brilliant polemic that changed the course of history. By saying that the Germans could not pay the reparations sketched out at Versailles, it practically ensured that they would not. Loaded with purple passages, including descriptions of the Big Four (Clemenceau, Orlando, Lloyd George, and Wilson, with whom the British adviser· Keynes seldom met), it is explained by its detractors as an attempt to justify to the Bloomsbury set Keynes's failure to join them as conscientious objectors during World War I or as a reaction to his intimacy with a German negotiator, Dr. Melchior of the Warburg bank in Hamburg. The overall conclusion that Germany might be able to pay $10 billion in reparations, but not an amount many times that, is undoubtedly just.

43. John Berry McFerrin, *Caldwell & Company: A Southern Financial Empire* (1939) (Nashville: Vanderbilt University Press, 1969). This is a sleeper. Written during the 1930s as a doctoral dissertation, it was published in 1939 by the University of North Carolina Press, went out of print, and then was reissued 30 years later in Tennessee, where the original investment house that failed with a bang in November 1930 had flourished. Caldwell & Co. was an aggressive issuer of municipal bonds that leveraged up by requiring the issuing city to maintain the money in its banks until used, and employed the funds in buying more banks and insurance companies. When municipal bonds fell after the stock market crash, Caldwell scrambled for cash for a year before his empire collapsed around him. A cautionary tale like the *Union Générale* of Bouvier, if not on the spectacular scale of the South Sea and Mississippi bubbles.

44. David S. Landes, *Bankers and Pashas, International Finance and Economic Imperialism in Egypt* (Cambridge, Mass: Harvard University Press, 1958). This book, somewhat like that of Iris Origo, below, originated in the discovery of a mass of (1860s) correspondence in Paris of a private bank (later absorbed into De Neuflize, Schlumberger et Cie.), between Edouard Devieu in Paris and Alfred André in Alexandria. The 1860s were a time of boom and bust in cotton, as the U.S. Civil War first took cotton off the market and then let loose a large accumulation. The completion of the Suez Canal in 1869 added complications. But the cupidity of the Egyptians and its exploitation by French, British,

and to some extent German bankers call to mind the 1970s boom and bust in oil.

45. Iris Origo, *The Merchant of Prato: Francesco di Marco Datini* (New York: Knopf, 1957). Prato is a town outside Florence. During the Black Death, started in 1347, Datini stayed in Florence and corresponded with his wife in Prato. He kept this correspondence, as well as his business letters to his correspondents in Avignon, Barcelona, elsewhere — more than 150,000 documents in all. These have been organized by an Italian archivist, Ruggero Nuti, and Iris Cutting Origo, an American woman married to an Italian, who, with advice from economic historians Raymond de Roover and Federigo Melis, wrote this fascinating account. Datini was more trader than banker, perhaps, but a prudent, infinitely patient man who refused to lend to kings or prelates, financed no wars, and stayed clear of political quarrels. The late Alexander Gerschenkron, to whom I recommended the book, was astounded that Datini would undertake complex multilateral transactions that were risky, took three years, and netted him only 10 percent overall, or close to 3 percent a year.

46. Ellis T. Powell, *The Evolution of the Money Market (1385–1915): An Historical and Analytical Study of the Rise and Development of Finance as a Central Coordinated Force* (1915) (New York: A. M. Kelley, 1966). This monograph has two points of interest, one substantial. The point of substance is that it is a history of the London financial market expressed in terms of natural selection and evolution, the survival of the fittest, with the gradual disappearance of organisms incapable of adaptation. The lesser point is that the copy in the Kress Rare Book Library at the Graduate School of Business Administration of Harvard University has had written on the inside cover: "This book was compiled by Powell from his notes on my historical lectures at the School of Economics, including even some of the little jokes with which I tried to keep the class awake (the lectures were delivered from 7 to 9 p.m.). Not a word of acknowledgement of course." Kenneth Carpenter told me that the handwriting on the note was that of H. S. Foxwell, an avid book collector as well as an economist, who sold one accumulation to the Goldsmith's Library of the University of London and a second to the Kress Library at the Business School.

47. Raymond de Roover, *Gresham on Foreign Exchange: An Essay on Early English Mercantilism* (Cambridge, Mass.: Harvard University Press, 1949). This is an account of the operations of Queen Elizabeth's "exchanger" who borrowed funds in Bruges and Antwerp and transmitted them to London. "Gresham's Law," that bad money drives out good, did not originate with Gresham, and was in fact ascribed to him by

McCleod in the nineteenth century entirely in error. But there is much of interest in this account of ways of remitting funds.

48. Raymond de Roover, *The Rise and Fall of the Medici Bank, 1397–1494* (New York: W. W. Norton, 1966). This is a fascinating account of banking (and trade) in the medieval period by the leading financial historian of the post–World War II era who taught at the Harvard Business School. Like earlier Italian bankers — the Ricciardi, the Bardi, Peruzzi, and the Aiaccuoli of northern Italy, so-called Lombards although they came especially from Tuscany — the Medici had networks of branches to serve domestic and international trade and the papacy. Like them, the Medici were brought down at the end of the century, after their heyday under Cosimo from 1429–64, by unauthorized loans to sovereign borrowers, notably the Duke of Burgundy. Additional troubles sprang from an unexplained depression. The spread of the bank was wide, with headquarters in Florence and branches in Rome, Venice, Naples, Milan, and Pisa, and in Avignon, Geneva, Lyons, plus, importantly, Bruges, and, of lesser significance, the provincial town of London.

49. Henry Thornton, *An Enquiry into the Nature and the Effect of the Paper Credit of Great Britain, together with the Evidence* (1802), edited with an introduction by F. A. Hayek (New York: A. M. Kelley, 1978). Henry Thornton was a Quaker, banker, Member of Parliament, friend of William Wilberforce, a fighter against slavery, who wrote one of the pioneering books in monetary theory. He was a member of the committee that wrote the *Bullion Report* of 1810 ascribing the depreciation of the pound sterling during the Napoleonic Wars (the high price of bullion while the pound was inconvertible) to overissue by the Bank of England, rather than to a series of particular circumstances such as bad harvests, the Continental blockade, and subsidies to British allies on the Continent. But *Paper Credit* is his classic statement, far ahead of the understanding of money and banking of his day, judicious in its unwillingness to side entirely with what would today be called the Keynesian view that money should expand with business, or with the Currency School that recommended a fixed supply. The book contains a well-developed theory of the lender of last resort, rationalized 70 years later by Bagehot. The book may be somewhat austere for reading after dinner, preceded by cocktails and followed by brandy. It is perhaps a better candidate for reading near the end of this list than at the beginning.

50. J. G. Van Dillen, ed., *History of the Principal Public Banks* (The Hague: Martinus Nijhoff, 1934). This symposium deals with the large public deposit banks starting with the bank of St. George in Genoa (1272), and has essays by leading economic historians of the time:

Heckscher on the Bank of Sweden (in its dealings with the banks of Amsterdam), Luzzato on the Bank of Venice, van Dillen, the editor, on the Bank of Amsterdam that flourished from 1619 to the French occupation of the city in 1795. The banks operated on the whole with 100 percent reserves, issuing deposits against all kinds of coin and bullion which they first assayed. Their contribution was to furnish a standard money and to spare merchants the trouble — called transactions costs in modern economics — of testing monies received. A distinction thus arose between bank money — liabilities of the deposit banks — and variegated coin, with different exchange rates.

NOTE

1. They are *The World in Depression, 1929–1939* (2d ed., 1986); *Keynesianism vs. Monetarism and Other Essays in Financial History* (1985); *A Financial History of Western Europe* (2d ed., 1993); and *Manias, Panics and Crashes, A History of Financial Crises* (3d ed., 1996).

Part 2

Economic History

Technological Diffusion: European Experience to 1850

Rates of economic growth have recently been explained in terms of "catching up" in technical capacity. One country pushes ahead in invention and/or innovation by some means, for example under the pressure of wartime demands, as the United States in World War II, and others, following peace and recovery from wartime destruction and dislocation, in due course catch up, i.e., learn and apply the leader's technology within the limits of economic appropriateness. The failure of the developing world to catch up with the standards of the most developed states is explained in terms of a lack of "social capability"—a deliberately vague expression which is roughly measured by a country's average years of education (Abramovitz 1986, 1990). Other concepts of comparable vagueness have been noted, and in some cases studied, to include social adaptability (Henderson 1969, p. 22), creativity (Mokyr 1990), national vitality,[1] capacity to transform (Economic Commission of Europe 1954), and even supply elasticity.

The diffusion of technological change is, of course, not a new topic, and in particular the diffusion of the industrial revolution from Britain to the Continent has been well studied.[2] A 1974 paper stated that diffusion used to be studied in terms of anthropology, sociology, and psychology (Saxonhouse 1974, p. 159), implying that analysis had turned or returned to more narrowly economic considerations such as the presence or absence of various types of natural resources, secure property rights, guilds, monopolies, and availability of foreign markets, high or low wages, capital availability, and the like. Different economists and economic historians have attached different values to different elements. Alexander Gerschenkron developed a theory that as one

This essay originally appeared in the *Journal of Evolutionary Economics* 5, no. 3 (1995): 229–42. It was printed again in Kurt Dopfer, ed., *The Global Dimension of Economic Evolution: Knowledge Variety and Diffusion in Economic Growth and Development* (Heidelberg: Physica-Verlag, 1995), pp. 49–62. Physica-Verlag owns the copyright and has granted permission for reproduction.

moved east from Britain which grew through its effective entrepreneurship, at one distance banks substituted for entrepreneurship, while still further east government took the lead in producing economic development (Gerschenkron 1962). Among the factors from other social sciences, including political science in addition to those listed earlier, have been cultural values, the openness of society, especially the presence of a robust middle class, the centralized or pluralist character of government, and many more.

Not only is social capability a somewhat crude concept; so are catching up and its corollary of income convergence. Catching up makes little allowance for independent spurts of economic growth through technological creativity. Britain's industrial revolution in the eighteenth century could possibly be interpreted as catching up with the Italian city-states and the United Provinces of Holland, but only in a few lines like shipping and textiles. A given country may be overtaken, and growth paths which converged may diverge again as the overtaken economy is left behind (Kindleberger 1978, pp. 185–236). Simple-minded catching up appears to rest on a model with only one output, whereas the theory of comparative advantage makes it virtually inevitable that if a country is ahead in all lines of industry, its lead in some outstrips that in others. Years of education may serve as a proxy for social capability between highly developed countries on the one hand and less developed countries on the other, but within either group it is likely that the capacity to catch up, insofar as it rests on education, will vary widely depending on the type. Education is not all of a piece. Simple literacy involving primary schooling may be more or less comparable, but secondary education may branch between classical and vocational, and higher education ramifies more widely. Even within a single institution like the Ecole Polytechnique there were pulls toward pure mathematics led by La Place, and a more applied branch of science represented by the founder, Monge, despite his profession as an analytical geometer (Fox 1975). The number, scope, and nature of educational institutions, moreover, are usually not exogenously given in the course of development, but are intimately related to it, being established in particular circumstances for particular purposes. The French created a series of institutions during and after the Revolution and the Napoleonic wars (Kindleberger 1976, pp. 3–39), as Prussia did after the 1806 defeat at Jena and the humiliating treaty of Tilsit (Ritter 1961). English technical education may be said to have been nonexistent in a formal sense until the realization following the Great Exhibition of 1851 that the country was falling behind in the application of science. The remarkable careers of engineers like Telford, Rennie, and Brindley, who were without formal education, produced in

Britain a strong bias against such education, much admired in France, some of which persisted into the twentieth century (Hughes 1966, p. 11). An educational system both changes the character and pace of economic growth, and is changed by them.

In addition, economic and social institutions may affect technological progress either positively or negatively. Guilds initially promoted high standards of workmanship and artisanal training, and thereby assisted economic development. At a later stage they restricted entry and output, and held standards too high in the face of cheaper but serviceable substitutes (Cipolla 1968, p. 137). The Venetian government, for example, refused to allow its weavers to meet British, Dutch, and French competition in the seventeenth century by relaxing the methods and standards that had served for six centuries, clinging to the over-optimistic belief that Venetian quality would prevail in the long run (Rapp 1976, pp. 154–55). Strict attention to individual property rights generally stimulates profit-seeking development, but it can also inhibit peasants from moving off the farm to industry, and get in the way of projects that necessarily involve cooperation, such as irrigation or rendering rivers navigable. Governments sometimes stimulate the wrong industries, destined to collapse when subsidies are withdrawn, as in the specialty factories of Frederick the Great's Berlin. And banks have not only been singled out as a crucial development institution, they have also been widely accused of diverting savings from profitable investment opportunities at home to speculative securities or adventures abroad.

This paper is addressed to the diffusion of British technology developed in the industrial revolution to the Continent, especially France and Prussia, ending about 1850 when the gap between England and Prussia which in 1800 had been estimated roughly as somewhere between 50 and 100 years had been more or less closed.[3] Little attention is given to the technology itself, widely studied in numerous books including those of Mokyr, Landes, Henderson already referred to, and of Nathan Rosenberg,[4] somewhat more to the transmission mechanism. It addresses the question whether diffusion was especially rapid, slow, or of varying speeds in different industrial lines, at different times and places. The thesis is that the economic growth of a country — and its absorption of foreign technology, given enough initial social capacity — tends to follow an S- or Gompertz or logistic curve, starting slowly, picking up speed, and eventually slowing down. The idea is not new. Alfred Marshall in *Industry and Trade* compares British and German industry, and cites that old business in an old country is in danger of underrating the advantages of that which is new (Marshall 1920, p. 103), and that German industry, being younger than British, naturally grows faster: a young boy grows very fast (Marshall 1920, p. 139). The model is of little value for forecasting since economies, unlike human beings, can be reborn economically, with new S-curves growing out of those that are slowing down or even declining absolutely. The analysis is broadly comparable with that of Walt Rostow in his *Stages of Growth* (Rostow 1960), without his preoccupation with the dating of turning points, and going beyond his last stage of "high level mass consumption," to later absolute or at least relative decline. Technological change, including imitation, adaptation, improvement, independent invention, and innovation, followed by a slowing down in technical creativity, is of course only one dimension of the growth curve, and is matched in rough parallel by comparable profiles in savings, productivity, responsiveness to market stimuli, monopoly formation, consolidation of economic interests, acceptance of risk, etc.

Before 1600 Britain was said to be parasitically dependent for its technology on the Continent (Harris 1972). The country depended on the skills of German miners, of Dutch engineers specialized in draining wetlands, and of French civil engineers and naval architects. In the 1680s Ambrose Crowley imported nailmakers from Liège in the Southern Netherlands to his plant then at Sunderland, whether to instruct North country workers in new skills or to piece out his labor supply is unclear (Flinn 1953, p. 244). The Revocation of the Edict of Nantes by Louis XIV in 1685 produced a diaspora of Huguenot artisans as well as financiers, and brought to Britain workers skilled in glass, clocks, silk, typically goods of high quality and cost, produced for the monarchy, the nobility, and the rich. Sometime during the seventeenth century, the transmission of technology became two-way. Nottingham manufacturers perfected the stocking knitting frame and in 1696 the British government enacted measures to prevent the export of the technique. After two years of spying in Italy, John Lombe acquired the plans for a silk-throwing mill à la Bolognese, from which his brother Thomas built a mill at Derby, the largest factory in Britain at the time, 1717 (Poni 1971). As early as 1719 the British government forbade the emigration of skilled artisans to the Continent, as the English were learning, with the help of tariffs, to reproduce Indian muslins and printed calicos (Rostow 1975, pp. 62–64). Dutch brothers named Eler came to England in 1688 to produce fine red and black earthenware. So anxious were they to preserve their secrets that they hired only idiots at the throwing wheel, before a Burslem potter, according to the story, posed as an idiot, obtained employment, in two years acquiring their secrets and setting up a rival pot works (Lord 1966, pp. 48–49). The Newcomen steam engine was developed in 1709, and by the end of the century there were 800 of them spread over Britain, but never more than 100 on the Continent (Geiger 1974, p. 72). Abraham Darby's puddling technique to burn carbon out of cast iron was discovered in the same year. It and John Kay's flying shuttle in 1730 for weaving made clear that British innovative qualities were on the increase. In 1750 the government renewed and extended the ban on the emigration of artisans. Before that date, however, John Kay who had failed to earn a patent for the flying shuttle left for France where he was helped by government to produce card-making machines for weaving and teach the use of his shuttle (Henderson 1954, pp. 11–13n). In 1750, too, John Holker, a Jacobite who had participated in the abortive revolt that ended in the defeat of the Young Pretender in 1745 at Carlisle, went to France to set up the first of a series of cotton mills in Rouen.[5]

Recent literature has questioned whether there was an industrial revolution in Britain, and if so when it occurred. The evidence against the revolution is the gradualness of the rise in income per capita (Crafts 1985; Cameron 1985). From the perspective of technology, however, the reality of revolution is clear. Before 1760 there were fewer than a dozen patents a year. The number rose to 31 in 1766 when James Watt patented his steam engine, and to 36 in 1769 when Richard Arkwright patented the water frame. Halévy observed that all the important innovations were crowded into the decade between 1766 and 1775 (Halévy 1924, p. 102). Whatever the macroeconomic numbers of overall growth per capita, there is no doubt of an industrial revolution in technology (Berg and Hudson 1992).

In Europe in the eighteenth century, artisans typically indulged in tramping or wandering, especially farm labor in the off-season. There is something of a dispute whether there is a difference between wandering in search of work, and travel undertaken more purposefully to acquire industrial knowledge. Redlich thought that the distinction could be over-drawn and that the two amounted to the same thing for an intelligent artisan. He went further and stated that the wanderings of handworkers and the travels of the industrially concerned aristocrat or leading business-man in the eighteenth century were "an important, perhaps the most important factor in early industrialization" (Redlich 1968, pp. 344–45).

Be that as it may, a substantial movement of wanderers and travel-ers to Britain and the Continent started practically simultaneously with the burst of inventions. The French government sent Gabriel Jars to England in 1765–66 to examine iron works and collieries. His instructions were drawn by the expatriate, John Holker, then Inspector General of Factories in France (Henderson 1954, p. 22n). He was followed by de la Houlière on an official mission in 1775, and by Constantin

Perier of the Paris machinery plant in 1777.[6] Claus Friederich von Reden, in charge of Frederick the Great's Mining Office in Silesia, made his first trip to England in 1776, visiting mines there and others in Germany and France on the way (Henderson 1958). His younger opposite number in West Prussia, Baron vom Stein, visited England in an extensive tour from November 1786 to August 1787 on a similar exploratory mission (Henderson 1958, p. 33). vom Stein irritated Matthew Boulton of the Boulton and Watt firm that produced Watt engines at Soho outside Birmingham by pressing a workman at the Barclay and Perkins brewery in London to let him inspect its steam engine (Henderson 1954, p. 140n). "Even a man of the rank and ethical greatness of vom Stein used dubious methods on his travels to England to obtain industrial knowledge" (Redlich 1968, p. 342n).

Perhaps the prize for visits was earned by Johann Conrad Fischer, a Swiss metallurgist, who visited Britain six times between 1794 and the Crystal Palace Exhibition of 1851. Fischer developed a method for crucible steel on his own after learning that the product had been made at Benjamin Huntsman's plant in Sheffield. At an early stage he marked his produce "B. Huntsman," excusing himself in his diary by saying that the suggestion that he do so had come from a Lyons merchant.[7] Another distinguished Swiss engineer, Johann Georg Bodmer, made an exploratory visit to the Midlands in 1816–17, and ultimately settled in London, something akin to the post–World War II "brain-drain." A capable inventor of a process for casting toothed wheels for cogged tracks, and a mechanical stoker, he ultimately gathered a group of Swiss engineers who came to his shop, then in Manchester, to learn their trade (Court 1938, p. 207). While Scotsmen studied on the Continent, notably at the University of Leiden, and German chemists visited the Conservatoire in Paris after 1815 to study with Gay-Lussac, there is little evidence that Continental industrialists and workers attended English educational institutions, as opposed to visiting and apprenticing, though *savants* attended meetings of the British Association for the Advancement of Science founded in 1831.

The gap opened up between British and Continental industry by the industrial revolution widened with the series of wars of the period: the Seven Years' War of 1756–63, the War of American Independence, 1775–83, the Fourth Anglo-Dutch War of 1780–84, and especially the Revolutionary and Napoleonic Wars from 1792 to 1815, with a brief intermission with the Treaty of Amiens in 1802. The Napoleonic Continental System or blockade from 1806 to 1814 somewhat reduced the considerable flow of manufactured goods and colonial products, and aided by the British embargo, of machinery, smuggled to the Continent, especially through Hamburg (Heckscher 1922). Liétvin Bauwens who had worked two years in England before the war to pick up tanning techniques for his father's business, later as a prospective textile manufacturer brought machinery, a steam engine, and some workers from London to Ghent, then a part of France, by way of Hamburg, though not without some losses of equipment and men (Dhondt 1955, p. 20). Charles Ballot's posthumous dissertation, completed by his colleagues after his death at Verdun, provides dramatic accounts of Bauwens's smuggling efforts for cotton machinery and homesick English workers, complete with storms, the firing of shots, picnic hampers covered with fruit, and the like (Ballot 1923, pp. 99–103). A French government official traveled from Paris to London by way of Mainz and the Netherlands in 1797, staying in England several months to satisfy his curiosity about British financial techniques, and especially the consequences, of which there were few, of the suspension of specie payments by the "Bank of London" (England) (Mollien 1845, pp. 186–90).

While the Napoleonic wars and blockade put no insuperable barriers in the way of purposeful imitation of British industrial development on the Continent, defeat of Prussia by Napoleon at Jena in 1806, and of Napoleon by the allies led by Wellington at Waterloo in 1815, stirred great interest in France and Prussia in pushing industrialization. One manifestation of this interest, largely distinct from imitation of the British path, was the establishment of schools, institutes, conservatories, universities for the promotion of science and technology. The pressure had begun earlier with the establishment of the Corps and Ecole des Ponts et Chaussées in France in 1747, and with schools of mines in Berlin and Paris in 1770 and 1783 respectively (Gillespie 1980). Parker has described the differences between the French and German styles of teaching mining, the one more theoretical, the other more practical, with French mining engineers requiring considerable on-the-job training before they were competent to run mines.[8] With first the Revolution and then Waterloo, there began a series of new educational institutions: the Conservatoire des Arts et Métiers in 1793, and the next year the Ecole Polytechnique, which Frederick Artz has called, perhaps hyperbolically, "in some ways the most significant advance in the whole history of higher education in Europe" (Artz 1966, p. 151). The Ecole Polytechnique was established as a reaction against the Sorbonne and the Catholic Church. It contained within it, as already stated, the clash between mathematics and applied science, and with the Restoration in 1815 came under attack by royalists and Catholics, which it weathered.

The Conservatoire evolved during the war into a vocational school at the popular level. Chaptal, Napoleon's Minister of the Interior, was troubled by the lead that the British had in spinning and weaving wool and linen. He brought to France one of the best constructors in Great Britain, one William Douglass, formed an establishment, and in a short time (*un peu de temps*) the French workers were able not only to undertake spinning but to manufacture the machines (Chaptal 1819, p. 16). In due course the Conservatoire became famous for its collection of machine models (which served as a prototype for Beuth in Prussia) and for chemistry, Chaptal's primary interest, with Gay-Lussac, whose laboratory attracted budding chemists from Germany.[9] The Ecole des Arts et Métiers evolved from a prerevolutionary school started by the Duc de la Rochefoucault for the children of his regiment of dragoons. The Ecole Central des Arts et Manufactures was started privately in 1829 by a number of industrialists unhappy with the supply of engineers.[10]

As in France, so in Prussia, upsets, including defeat at Jena, led to major resolves to establish further institutions of largely practical training. Secondary schools increased in number, the system of gymnasiums was revised, new universities created (Berlin, 1810, Breslau, 1811, Bonn, 1818). Established universities like Halle and Göttingen changed direction, with a de-emphasis on religion and philosophy and increased attention to science. All universities emphasized the connection between research and teaching as advocated by Wilhelm Humboldt (Ritter 1961, p. 25n). Among the most effective institutions advancing industrialization was the Gewerbeinstitut and the related Gewerbeschule, also known as Technische Hochschule, started by Peter Beuth. Beuth had become interested in industry while billeted during the Napoleonic wars with the Prussian army at William Cockerill's machinery plant at Liège. As head of the Department of Trade and Industry of the Ministry of Finance from 1816, Beuth established what would today be called an industrial policy for Prussia, traveling himself to inspect industrial establishments in France, Belgium, Holland, and England, as well as in other German provinces. He trained young men between the ages of 12 and 16, chose outstanding students among them for voyages abroad as travelers or workers in foreign plants, bought foreign machinery models, and after having them copied, passed the originals on to Prussian entrepreneurs. Leading political figures, scholars, and manufacturers met under his auspices on a continuous basis, published volumes of their transactions dealing with foreign inventions and construction projects. Among the industrialists he helped get started with government subsidies were William and James Cockerill, sons of the English machine builder of Liège and Seraing in Belgium, F. A. J. Egells who built steam engines, and August Borsig, who dedicated his twenty-fifth locomotive to Beuth (Benaerts 1933a; Henderson 1958). The Gewerbeinstitut also followed

French practice in holding industrial exhibitions with prizes and honors. Funds for the purchase of foreign machines were provided by *Seehandlung,* a corporation set up to promote Prussian overseas trade.

The passion for education was not limited to the middle and upper clases. An anthropologist has characterized the German workman as having "an insatiable lust for learning," and being "culture greedy." Much of this was general rather than vocational education, relying on German classical writers like Schiller. It constituted nonetheless a break with traditional society (Lowie 1946, pp. 71–73).

As in France, the technical institutes were not universally admired in Germany. At the time of the 1848 abortive revolution, many conservative government officials regarded them as enemies of religion and authority, and sought to restrict their privileges. Some recovery in esteem was made under the enlightened leadership toward the end of the nineteenth century, but university professors as late as the Weimar Republic after World War I occasionally referred to the Technische Hochschule as "plumbers' academies" (Ringer 1969, p. 482n). Opposing views were not lacking. Michel Chevalier who attended the Ecole Polytechnique and the Ecole des Mines wrote that the French bourgeoisie raised their sons as if they were destined to become, some of them, members of the French Academy or the Academy of Science. This would be satisfactory for the sons of grand seigneurs, called to enjoy 100,000 francs of rentes, but was too much education for young people destined to take their place among the upper middle classes (Chevalier 1838, p. 17). Mathematics, Chevalier added, cannot claim to govern or administer the state, and experience, once again, is worth all the $(a + b)$ in the world (Chevalier 1838, p. 270).

With the war over in 1815, there came a flood of visitors from the Continent to Britain for pleasure and for education. Among the tourists were economists Jean-Baptiste Say, his son Horace, Sismonde de Sismondi, Adolphe Blanqui, mostly impressed by the rapid growth of England and depressed by the slums of the larger cities. Jean-Baptiste Say met Thomas Malthus, David Ricardo, perhaps John Stuart Mill, sat in Adam Smith's chair at the University of Glasgow, and noted that the purpose of his trip had been to measure the lever by which Britain had more than once lifted the Continent (Jones 1930, pp. 126–27). Other savants and engineers were de Gallois of the Corps des Mines, Dutens of Ponts et Chausées, Dupin of Arts et Manufactures who made repeated voyages and wrote a six-volume book on British industry (Jones 1930, chap 8). De Gallois's description of wooden tramways for carrying coal from the pithead to the loading docks caused a sensation in France, though the Anzin coal mine was slow to adopt the technique, continuing with carts and roads until 1830 when a shift to wooden rails produced a riot among the carters who would be displaced (Geiger 1974, pp. 169–70).

Particularly interested in visiting Britain and studying its methods were the owners of the larger iron and steel plants. One issue was puddling, another the shift from charcoal to coal, and then to coke. Entry into the industry as a *maître des forge* had been governed by the ownership of forests for the production of charcoal. As late as 1825 half of the forges in France using coal were owned by the British, who had to contend with resistance of their workers to the change from charcoal (Vial 1967, p. 132). The owners of the larger plants—Benoist d'Azy, Boigues, Cabrol, Dubost, Dufaud, Martin, Rambourg, Schneider, and Wendel—took trips to England, Rambourg working there as a laborer and reporting back on rolling and puddling (Vial 1967, p. 181). Benoist made a number of trips between 1839 and 1849, visiting British plants, occasionally as many as seven (Locke 1978, p. 50). In 1837, Emile Martin went to Britain to visit establishments and bring back workers (Locke 1978, p. 47). Martin noted in his diary on a trip to England and especially Wales that the British workers there really knew how to puddle, and that the ones sent to France were leftovers (Thuiller 1959, pp. 224–25).

Trips to England, Scotland, and Wales to study British methods were frequently combined with enlistment in the grandes écoles, if not for the *maître des forges,* then for his son, leading to the adoption of newer technology if not immediately, with a lag. Many did both. Of those noted by Vial to have traveled to Britain, Cabrol, Dufaud, Martin, and Wendel were polytechniciens. A classic case is that of Ernst Gouin, first in his class at the Polytechnique, who went on to Ponts et Chaussées and then to England to complete his education. He ordered locomotives from Sharp in Manchester for the Paris to Orleans railroad before beginning to build locomotives himself at a plant in Batignolles (Ecole Polytechnique 1895, p. 378). The contrast is with the Berlin locomotive builder Borsig, whose education was limited to two years at the Gewerbeinstitut, and who had not visited England though his teacher and an early employer both had (Benaerts 1933a, p. 27).

In addition to visits by Continental industrialists and artisans, and the former seeking to recruit British skilled persons at various levels, a good many British individuals sought out business opportunities on the Continent on their own behalf. The movement started as early as 1747, as noted for John Kay and John Holker, and kept up with Wilkinson in iron and steel, Cockerill in machinery, Manby and Wilson in iron and steel, plus many more. Many individuals started as builder of a high furnace, or installer of machinery and stayed on to make a career in a

European plant. The movement of especially French and Belgian entrepreneurs into Germany in the 1850s, at a time when German economic growth was picking up speed, drew an impassioned protest from the banker Gustav Mevissen, charging "Uberfremdung" or overforeignization (Benaerts 1933b, p. 353).

The various methods of technology transfer from Britain to the Continent — espionage, travel, machinery imports, whether open or smuggled, the hiring of artisans, the attraction of entrepreneurs — do not exhaust the list, and indeed may omit the primary one in a world of educated people who know foreign languages — called by Timo Myllyntaus, "natural diffusion."[11] Natural diffusion is that by means of the press, foreign and domestic, journals, scientific and trade literature, business correspondence, and exhibitions. It is low cost, and relies heavily on "natural curiosity" as a motivating factor (Myllyntaus 1990, pp. 65–66). Along with years of education, and training in foreign languages, natural curiosity — difficult to measure — may be an important element in social capability.

There is some disagreement whether the technological catching up to Britain by the Continent in the seventy-five or so years from the industrial revolution to 1850 was fast or slow. In agriculture most economic historians view technical imitation of leaders as a drawn-out process. It took seventy-five years, for example, for the replacement of the sickle by the scythe in the harvesting of wheat in France, although Theodore Schultz blames this not on the lack of social capability of peasants, but on the absence of stabling which reduced the value of straw (for bedding) and made it efficient to leave the straw in the fields.[12] Farmers and peasants were typically not in close contact with their peers, nor did they read. New techniques in farming move mostly along roads and then slowly.

Industrial technology moves rapidly or slowly in the eyes of different beholders, depending on the implicit counterfactual they have in mind. In *The Lever of Riches,* Joel Mokyr expresses surprise how rapidly the Continent picked up British technology (and new technologies moved within Europe) (Mokyr 1990, pp. 46, 49, 69, 105, 109, 130, 139); in *Unbound Prometheus,* David Landes emphasizes how long it took (Landes 1965, pp. 354, 368, 371, 396, 407, 408). Dealing only with the British–French comparison, J. H. Habakkuk took the view that French imitation of British industry was slow. He suspects that the price differential between coke and charcoal was so narrow, and the risks of change so high, that conversion was uneconomic. He further blamed the family firm, narrow markets for high quality rather than mass-produced goods, and labor immobility. Finance may have slowed down railway building but was not otherwise of critical importance (Habakkuk 1955). An intermediate view is that dramatic new machines were transferred quickly from Britain to the Continent, but that diffusion on the Continent was slow so that the gap between best practice and the average was narrow in Britain, wide across the channel (Mathias 1975, p. 95). Another possible hypothesis is that diffusion is faster in higher technology industries: in chemistry, aniline blue was first patented in France, but within a year 10 firms in England, Germany, France, and Switzerland were producing it. This result, however, may have been caused by the peculiarity of the French patent system which ran to the product rather than the process (Beer 1959, p. 59).

If technological change follows a Gompertz or S curve, with different S curves in different industrial lines, and perhaps in different regions, one would expect catching up to be slow in initial stages, to speed up later, perhaps slow down again, but with considerable variance. Germany adopted policies for industrial development in Prussia in the 1780s, but accumulated speed primarily in the 1840s and 1850s, after its lines of communication had been developed with canals and railroads. In twenty years, as noted, it is said to have made up an industrial lag compared with Britain of 50 years (Benaerts 1933b, p. 368). France started somewhat earlier, and industrialized somewhat more evenly in the face of economic and social resistances. The Revolutionary and Napoleonic wars both stimulated economic expansion through high prices, and retarded it by reduced ability to acquire the necessary inputs (Crouzet 1964). Over the longer period, however, it enlarged social capability by stimulating the establishment of technical and practical education. Writing in 1819, Chaptal makes somewhat exaggerated claims for French success: when France had to fall back on her own resources in wartime, she "astounded Europe by showing what an enlightened nation could do in a short time when its independence was threatened." His rosy view of the position may have had its origin in his primary interest in chemistry, in which France led both Britain and the rest of the Continent, with textiles a secondary concern, and machinery after that.[13] Visits, machinery imports, direct investment, and especially schooling in the decades after 1815 set the stage for a substantial spurt which came, however, mostly after 1851.

It is worth noting that Holland and Italy took little part in the drive for industrialization in the first half of the nineteenth century, having slowed down after earlier rapid growth based on flourishing trade, significant export handicraft industries, especially shipping. This experience has been called "failed transitions," but could readily be known as failed catchings-up, with delays in modernization, or participation in the industrial revolution, until the 1890s (Krantz and Hohenberg 1975). Sweden had an early spurt in industry in the seventeenth century based on imported technology in copper and iron and steel, originating in the Low Countries, and led by foreign entrepreneurs in general and Louis de Geer and the Trip family in particular. "Almost every innovation in the Swedish economy had its origin in the initiatives of foreigners" (Heckscher 1952). Basic transformation in the Swedish economy was limited, however, and the country was looked upon in the middle of the nineteenth century as an "impoverished sophisticate," impoverished, or at least poor, compared with western Europe, sophisticated because of a high degree of literacy in its population (years of schooling) and the beginnings of a banking system which, with the help of buoyant exports, would power rapid economic development after 1860 (Sandberg 1979).

Social capability on this showing is more complex than a simple total of years of schooling. Like individual creativity it follows a profile through time, starting usually slowly, picking up speed, ultimately slowing down, following an S or growth or logistic curve. Unlike individuals, countries do not die. The Italian city-states and the United Provinces of Holland reached the peaks of their growth curves during the commercial era, and had little creativity left for some years despite high levels of literacy and distinguished universities. Their industrialization came only after an extended period of quiescence. In 1860, despite widespread literacy, Sweden had not really started. The creative surges in British industry in the second half of the nineteenth century after some slowdown came from foreign individuals — "Italians like Marconi and Ferranti, Germans and Swiss like C. F. Beyer, Sir William Siemens, Hans Renold, Heinrich Simon, Ivan Levinstein, Ludwig Mond and others". . . and "foreign firms, Mannesmann Brothers, United Shoe, British Westinghouse, Thomson Houston and later Ford" (Cardwell 1972, pp. 193–94). In the twentieth century, Britain experienced a certain amount of dualism, with decay in the north in textiles, coal, and steel, and growth in the south in durable consumers goods (Sayers 1950).

Joel Mokyr is fascinated by what he calls "Cardwell's Law" — that no nation has been technologically very creative for more than a short period. As Mokyr points out this is only an empirical law for which Cardwell gives no economic or social reasons (Mokyr 1990, p. 207). Cardwell goes on to say that when one country goes down, another has risen "inside the wider culture of Europe — for Europe is the true home of technology, making possible the continuous growth of technology over the last 700 years" (Cardwell 1972, p. 210). Written in 1972, this seems a little less than generous to China and the Arab countries up to 1600, and to American, Japanese, Korean technology since World War

II. It does suggest, however, like the spread of British technology to the Continent after the industrial revolution, that linear and strictly economic explanations of technological transmission may be inadequate. Moreover, there is innovation and innovation. Purely empirical innovations achieved by trial and error work some of the time, as in Britain in the eighteenth century. At other times, a scientific approach, best combined with hands-on experience, is called for. In either instance, the acquisition of technical capacity is likely to start slowly, build, speed up, and ultimately slow down. Shirt-sleeves-to-shirt-sleeves (or clogs-to-clogs) in three generations is another and analogous empirical law. The system can be jolted. Postan attributed the economic surge of Europe outside Britain after World War II to "new men" (Postan 1967). Marshall of Leeds in flaxspinning offers a classic example: the leading firm in the industry in 1848 ran into the ground under the leadership of the founder's sons, and had to be liquidated by his grandsons (Rimmer 1960). The export of woolens from the same city required new men when the market shifted from Europe to America; by 1830 only 21 merchant houses retained links to the 135 that had been flourishing in 1782 (Wilson 1971, pp. 115–16).

Cardwell's law may be overcome by institutionalized research and development in government, industry, and as spin-offs of academic research. Such institutions have the opportunity for constant renewal through youthful intake. The risk of resistance to change is omnipresent, however. The returns are far from in, but the hypothesis that the creativity curve of a nation in technology — starting with imitation — is S-shaped and ultimately bends down is sufficiently plausible to require constant monitoring of what is happening.

NOTES

1. The Institute for European and International Studies of Luxembourg has embarked on a study of the "Vitality of Nations."
2. See esp. Henderson (1954); Landes (1965); Mathias (1975); Mokyr (1990).
3. Benaerts (1933) asserts that Germany in 20 years made up an industrial lag of more than 50 years.
4. See for example Rosenberg and Birdzell (1986).
5. Henderson, Britain: p. 14. Holker's role in spreading technology in France is discussed on pp. 14–24.
6. Communicated to me from a French source by Olivier Blanchard. Jacques-Constantin and Auguste-Charles Perier erected the first Watt steam

engine to pump water from the Seine for Paris, and began to manufacture Watt engines in their Caillot shops in 1780 (Geiger 1974, p. 73n).

7. W. O. Henderson (1966), p. 5. For more on German copying of English trade marks, and, in silk, French styles, see Friederich Zunkel (1962), p. 38. Even Krupp sold some steel as English made.

8. Parker (1959). For a comparison of French and German science and technology in the nineteenth century, which finds them surprisingly similar, see Peter Lundgreen (1980).

9. Paul M. Hohenberg (1967). Hohenberg writes (p. 68) "The men who organized and directed early chemical education in Germany, from Liebig to Kekulé, studied in Paris, because they preferred the practical, laboratory-centered approach to the sterile idealism of German universities at that time."

10. Prost observes that the Ecole Polytechnique graduates were going into the service of government, leaving few available for industry (Prost 1968, p. 302).

11. Myllyntaus (1990, table 1, p. 102). Myllyntaus lists six main channels of technology transfer in the nineteenth century: importing foreign machinery and equipment; direct foreign investment; foreign licenses and patents; recruiting skilled workers, artisans, engineers, teachers, and consultants from abroad, or permitting mass immigration; encouraging and supporting journeys abroad for study and training; and "natural and low cost diffusion." The last was handicapped for Finland because whereas 70 to 98.5 percent of the population in the second half of the nineteenth century was literate, most were so only in Finnish or Swedish (p. 116).

12. Chatelain (1958). Professor Schultz's economic explanation was given me in a private communication.

13. Chaptal (1819) ([industrie], p. 37). The expression "in a short time" (en peu de temps) occurs on pp. 16 and 43.

REFERENCES

Abramovitz, M. (1986) Catching up, forging ahead, falling behind. *J Econ Hist* 46:365–406.
Abramovitz, M. (1990) The catching up factor in postwar economic growth. *Econ Inquiry* 18:1–18.
Artz, F. B. (1966) *The development of technical education in France, 1500–1850.* Cambridge, Mass.: MIT Press.
Ballot, C., and C. Gevel. (1923) *Introduction du machinisme dans l'industrie française.* Paris: Rieder.
Beer, J. J. 1959. *The emergence of the German dye industry.* Urbana, Il.: University of Illinois Press.
Benaerts, P. (1933a) *Borsig et les débuts de la fabrication des locomotives en Allemagne.* Paris: Turot.
Benaerts, P. (1933b) *Les origines de la grande industrie Allemande.* Paris: Turot.

Berg, M., Hudson P. (1992) Rehabilitating the industrial revolution. *Econ Hist Rev* 45:24–30.

Cameron, R. (1985) A new view of European industrialization. *Econ Hist Rev* 38:2.

Cardwell, D. S. L. (1972) *Turning points in Western technology*. New York: Neale Watson Science History Publication.

Chaptal, Count (1819) De l'industrie Française, vol. 2, Paris: Renouard.

Chatelain, A. (1958) Dans les compagnes françaises du XIXe siècle: la lente progression de la faux. *Ann Econ Soc Civil* 11:373–85.

Chevalier, M. (1838) *Des intérets matériels en France: travaux publics, routes, canaux, chemins de fer.* Paris: Charles Gosselin et W. Coquebert.

Cipolla, C. M. (1968) The economic decline of Italy. In B. Pullan (ed.) *Crisis and change in the Venetian economy in the sixteenth and seventeenth centuries,* p. 137. London: Methuen.

Court, W. H. B. (1938) *The rise of Midland industries, 1600–1838.* London: Oxford University Press.

Crafts, N. F. R. (1985) *British economic growth during the industrial revolution.* London: Oxford University Press.

Crouzet, F. (1964) War, blockade and economic change in Europe, 1792–1813. *J Econ Hist* 24:567–88.

Dhondt, J. (1969) The cotton industry at Ghent during the French regime. In F. Crouzet, W. H. Chaloner, W. M. Stern, (eds.) *Essays in European economic history,* p. 20. New York: St. Martin's Press.

Ecole Polytechnique (1895) *Livre du centenaire, 1794–1894.* Paris: Gautier–Vilias.

Economic Commission of Europe. (1954) *Growth and stagnation in the European economy.* Geneva: EEC.

Flinn, M. W. (1965) In H. G. J. Aitken (ed.) *Explorations in enterprise,* p. 244. Cambridge, Mass.: Harvard University Press.

Fox, R. (1975) Science policy in restoration France, 1915–30. Seminar, MIT Technological Studies Program, Kindleberger notes. Cambridge, Mass.: MIT University Press.

Geiger, R. D. (1974) *The Anzin coal company: Big business in the early stages of the French industrial revolution.* Newark: University of Delaware Press.

Gerschenkron, A. (1962) *Economic backwardness in historical perspective.* Cambridge, Mass.: Harvard University Press.

Gillespie, C. C. (1980) *Science and polity in France at the end of the old regime.* Princeton: Princeton University Press.

Habakkuk, H. J. (1955) The historical experience on the basic conditions of economic progress. In L. H. Dupriez (ed.) *Economic progress,* pp. 149–69. Louvain: Institut de Recherches économiques et sociales.

Halévy, E. (1937) *A history of the English people in 1815, Book II. Economic Life.* Harmondsworth, Middlesex: Penguin.

Harris J. H. (1972) Industry and technology in France and Britain in the eighteenth century. Presented at the Economic History Society Conference at the University of Kent (Kindleberger notes).

Heckscher, E. F. (1922) *The continental system: An economic interpretation.* Gloucester, Mass.: Peter Smith.

Heckscher, E. F. (1952) *An economic history of Sweden* (translated by Goran Ohlin). Cambridge, Mass.: Harvard University Press.

Henderson, W. O. (1954) *Britain and industrial Europe, 1750–1870: Studies in British influence on the industrial revolution in Western Europe.* Liverpool: Liverpool University Press.

Henderson, W. O. (1966) *J. C. Fischer and his diary of industrial England.* London: Frank Cass.

Henderson, W. O. (1967) *The state and the industrial revolution in Prussia.* Liverpool: Liverpool University Press.

Henderson, W. O. (1969) *The industrialization of Europe, 1870–1914.* New York: Harcourt Brace.

Hohenberg, P. M. (1967) *Chemicals in Western Europe, 1850–1914.* Chicago: Rand McNally.

Hughes, T. P. (1966) Introduction to *Selections from lives of the engineers,* by S. Smiles, p. 11. Cambridge, Mass.: MIT Press.

Jones, E. (1930) *Les voyageurs français en Angleterre de 1815 à 1830.* Paris: Boccard.

Kindleberger C. P. (1976) Technical education and the French entrepreneur. In E. C. Carter II, R. Foster, and J. N. Moody (eds.) *Enterprise and entrepreneurs in nineteenth and twentieth-century France,* pp. 3–39. Baltimore: Johns Hopkins University Press.

Kindleberger, C. P. (1978) Germany's overtaking of England, 1806–1914. In C. P. Kindleberger (ed.) *Economic response: Comparative studies in trade, finance and growth,* pp. 185–236. Cambridge, Mass.: Harvard University Press.

Krantz, F., and P. M. Hohenberg (1975) *Failed transitions to modern industrial society: Renaissance Italy and seventeenth century Holland.* Montreal: Interuniversity Centre for European Studies.

Landes, D. S. (1965) Technological change and development in Western Europe, 1750–1914. In H. J. Habakkuk and M. Postan (eds.) *The Cambridge economic history of Europe,* vol. 6. *The industrial revolution and after: Incomes, population and technological change* (1), pp. 274–601. Cambridge: Cambridge University Press.

Locke, R. R. (1978) *Les fonderies et forges d'Alais et l'époque des premiers chemins de fer.* Paris: Marcel Riviere.

Lord, J. (1966) *Capital and steam power, 1750–1800.* 2d ed. London: Frank Cass.

Lowie, R. H. (1946) *The German people: a social portrait to 1914.* New York: Rinehart.

Lundgreen, P. (1980) *The organization of science and technology in France: A German perspective.* In R. Fox and G. Weisz (eds.) *The organization of science and technology in France, 1808–1914.* Paris: Cambridge University Press, Cambridge and Editions de la Maison des Sciences de l'Homme.

Marshall, A. (1920) *Industry and trade.* London: Macmillan.

Mathias, P. (1975) Skills and the diffusion of innovations from Britain in the eighteenth century. *Transact R Hist Soc 5th Ser* 23:93–113.

Mokyr, J. (1990) *The lever of riches: Technological creativity and economic progress.* New York: Oxford University Press.

Mollien, F. N. (1845) *Memoires d'un ministre du trésor publique, 1780–1815, Vol. 1.* Paris: Fournier.

Myllyntaus, T. (1990) The gatecrashing apprentice: industrializing Finland as an adopter of new technology. Communications of the Institute of Economic and Social History. University of Helsinki, Helsinki.

Parker, W. N. (1959) National states and national development: French and German ore mining in the late nineteenth century. In H. G. J. Aitken (ed.) *The state and economic growth,* pp. 201–12. New York: Social Science Council.

Poni, C. (1971) Archeologie de la fabrique: La diffusion des moulins à soie "alla Bolognese" dans les états Venétiens du XVI ème au XVIIIème siècles. Monograf, Bologna.

Postan, M. M. (1967) *An economic history of Western Europe, 1945–1964.* Part 2. London: Methuen.

Prost, A. (1968) *Histoire de l'enseignement en France, 1800–1967.* Collection "U," Paris.

Rapp, R. T. (1976) *Industry and economic decline in seventeenth-century Venice.* Cambridge, Mass.: Harvard University Press.

Redlich, F. (1968) Frühindustrielle Unternehmer und ihre Probleme im Lichte ihrer Selbstzeugnisse. In W. Fischer (ed.) *Wirtschafts- und Sozialgeschichte. Probleme der frühen Industrialiserung,* pp. 344–45. Berlin: Colloquium Verlag.

Rimmer, W. G. (1960) *Marshall of Leeds, Flax-spinners, 1788–1886.* Cambridge: Cambridge University Press.

Ringer, F. K. (1969) *The decline of the German mandarins: the German academic community, 1890–1933.* Cambridge: Harvard University Press.

Ritter, U. P. (1961) *Die Rolle des Staates in den Frühstadien der Industrialisierung.* Berlin: Duncker and Humbolt.

Rosenberg, N., and L. R. Birdzell Jr. (1986) *How the West grew rich: The economic transformation of the industrial world.* New York: Basic Books.

Rostow, W. W. (1960) *The stages of economic growth.* Cambridge: Cambridge University Press.

Rostow, W. W. (1975) *How it all began: Origins of the modern economy.* London: Methuen.

Sandberg, L. G. (1979) The case of the impoverished sophisticate: human capital and Swedish economic growth before World War I. *J Econ Hist* 39:225–41.

Saxonhouse, G. (1974) A tale of Japanese technological diffusion in the Meiji period. *J Econ Hist* 34:159.

Sayers, R. S. (1950) The springs of technical progress in Britain, 1919–1939. *Econ J* 60:278–91.

Thuiller, G. (1959) *Georges Dufaud et les débuts du grand capitalisme dans la métallurgie, en Niverais, au XIXe siècle.* Paris: S.E.V.P.E.N.

Vial, J. (1967) *L'industrialization de sidérurgie française 1814–1864.* Paris: Mouton.

Wilson, R. G. (1971) *Gentlemen merchants: The merchant community of Leeds, 1700–1830.* Manchester: Manchester University Press.

Zunkel, F. (1962) *Der Rheinisch-Westfälische Unternehmer, 1834–1879. Ein Beitrag zur Geschichte des deutsche Bürgertums im 19. Jahrhundert.* Köhn Opladen, Westdeutscher Verlag.

10

The Merchant as Entrepreneur

In honoring Herman van der Wee, I have some difficulty in writing about entrepreneurship for two reasons: one, because he knows so much more economic history than I can hope to learn, and two, because I have dealt with entrepreneurship in western Europe — which is the only domain of which I know some economic history — on three previous occasions, and have a hard time thinking of anything more to contribute on industrial entrepreneurship. In 1964, I produced a chapter on the entrepreneur in France and Britain after 1851.[1] In 1975, a paper on "Germany Overtaking England, 1806–1914"[2] touched on entrepreneurship in gently chiding Alexander Gerschenkron for his theory of backwardness. In that classic and widely cited work Gershenkron suggested that while England developed mainly through entrepreneurship, late-starting countries to the east did so otherwise, the nearer ones, France and Germany, through the leadership of banks, and those further off, notably Russia, through government,[3] when in my view banks had played only a small role in France and the role of government in what we would call today "industrial policy" was substantial. About the same time a paper of mine on "Technical Education and the French Entrepreneur" devoted a few pages to a "staple theory" of entrepreneurship, patterned after Harold Innis's staple theory of economic development.[4] My thought held that different industries were associated with different types of entrepreneurs, for example, textiles with merchants, metallurgical industries with artisanal occupations involving manual dexterity and spatial imagination, and industries of high technology with complex skills like clockmaking or locksmithy, or from the shop of the apothecary.[5] I had thought to develop one or more of these ideas further, but quickly encountered diminishing returns. In consequence, I propose to turn back, if you will, to the merchant as entrepreneur, and ring some of the changes on his evolving role. Much of this

This essay originally appeared in Paul Klep and Eddy Van Cauwenberghe, eds., *Entrepreneurship and the Transformation of the Economy (10th–20th Centuries), Essays in Honour of Herman Van der Wee* (Leuven: Leuven University Press, 1994), pp. 401–10. Reprinted with permission of Leuven University Press.

brings together bits of analysis that I have used in disparate studies, but, I hope, in more coherent form.

Adam Smith recognized in human nature a "propensity to truck, barter and exchange one thing for another." This trait is presumably present in degree in all mankind, more in some persons, less in others, and it constitutes the dominant characteristic of the merchant. Dr. Smith is not always reliable on the merchant's role. He is readily believed when he distinguishes between the ordinary merchant who makes a fortune even in great towns, only by "a long life of industry, frugality and attention," and speculative merchants who may make sudden fortunes, speculating now in one commodity, then in another. "A bold adventurer may sometimes acquire a considerable fortune by two or three successful speculations; but is just as likely to lose one by two or three unsuccessful ones."[6] It is hard, however, to accept his view that a little grocer in a seaport town must have all the knowledge that is necessary for a great merchant — ability to write, read, and account, and be a tolerable judge of perhaps 50 or 60 types of goods, their qualities, prices, and the markets where they are to be had cheapest — except for sufficient capital.[7] The list ignores foreign languages, an understanding of foreign exchange, including credit instruments, and a knowledge of a wider list of goods than those entering local consumption. Moreover the Smithian view, expressed following a cogent discussion of the capital employed in foreign trade, that "the carrying trade is the natural effect and symptom of great national wealth, but it does not seem to be the natural cause of it"[8] is not easy to accept. Nor is the idea plausible that the Dutch merchant delivering grain from Koenigsberg to Lisbon stops off in Amsterdam and unloads it, before reloading and proceeding, because he is uneasy far from his capital and wants the goods under his view and command.[9] This overlooks the stapling functions of merchants in breaking bulk, grading, packing — perhaps against spontaneous combustion — storing commodities, and the economics of scale of an entrepot center.

In what follows, I ignore the retail merchant to focus on the wholesaler, jobber, putter-out (in German *Verleger*) of cottage industry who puts out cotton, wools, and flax and/or their yarns to be spun and woven, collects the output, and sells it in the market, plus the "great merchant," the "First Hand" in Dutch parlance, the *négociant* in French or *Kaufman* in German, who deals in "distant trade."

I ignore the youth or apprentice making a start as a merchant in some trade. My concern is what happens after he has a start. The role is not always a static one. In discussing the "commercial revolution" of the thirteenth century, N. S. B. Gras describes the transition of the traveling merchant, who sailed with his goods to foreign ports, this time to keep an eye on them in case of jettison or barratry, to the sedentary one who remained in his warehouse and accounting office, to supervise a variety of shipments, and in part to supervise the production of goods he sold to ensure their quality.[10] This was a backward linkage, in Albert Hirschman's terminology, from merchant to manufacturer.[11] In due course, the putter-out in textiles became a manufacturer, as the industry moved from the cottage to the factory. In one view, this transition was motivated by the desire of "bosses" to hold down wages.[12] Few find this persuasive. In general the merchant wanted direct supervision of the spinning, weaving, finishing, and/or dyeing processes for quality control, to take advantage of a water-power site, later the economies of scale of a steam engine, to limit embezzlement of materials or final output by workers, or, as technological progress was made, to safeguard industrial secrets. The start of or transition to a factory might be led by a spinner, weaver, fuller, bleacher, dyer at the artisanal level. It was more likely, especially in western Prussia, to be directed by a merchant. In England, entrepreneurs were mostly technically oriented, whereas in Rheinisch-Westphalia, merchants played at least an equal role, though it is difficult to make confident estimates. Merchant skill, it was said, was more important than those of the artisan at this early stage, because access to raw materials and assurance of market outlets in the Ruhr area were more important than production.[13]

Even in firms started by technically oriented artisans — workers in wood and iron, instrument makers, clockmakers, locksmiths, and technically trained persons — merchants were needed even though they may not have constituted the entrepreneur who made decisions. Josiah Wedgwood produced his fine tableware in the plant Etruria outside Birmingham, but he had a showroom in London run by Thomas Bentley.[14] Boulton and Watt had their merchant Fothergill. The Marglin view that a single worker could achieve division of labor by performing one function at a time for extended periods each — drawing the wire for pins for several days, fashioning now the heads, then the pins, and so on — overlooks at a minimum that merchants are needed to sell the output at a distance from the worker's cottage.

In one instance in the Ruhr, Wuppertal, that grew from the joining of the separate towns of Elberfeld and Barmen as they encroached on the bleaching fields between them when chemicals replaced sunlight, the two towns specialized, to a considerable extent, Elberfeld in trading, and Barmen in weaving, first in cloth, ultimately in ribbon, braid, and lace. Barmen had few merchants, apart from local shops; Elberfeld had six times as many wholesalers, forwarders, and bankers as Barmen. In due course, however, Barmen stopped buying yarn for specialized needs through Elberfeld merchants, going directly abroad.[15]

A merchant may enter industry as an entrepreneur through the provision of capital. In partnerships, as Postan observed, the capitalist may hire the worker or the worker may hire the monies of the capitalist.[16] Much depended on the size of the capital requirement. In textiles, apart from an occasional large mill such as that of Thomas Lombe in silk-throwing in Derby, or of Benjamin Gott in wool near Leeds, little capital was required at the start, and that could be provided from self-financing, informal loans from friends and relations, plus trade credit and occasionally bank credit. In metallurgy, mining, and after the middle of the nineteenth century shipping, larger amounts of capital were needed. Some was furnished by merchants, through retained profits or inheritance, some by banks which may have been started by merchants.

One form of vertical integration akin to the merchant investing in a textile factory was into shipping, either as owner, in whole or part, or outfitter (*armateur* in French), i.e., supplying everything for a particular voyage save for the vessel, akin to today's bareboat charter. Another was marine insurance. Ship captains and their crew originally reversed this process and became merchants to a small extent as they carried their own "ventures" on board. Some small ships in fact were owned in whole or in part by seamen, particularly a captain — one of the few avenues from the lowest to the middle ranks of society in Britain before the twentieth century.[17] I have not encountered in the literature examples of mariners who made their way into shipownership by "a long life of industry, frugality and attention," or going the other way, becoming a great merchant.

A major entrepreneurial avenue for the great merchant was into banking. Merchant banking is one form, with a rather exacting definition today, but one which involved many firms moving slowly from trading in commodities, generally internationally, to lending on commodities, and ultimately doing a general banking business, including issuing securities for clients. Baring Brothers evolved from producing and trading serges in Exeter to merchant banking in London and speculation in cotton and Argentine mortgages. Hope and Company in Amsterdam continued to trade and speculate in commodities long after it was known as a banker and security dealer.[18] French merchants before 1789, and to a lesser extent British merchants under the Tudors and Stuarts, would buy offices at the local, departmental, or central governmental level, farm taxes, buy monopolies such as those in tobacco or sweet wine, the tax farmers using the monies collected for the crown in varied credit operations. In France this activity came to an end with the beheading of 28 *officiers* and *financiers* in 1793 in the Terror.[19]

Merchants were not, of course, the only source of bankers, although the principal one. Economics textbooks have exaggerated the role of goldsmiths who evolved into banks, primarily because many of the surviving London banks in the nineteenth and twentieth centuries started in this fashion centuries earlier.[20] Along with merchants and goldsmiths evolving into bankers were scriveners, notaries in France, industrialists who issued notes to pay for goods and wages, and others.

The move from distant trade into banking, except where merchant bankers continued to speculate in commodities, had its roots in efforts to minimize risk. Bankers diversified. While insurance developed gradually, it matured in financial terms after about 1660, and insurance, as noted earlier, was another outlet for merchant fortunes. William Braund first traded woolens to Portugal, then bought export bills of other woolen exporters, brought back gold, moved into marine insurance, the "Climax of the slow road to pure finance followed by so many merchants of his time."[21] That many merchants quit distant trade and the sea for the life of finance, a rentier, and a country gentleman gave rise to complaint, especially as they bought titles, stately homes, *chateaux,* and to the extent that the rigid German social system permitted, *Güter.* As early as 1612 it was said in Venice of the nobility: "their former course of life was merchandising; which is now quite left and they look to landward, buying house and land . . . their wont was to send their sons upon galleys into the Levant to accustom them to navigation and trade. They now send them to travel and to learn more of the gentleman than the merchant." In Amsterdam in 1652, it was said that "the regents were not merchants, that they did not take risks on the seas, but derived their income from houses, lands and securities, and so allowed the seas to be lost." After quoting these statements, Peter Burke goes on: "the shift was from sea to land, from work to play, from thrift to conspicuous consumption, from entrepreneur to rentier, from bourgeois to aristocrat."[22]

One reason to move out of distant trade was that it was difficult to manage change. The woolen merchants of Leeds, already gentlemen, found it difficult to redirect their exports from the Continent by way of Amsterdam to new markets in America. The outbreak of the American War of Independence added confusion. By 1830 only a handful of the 137 merchant houses existing in 1782 still survived. Some families had become rentiers in landed estates, government securities, canals, and turnpikes, with sons of the original great merchants passing their days and nights in hunting and balls, rather than overseas selling. The change of markets required a change from rapid to slow turnover, and from short to long credits with slow payback.[23] The construction of the great woolen mill, Bean Ing, should not be taken as an indication that great merchants as a rule moved into manufacture. Gott was almost alone.

Most merchants participated in the finishing stages to maintain quality, and one Thomas Lloyd ran a fulling mill. It was said of Lloyd, however, that he would not have dreamed of manufacturing cloth.[24]

There is an important contrast between Venice and Amsterdam. As the sea was lost, the Venetian nobility which had represented the mercantile oligarchy of the city transformed itself into a class of landed proprietors on *terra ferma*.[25] With limited available land, the bulk of Dutch merchants were unable to follow suit. One exception was John Hope, of Scottish origin. He was a director of the Dutch East India Company, a banker who issued foreign loans, but at the same time traded at first and second hand in Amsterdam in "money, grain, colonial produce, ships' articles, gold, silver, drysaltery, ordnance, textiles, tobacco, wine, flower bulbs, in short, anything that could be traded at a profit."[26] At the same time, he bought a number of estates in the United Provinces, among which he traveled incessantly.[27] Even less attracted to the life of the aristocracy than the bulk of Dutch merchants, the merchants of Hamburg kept their sons in the family mercantile business, and sought to prevent their daughters from marrying either Junkers or state officials. The facts that the son of a first Burgomeister had entered government service and that a number of daughters of the highest society had married Prussian officers were regarded as unseemly.[28] In these attitudes, Hamburg was different not only from Augsburg where merchants were anxious to be ennobled with a diploma,[29] but from the inland trading city of Frankfurt, where families that had lived in the city for more than a hundred years were treated as nobles.[30]

Merchant communities — Venice, Amsterdam, Hamburg, London — suffered not only from competition with one another, but from direct trading by producers who came in due course to dispense with entrepot centers and ship goods directly to their final destination. The process is akin to financial disintermediation which occurs when institutions collecting large bodies of savings lend directly to industrial firms without going through banks. Venice tried vainly to keep a monopoly of trade between the Levant and Europe north of the Alps. A "navigation act" passed in 1602 to require goods coming to and leaving Venice to be carried in Venetian bottoms backfired, as the British exported woolens directly to the Eastern Mediterranean in British ships, while Flemish, French, and English ships brought silk, spice, cotton, and other eastern commodities to Flanders and Marseilles to be shipped to Frankfurt and other German fairs, rather than through the Fondaco dei Tedeschi (house of German merchants) in Venice.[31] In due course, French and British shipping, even Dutch ships between the Bay of Biscay and the Baltic, cut out Amsterdam. Bordeaux exports of wine to the United Provinces fell from 67 percent of the total in 1717 to 10 percent in 1789, those to the North Sea and Baltic rose from 13 to 46 percent over the same period.[32] Holland's proportion of British exports fell from 42 percent in 1696–97 to 13 percent, while British imports from Holland declined over the same period from 13 percent to 4 percent.[33] The diseconomy seen by Adam Smith in double loading and unloading comes into its own when mercantile knowledge of what is available where and wanted where is widely diffused.

Elimination of the merchants' relaying function can take place in stages. In an illustration I have used before, serges manufactured in Exeter in Devon first went to London for transhipment to Amsterdam, whence they were sent on to Hamburg for Germany and to Cadiz for Spanish colonies. They were originally finished in Holland. Later the finishing stage was moved to London, and still later to Exeter. While all this was taking place, Exeter serges went out of fashion and Norwich worsteds took away the demand.[34]

One particular breed of merchant who lost out to direct trading was the foreign agent. These from the Italian city-states used to reside in the Levant, Bruges, Lyons, and Spain; from the Hansa in Bruges and London, from Rotterdam and Germany in Bordeaux, and from all over Europe in Seville and later Cadiz. Bordeaux, for example, was a convenient place to tranship French colonial goods to other European ports, as well as the outlet for Bordeaux wines and brandies. In the seventeenth and eighteenth centuries, it housed a colony of especially British, German, and Dutch merchants in the Chartrons district. The British were to a considerable extent Jacobin Catholics from Ireland and imported especially the celebrated Irish salt beef.[35] In 1702 Cadiz, which commanded a monopoly of Spanish overseas trade, had at one time 84 commercial houses of which 12 were Spanish, 26 Genoan, 11 French, 10 English, and seven from Hamburg.[36] By the end of the century, there were 8,700 foreigners resident in Cadiz, 5,000 Italian, 2,700 French, 275 German and Flemish, and 270 English.[37] If the South Sea Company had used its *asiento* obtained in 1713 to trade to Buenos Ayres, instead of in British government debt, direct trading to Spanish overseas possessions, instead of relaying through Cadiz, might have proceeded a good deal faster.

Alfred Chandler has pointed out that as they rose above the local and regional to the national scale, American firms tended to take the marketing and purchasing functions into the firm, rather than depending on wholesalers and jobbers.[38] This is a form of direct trading that economizes on transport and commissions, and may guard against interruptions in supplies and possible interruptions in sales. Dealing directly with the user also may have the advantage of accelerating worthwhile technical change. The reliance of Oldham and Bolton cotton spinners on a highly organized market in yarns led to a proliferation of distinct qualities, cutting down on economies of scale, many of which grades of yarn could have been abandoned if the spinners had dealt directly with the weavers.[39] Somewhat contrarily, an active market for machine tools in Britain forestalled the development of special tools for special purposes as the wholesalers in the middle formed a communication barrier between the producers and the users.[40]

Too few merchants of local origin, and too weak, as in Seville and Cadiz, or in Silesia where linen exports through Hamburg were mostly handled by foreigners, can stunt the development of industry and the modernization process, but so can too many and too strong. This is true not only in the organization of the market place, as the intermediaries keep producers and users apart, and thereby impede technological change, as noted for cotton yarns and machine tools in Britain. Political domination of Holland by the mercantile community led to low or no duties on traded commodities, and heavy taxes on items of general domestic consumption, making for high wages and a competitive handicap to industrial production.[41] When direct trading reduced the profits from stapling, Holland was ill placed to industrialize, especially in competition with Belgium which used protective tariffs. Like the Italian city-states, where merchants first dominated political decision making and then deserted trade for the agricultural mainland, the Dutch case is regarded as one of a "failed transition" to modern industry.[42] The displacement of great merchants into banking and rentier ranks was satisfactory for those involved, and Dutch agriculture thrived after British markets opened up in the 1850s, but industrial production was excruciatingly slow in developing until the end of the nineteenth century.

I conclude that merchants as entrepreneurs — whether new entrants, continuing as merchants, moving into industry, or into finance — must move with times, unless they are so fortunate for themselves — though not necessarily for their progeny — to become rich and idle.

NOTES

1. C. P. Kindleberger, *Economic Growth in France and Britain, 1851–1950* (Cambridge, Mass., 1964), chap. 6.
2. C. P. Kindleberger, reprinted in *Economic Response: Comparative Studies in Trade, Finance and Growth* (Cambridge, Mass., 1978), chap. 7.

3. A. Gerschenkron, *Economic Backwardness in Historical Perspective* (Cambridge, Mass., 1962), esp. chap. 1.

4. H. A. Innis, *Problems of Staple Production in Canada* (Toronto, 1930).

5. C. P. Kindleberger, "Technical Education and the French Entrepreneur," in Edward C. Carter II, Robert Forster, and J. N. Moody, eds., *Enterprise and Entrepreneurship in Nineteenth and Twentieth-Century France* (Baltimore, 1976), pp. 3–39.

6. Adam Smith, *The Wealth of Nations* (New York, 1937), pp. 113–14.

7. Ibid., p. 112.

8. Ibid., p. 354.

9. Ibid., p. 422.

10. N. S. B. Gras, "Capitalism — Concepts and History," in F. C. Lane and J. C. Riemersma, eds., *Enterprise and Secular Change* (Homewood, Ill., 1953), pp. 66–79.

11. A. O. Hirschman, *The Strategy of Economic Development* (New Haven, Conn., 1953).

12. S. A. Marglin, "What do Bosses Do," part 1, *Review of Radical Political Economy* 6 (1974): 60–112.

13. F. Zunkel, *Der Rheinische-Westphälische Unternehmer, 1834–1879* (Cologne, Opladen, 1962), p. 25.

14. Julia Wedgwood, *The Personal Life of Josiah Wedgwood* (London, 1915), p. 123.

15. W. Köllmann, *Sozialgeschichte der Stadt Barmen im 19. Jahrhundert* (Tübingen, 1960), pp. 17–33.

16. M. M. Postan, *Medieval Trade and Finance* (Cambridge, 1953), chap. 3.

17. Ralph Davis, *The Rise of the English Shipping Industry in the Seventeenth and Eighteenth Centuries* (London, 1962), p. 151.

18. M. G. Buist, *At Spes Non Fracta: Hope and Company, 1700–1815, Merchant Bankers and Diplomats at Work* (The Hague, 1974), chap. 7.

19. J. F. Bosher, *French Finances, 1770–1795: From Business to Bureaucracy* (Cambridge, 1970).

20. R. H. Tawney, Introduction to Thomas Wilson, *A Discourse on Usury* (New York, 1925).

21. Lucy Stuart Sutherland, *A London Merchant, 1695–1774* (London, 1933), pp. 98, 102.

22. Peter Burke, *Venice and Amsterdam: A Study of Seventeenth Century Elites* (London, 1974).

23. R. G. Wilson, *Gentlemen Merchants: The Merchant Community of Leeds, 1700–1830* (Manchester, 1971), chaps. 4, 5, and 6.

24. Ibid., pp. 60, 95.

25. S. L. Woolf, "Venice and the Terra Ferma: Problems of the Change from Commercial to Landed Activities." in Brian Pullan, ed., *Crisis and Change in the Venetian Economy in the Sixteenth and Seventeenth Centuries* (London, 1968), pp. 175–203.

26. Buist, *At Spes Non Fracta,* p. 33.

27. Ibid., p. 18.

28. Julius V. Eckardt, *Lebenserinnerungen* (Leipzig, 1910), pp. 200–201.

29. Percy Ernest Schramm, "Hamburg und die Adelsfrage (bis 1806)," *Zeitschrift des Vereins für hamburgische Geschichts* 55 (1969): 82.

30. Helmut Böhme, *Frankfurt und Hamburg, des deutsches Reiches Silber- und Goldloch und die allerenglische Stadt des Kontinents* (Frankfurt, 1968), pp. 36–40.

31. Domenico Sella, "Crisis and Transformation in Venetian Trade," in Brian Pullen, ed., *Crisis and Change in the Venetian Economy,* p. 91.

32. François Crouzet, *"Economie et société* (1715–1719)," in François-George Pariset, ed., *Bordeaux au XVIII siècle,* vol. 6 (Bordeaux, 1968), p. 250.

33. Reference misplaced.

34. W. G. Hoskins, *Industry, Trade and People in Exeter, 1688–1800, with Special Reference to the Serge Industry* (Manchester, 1935), chaps. 2 and 3.

35. Crouzet, *Economie et société,* chap. 2.

36. Clarence Henry Haring, *Trade and Navigation between Spain and the Indies in the Time of the Hapsburgs* (Cambridge, Mass., 1918), p. 113.

37. François Dornic, *L'industrie textile dans la Maine et ses débouches internationaux (1650–1815)* (Le Mans, 1955), pp. 83–86.

38. Alfred D. Chandler, Jr., *Strategy and Structure: Chapters in the History of American Industrial Enterprise* (Cambridge, Mass., 1962).

39. R. Robson, *The Cotton Industry in Britain* (London, 1957), pp. 92–95.

40. M. E. Beesley and G. W. Throup, "The Machine-Tool Industry," in D. L. Burn, ed., *The Structure of British Industry* (Cambridge, 1958), 1:380 et seq.

41. H. R. C. Wright, *Free Trade and Protectin in the Netherlands, 1816–30* (Cambridge, 1955).

42. Frederick Krantz and Paul M. Hohenberg, eds., *Failed Transitions to Modern Industrial Society: Renaissance Italy and Seventeenth Century Holland* (Montreal, 1975).

11

Long Waves in Economics and Politics:
A Review Article

Paul Kennedy, *The Rise and Fall of Great Powers: Economic Change and Military Conflict from 1500 to 2000* (New York: Random House, 1987); and Joshua S. Goldstein, *Long Cycles: Prosperity and War in the Modern Age* (New Haven: Yale University Press, 1988).

These books are alike in covering half a millennium from 1500 (in Goldstein's case from 1495), and in exploring the interaction of economics and politics. They differ in that one is by a historian, the other by a political scientist, the historian interested in narrative and detail, the political scientist in sweeping generalization. The Kennedy book has been on the best-seller lists for months, widely reviewed and quoted, and is less in need of attention than the more austere and less accessible effort of Goldstein. I choose therefore to dismiss *The Rise and Fall . . .* quickly and concentrate on the more elusive monograph that attempts to wrap up related long waves in prices, production, war, and hegemonic dominance in a single package.

I should perhaps say at the start that the Kennedy book makes important points about the fall of great powers that may spend unduly on military preparation or adventure. His analysis is somewhat monocausal, however, and neglects other aspects of the rise and fall of nations such as consumption (and its corollary, saving), innovations in product and process that are central to increases in productivity, and social cohesion or blockage, all aspects of the problem that he associates primarily with military expenditure. His historical exploration of spending for arms is apposite for the United States today, as he intended it to be, but the book deflects attention from other dimensions of our present problem in this country.

Goldstein, on the other hand, paints a broad canvas. The book is di-

---

    This essay was reprinted with permission from *Economics and Politics* 1, no. 1 (July 1989): 201–6.

vided into parts dealing with theory — largely a review of the literature — with statistics, and with history, each covering prices, production, investment, war, and the political standing of nations as affected by war. In all of these he finds what he is looking for, a 50-year cycle with regular patterns of sequence, cause, and effect. I confess I am partial to the notion that one country after another is likely to achieve a leading position in the world economy, only to decline thereafter, but I would argue that such "hegemonic cycles," to use his vocabulary that I dislike, are not regular, nor similar in causation, do not succeed one another as an immediate result of war, but occasionally have long and disorderly transitions. Along with most economists, I do not have much respect for the Kondratieff 50-year cycle. One must give Goldstein credit that his claims are guarded: the Kondratieff cannot be used for forecasting, as some modern scholars do. The future is indeterminate (p. 376), though he offers a "projection" that calls for a production upswing from 1995 to 2020, an outbreak of war or wars from 2000–2005 to 2025–2030, followed by price increases from 2010–2035 (p. 353). Presumably the period from the present (or 1980) is one of downswing (as Jay Forrester believes, while W. W. Rostow forecast an upswing from 1979). His candidates for participation in the war of the upswing are the USSR and the United States, but he recognizes that the hydrogen bomb may make such war less likely.

After this summary, let me start with the Kennedy book. His villain in economic decline is military expenditure. This is surely relevant to the parallel that he and others see between sixteenth- and seventeenth-century Spain and the United States today. Louis XIV on his deathbed regretted "Too many palaces; too many wars." The palaces represented conspicuous consumption that is the prime factor of decline in Carlo Cipolla's analysis in *The Economic Decline of Empires* (London: Methuen, 1970). Cipolla observes justly that all cases have aspects of originality, but he is concerned with rising standards of living in a growing economy. At home they lead more and more people to demand a share in the benefits (foreshadowing the analysis of Mancur Olson), and as prosperity spreads abroad, neighboring countries tend to become a threat, requiring the empire to enlarge its military program (back to Kennedy). Public consumption in mature empires thus rises sharply and outstrips production. To right the position, the empire needs to develop new methods of enlarging production, but as a mature economy it resists change. Prices and inflation are no necessary aspect of this analysis.

Mancur Olson's views (*The Rise and Decline of Nations: Economic Growth, Stagflation and Social Rigidities* [New Haven: Yale University Press, 1982]) focus on the connections between income distribution and inflation. With long periods of peace, or even after wars that do not profoundly disturb relations within a country, economic and class groups that he calls "distributional coalitions" dig in, especially to resist taking undue or even a due share of the burdens of the time — perhaps a program of military expenditure, of reconstruction, or the payment abroad of reparations as in the case of Germany in the 1920s. These groups resist the imposition of taxes on them, raise prices or wages to the extent they have oligopolistic power, respond to increases in foreign-trade prices as a consequence of exchange depreciation by pushing harder for higher wages. The theory was not completely original with Olson; a model much like it was worked out for France immediately after World War II by Henri Aujac, and it is the essence of the notion of "structural inflation," first applied to Latin America by Albert O. Hirschman and David Felix, and later generalized by Fred Hirsch. Olson suggested that distributional coalitions impede growth and spur inflation by blocking agendas for corrective change. He explains the miracle growth after World War II of such countries as West Germany and Japan by the fact that their interest groups had been destroyed by the dictatorships of the 1930s and defeat in war. The inflationary aspect of the analysis can be reduced to a simple statement: if 100 percent of the population demands 110 percent of the national income, one means of satisfying them in the short run is to pay them 110 percent of national income and let the various groups fight out which gets the short end. In this way of looking at the matter, money creation is not an exogenous result of bad economic policy, but an endogenous means of temporizing to postpone social discord.

A few analysts find the key to growth and decline in spurts and lapses in productivity. Joseph Schumpeter developed a business-cycle theory that emphasized the effect of depression in stimulating innovation. Gerhard Mench believes that there are 50-year long waves in innovation, but that it flourishes in upswings rather than in depression (Goldstein, pp. 50ff.). Jay Forrester of MIT is a strong believer in the 50-year Kondratieff cycle, finding the key in waves of capital investment.

Paul Kennedy is a consummate historian and his book is a good read. But the wars that cause the trouble are exogenous, not events that fall out of the economic system, as Goldstein believes. The wars of the Habsburgs and Spain were to a great extent religious in origin, the Counter-Reformation's attempt to defend the Catholic faith against the inroads from Lutherans and Calvinists. Other wars were dynastic. For Goldstein, on the other hand, both economics and politics are shaped by long cycles of approximately 50 years — cycles in prices, production, wars, and hegemonic rise and fall.

The Goldstein book started as a doctoral dissertation in political science at MIT, under Professor Hayward Alker, Jr. It is enormously ambitious in trying to integrate economics and politics in 50-year cycles, with data stretching back from the 1790s, when Kondratieff's observations of prices began, to 1495. Goldstein candidly admits that most economists are deeply skeptical of long cycles—he early quotes Paul Samuelson who called the Kondratieff cycle "science fiction" (p. 21). Moreover, he makes use of Forrester's system dynamics, derived from electrical circuitry, with positive and negative feedback loops, while admitting that most liberal economists reject that style of reasoning (p. 49, n. 3). The language is everywhere guarded: for example, he states that his theory of long waves is not necessarily true, only "that it is plausible, that it might be true, and that if true it would have interesting and important ramifications" (p. 13). It is, however, evident to me that he wants to believe his all-encompassing economics-cum-politics theory is true, and that he wants to persuade the reader that it is true.

The theory holds that 50-year cycles exist in the realm of economics, affecting prices, production, innovation, and investment. On the political side there are 50-year cycles of wars, up and down, but large hegemonic wars among core countries from time to time that yield hegemonic cycles of more nearly 150 years. The hegemonic wars typically last an entire generation—the Thirty Years' War from 1618 to 1648, culminating in the economic dominance of the Netherlands, the French revolutionary, and Napoleonic wars from 1792 to 1815, ending in Great Britain at the apex of the world economy, and the combined World Wars I and II, from 1914 to 1945 that led to the United States taking over as the world's leading economic power. This scheme is borrowed from Immanuel Wallerstein's *The Modern World-System II: Mercantilism and the Consolidation of the European World Economy, 1600–1750* (New York: Academic Press, 1980) on which, along with the work of Fernand Braudel, he relies for his history from 1495 to 1789. Detailed data on wars come from Jack Levy's list of 119 wars from 1495 to Vietnam (1965–1973), complete with measures of intensity. Economic data for establishing the long cycles are the standard series, rather patchy and for limited periods before 1850: 28 series on prices, 10 on production, four on innovations, three on patents, and two each on capital investment (for the United States only) and real wages (table 8.1, p. 182).

Long waves are divided into upswings and downswings that range from as few as 10 years to as many as 39. The dating takes off from the cycles in prices, which is where Kondratieff started. One could quarrel with Goldstein's choices of individual years based upon the general information carried in the heads of economic historians. The upswing in the middle of the nineteenth century is stated to end in 1871, rather than the usual date of 1873 after the bursting of the German-Austrian bubble that followed payment of the Franco-Prussian indemnity. The "Great Depression," normally thought of as running from 1873 to 1896, is given an ending in 1892. These small differences can be overlooked. There is a problem, however, in measuring the last cycle, beginning after World War II. Table 11.5 (p. 247) gives the upswing as from 1940 to 1967, followed by a downswing from 1968 to 1975. Elsewhere the turning point is stated to be 1980, rather than 1968, making for a 40-year upswing, and presumably a downswing starting in 1980. But 1980 produced a slowdown in price increases, not a decline, and the downswing that many economists anticipated after the deflationary steps of 1979–81 never really developed. The transition from the 1960s boom to the 1995–2020 upswing of the Goldstein projection mentioned earlier is muddy in the extreme.

Prices are used for dating the long swings, but they are not crucial to the theory of long waves that is essentially directed to the relations between production and war. The use of prices for dating is explained by the fact that the data are better, evoking the story of the lost ring and the street lamp which I forebear repeating. With the weaker data on production, Goldstein establishes that production cycles lead price cycles by 10 to 15 years, or about one-quarter of the full 50-year cycle. With still weaker data on wars, normalized by severity based on casualties, he accepts the hypothesis of a 50-year cycle in war. There is a weak 26-year cycle in war severity from 1815 to the present, primarily imposed by the experience of World Wars I and II, but when the data are extended back to 1495 a 50-year cycle emerges (p. 244). Thirty-one wars occurred in price upswings, 27 in downswings, and seven were seriously overlapping. War leads prices by about one to five years (p. 254), so that production upswings are followed by war on an average of 10 years. An elaborate statistical technique called Granger causality "proves" that war leads to price increases, not vice versa, although the result is stronger for the nineteenth and twentieth centuries and insignificant before 1648. The biggest wars occur when core countries have full treasuries and can afford them. The smaller ones may result from competition for markets, population pressure, colonial expansion, and the like (pp. 261, 263).

This gets close to historical nonsense if it is meant as a generalization. Kennedy's account of Spain's Eighty Years' War against Holland in the interest of the Catholic faith and Spanish prestige records more than half a dozen bankruptcies, interrupted by heavy borrowing from bankers. The Prussian legislature's refusal to vote Prince Bismarck taxes for the 1866 attack on Austria led him to sell the government-owned Cologne-Minden railroad to raise the necessary cash. The Netherlands and England used to fight wars with allies that would fight only so long as they received subventions; France and Germany, on the other hand, were kept going in the field by indemnities extracted from defeated enemies, and lived off the land as they went along. In my judgment, it is impossible to establish a plausible general relationship between economic growth, with or without rich treasuries, and the outbreak of war.

Exhaustion by war leads to the production downswing after the price peak, according to the theory. But not always. World War I hurt Germany and France, but stimulated the United States and (he claims) the United Kingdom (p. 265). I have a personal theory that war is a hothouse, stimulating faster growth in rising economies, wilting those in decline.

Major wars produce changes in hegemonic leadership. Before the twentieth century, they were fought among the countries of Europe. Now the list must be broadened to include the United States and the Soviet Union, in the future possibly Japan. But the outcome of the war does not directly determine where the mantle of the hegemon ends up. The leading warring challenger in the sixteenth and seventeenth centuries, Spain, failed to win the role of hegemon, nor did France emerge on top at the turn from the eighteenth to the nineteenth, or Germany in the twentieth. Life cycles occur among leading economic powers, war plays a role in the process, but the connections are both loose and complex. Equally complex is the dating. When did Holland cease to be the leading economic power in Europe? Wallerstein is quoted as giving a date of 1672, Maddison 1780. Dutch military leadership was short lived, ending about 1672, a date Simon Schama also chooses for the end of Dutch "exceptionalism," after which the United Provinces were simply one among a number of European countries (1988, pp. 224, 282–86). Dutch virtuosity in production (shipbuilding, fishing, whaling, textiles) went on for a couple of decades, in trade to about 1730, and in finance to 1784 when it collapsed in the Fourth Anglo-Dutch war, one, as it happens, not included in Jack Levy's list. The Dutch Golden Age went out in stages, and with a whimper rather than a bang.

Hegemonies, to use that disliked term, rise and fall, but do so in complex ways that do not lend themselves readily to model-building that can be statistically tested. If there is any general model in the world of economic growth, it is the S-curve, the curve of material transformation, that suggests that there is first nucleation, then growth that starts slowly, picks up speed, meets some resistance, and then slows down, levels off, or even declines. Since new S-curves can grow out of slowed portions of old ones, and since the nucleation of new S-curves is difficult to detect until some time afterward, prediction or even projection is hazardous. "Unexpected" as well as "unintended" results occur frequently in conditions close to chaos. William McNeill, the Chicago historian, has asserted that population pressure — a factor almost entirely neglected by Goldstein, though prominent in W. W. Rostow's explanation of the Kondratieff cycle — produced the industrial revolution in England, the storming of the Bastille in France, and today's religious wars in the Middle East (MIT Seminar in Science, Technology, May 8, 1985). One can add that Dutch urban growth led first to land reclamation and then to imports of grain from the Baltic, and population growth under some circumstances leads to family limitation. One source of evidence for Kondratieffs, I suspect, is to correct an S-curve for trend. A flattened curve with the trend removed looks like a downswing followed by an upswing. But I can conceive of no reason that the S crossings of the trend line should occur at 25-year intervals.

 **trend removed**

The Goldstein monograph is a performance of great social-science virtuosity. His reading is enormous — in political science, economics, and history — his statistical technique is formidable, his reasoning in defense of his thesis acute. While his history before 1789 relies too much for my taste on the Marxist interpretations of core and periphery of Wallerstein (and to a lesser extent Braudel), he can surely be forgiven for using secondary sources. But in my view, the attempt to fit 500 years of economics with fragile data, and politics, into the Procrustean bed of 50-year linked cycles in production and wars, dated by cycles in prices, is excessively ambitious. One can admire the performance but deplore that so much talent should be expended chasing a will o' the wisp. As I read the book, I found myself recalling the story of Samuel Johnson at a violin performance by Pagannini, responding to a friend's remark that a particular piece was very difficult. Johnson's reply: "I wish it were impossible."

REFERENCES

Cipolla, Carlo. 1970. *The Economic Decline of Empires.* London: Methuen.
Olson, Mancur. 1982. *The Rise and Decline of Nations: Economic Growth, Stagflation and Social Rigidities.* New Haven, Conn.: Yale University Press.

Schama, Simon. 1988. *The Embarrassment of Riches: An Interpretation of the Dutch Culture of the Golden Age.* New York: Knopf.

Wallerstein, Immanuel. 1980. *The Modern World-System II: Mercantilism and the Consolidation of the World Economy, 1600–1750.* New York: Academic Press.

12

Types of International Economic History

It may not be readily apparent why anyone should attempt a taxonomy of international economic history. Do we study economic history because of curiosity? To test economic theories? To guide policy? All or none of the above? Or some variously weighted combination of each? Even in the absence of clear purpose, however, there may be advantage in an ordering of various types of economic history, limited to those dealing with more than one country, and their strengths and weaknesses. In an earlier collection of essays, I included an introduction on "Comparative Economic History."[1] The present essay, to honor Paul Bairoch, an ingenious and lively expositor of comparative history, is to some extent merely an exercise in bringing that paper up to date.

Comparative economic history may be classified in various ways, some common to all history: by area, time period, function, explicit or implicit model, if any, dependence on statistics and statistical method, and whether the work is produced by one head or a number. Few economic historians are as daring as R. Cameron, who has produced a successful textbook.[2] At the opposite end of the spectrum one might perhaps cite F. C. Spooner's book.[3]

P. Bairoch belongs to a distinguished class of economic historians who go in for statistical collection and ordering, as contrasted with what might be called descriptive — or more pejoratively literary-history. The latter is by no means bare of tables and charts, but does not rely on them to the extent that do M. Abramovitz, E. Denison, C. Feinstein, G. Fua, R. Goldsmith, W. Hoffmann, S. Kuznets, A. Maddison, J. Marcewski, T. J. Markovitch, R. C. O. Matthews, and J.-C. Toutain, inter alios. R. Goldsmith once adapted Lord Elgin's remark on measurement to say that if one cannot measure something, it does not exist. That goes far, in my judgment too far. Moreover, back a certain distance in time, data

---

This essay originally appeared in Bodina Etemad, Jean Batou, and Thomas David, eds., *Towards an International Economic and Social History: Essays in Honour of Paul Bairoch* (Geneva: Editions Passe Present, 1995), pp. 33–46. Reprinted with permission of Editions Passe Present.

collection is fraught not only with difficulty but with evident sources of distortion. E. J. Hamilton collected his prices for sixteenth-century Spain from hospital records, which managers had little reason to keep accurately, and which are implausible. The numbers on silver imports for his study came from the Casa de la Contratacion in Seville whereas considerable amounts escaped official surveillance in Lisbon, at Cadiz, and in smuggling.[4] Ingenious attempts have been made to use official and private statistics of the nineteenth century and earlier to measure the earnings of sailors, but they have difficulty in allowing for deaths, desertions, maroonings, excessive charges, and fines, etc.

Much painstaking work goes into first collecting and then testing the validity of historical statistics. At the comparative level, W. Fischer has edited a German series of so-called Handbooks which attempt to draw together comparable data for various countries for various periods. I once expressed amusement to him over a seven-volume work published in Berlin called *Die Welt in Zahlen*, only to have him say that it was a very useful compendium as it was devoted to making statistics of various countries comparable, for example kilometers of railroads, initially collected on differing national bases: private, public, standard gauge, narrow gauge, wide, etc.

In a number of cases, projects have been undertaken to study data on, say, economic growth, in a number of countries, each by a different author. One such series is that on national income under the direction first of S. Kuznets, then of M. Abramovitz, covering major industrial countries; another, under the guidance of L. Reynolds of Yale University, dealt with developing countries, and produced a series of books by different authors, and a covering volume by L. Reynolds.[5] W. Fischer undertook to edit a series of volumes of world economic history by decades, more or less, from 1890 to 1980.[6] Similar studies have been undertaken in European banking, on wealth and the wealthy, landed elites, and so on.[7] With various authors there is gain in wider coverage, loss in lack of comparability since each economic historian tends to emphasize aspects of the subject that particularly interest her or him. In addition, different authors work at different speeds, so that completion of the series or volume often loses unity. When studies of separate regions, countries, or continents go through a single mind, comparability is gained, occasionally at the expense of width or depth of coverage. P. Bairoch belongs among the stars of the single-mind school, along with especially R. Goldsmith in financial development, and A. Maddison in economic growth.

Beyond the distinction between statistical and descriptive, there are questions of area and time period, and general economic history vs. particular functions.

On area, as noted, I omit listing studies of single cities, regions, or countries. Some comparisons run between two countries, some cover wider areas, notably Europe, and some the world. Few have the equipment to tackle Asia, Africa, the Middle East, the Western hemisphere, and Europe, though E. L. Jones, now in Australia, is one,[8] along with R. Cameron, noted above, and W. W. Rostow, whose books cut wide swaths.[9] Two series deal with European economic history, *The Cambridge Economic History of Europe* in eight fat volumes, with various editors and various authors, and the *Fontana Economic History of Europe,* under the editorship of C. M. Cipolla and in paperback, both going back to the Middle Ages. Europe is sometimes divided, as in A. S. Milward and S. B. Saul's two-volume study of continental Europe, which omits Britain, one from 1780 to 1870, the other from 1850 to 1914.[10] A. S. Milward also has a study of economic reconstruction of Western Europe after 1945,[11] an area of greater comparability than Europe as a whole, also tackled in my own financial history over several centuries.[12] Europe can be divided north-south as well as east-west, as in F. Braudel's book,[13] which stretches beyond Europe to the Levant and the Maghreb. With a quasi-Marxist interpretation of economic history, I. Wallerstein links up the core and the periphery, the core consisting of the hegemonic colonial powers of Europe, and the periphery of the colonies in other continents.[14] Some of the smaller noncolonial nations in Europe fall into a semiperiphery, also exploited by the core of Italy, Spain, France, Germany, and Great Britain.

Considerable illumination of economic processes can be derived by comparing pairs of countries, regions, cities. Sir J. Clapham's study is something of a disappointment in this respect as France and Germany are treated in separate chapters and comparison is left largely to the reader to draw.[15] An outstanding classic in binary comparison is the one by C. Wilson.[16] The Low Countries lend themselves to comparison fairly generally, as illustrated by J. A. Van Houtte for early modern trade and finance, and by J. Mokyr on industrialization.[17] Comparison in economic growth between France and Britain is frequently made, for example in detailed particulars by F. Crouzet, and more generally by P. O'Brien and C. Keyder and by me.[18]

Division of comparative economic history by period is contained in a number of studies already cited, not least in the *Cambridge History* to which P. Bairoch made a notable contribution on European trade policy in the nineteenth century.[19] Without going back to the Dark Ages, one can cite R.-H. Bautier, J. Day, H. A. Miskimin, the U.C.L.A. Center for Medieval and Renaissance Studies, with a series of scholarly articles, largely on Europe, but reaching to the Islamic world.[20] Particular attention has been paid to the early modern period, in, for example, J. de Vries,[21] and a collection of papers from the periodical *Past and Present* on much of the same period, edited by T. Aston.[22]

Coming further down to the present are studies on the spread of industrialization from Britain to the Continent, especially the work of W. O. Henderson in a collection of papers.[23]

Beyond general economic histories covering two or more areas and a particular period, one comes to focus on one or more aspects of an economy: growth, factors of production, sectors, trade, finance, institutions, or a single event or change such as the industrial revolution, the inflations of the early 1920s, or the great Depression that started with the collapse of the New York Stock Market in October 1929.

Growth economics has been mentioned both for the industrialized and the developing countries. Statistical studies investigate trends in population, income and wealth, their distribution, capital formation, consumption, savings, balances of international payments. In recent years attention has been turned to economic decline. An economist such as M. Abramovitz in discussing growth examines factors of production — land, labor, capital, and entrepreneurship — sometimes the sectors of an economy — agriculture, industry, services — including especially trade, transport and finance — and government activity and policy. All this proves not to be enough to explain especially the differences between the industrialized and the nonindustrialized countries, and resort has been taken to the elusive concept of "social capability," for which a crude proxy is years of education. This is sometimes called investment in human capital, by analogy with fixed capital and inventories. When social capability is probed more deeply, education can be broken down by type — basic literacy, secondary-school training, higher education, and various qualities of the latter two, technical training and classical education at the secondary level, classical, scientific, and professional education at the highest. In addition, social capability can be pushed in different directions to explore what the French call *"mentalités,"* a concept derided by some economic historians who seek parsimonious explanations for economic outcomes in narrowly economic concepts. It may be defended by pointing to different value-systems in different societies — the amateur tradition in Britain with its "spirit of association," missing in France, and the more professional attitudes of managers in France, Germany, and the United States.

Within the field of growth, an important area is technological change which is the subject of a classic study by D. S. Landes, others by

N. Rosenberg and by J. Mokyr.[24] Studies of technical change in particular industries abound, from P. M. Hohenberg's wide-ranging study on
chemicals to Landes's narrowly focused book on clock-making.[25]

The usual factors of production — land, labor, and capital — are developed in elementary theory in "a given state of the arts," as a fixed
technology used to be called. Land is shorthand for natural resources in
general: arable land of various kinds — plains, downs, land cleared or
drained, and the like — forests, mineral veins, oil and gas fields, even
navigable rivers and natural ports, or advantageous locations near to
markets. Coal was considered a particularly advantageous resource,
after technology made possible its substitution for charcoal in iron-
smelting, and later usefulness in the age of steam. From time to time,
economic historians divided themselves between those who emphasize
coal (resources) or culture (social capability). Among the former is
W. N. Parker.[26] One of his conclusions from his study of the coal fields
that stretch from the Pas-de-Calais in France through Belgium to the
Ruhr is that economic history should not focus exclusively on nations,
but on regions, including those that run across national boundaries. The
alternative emphasis on culture normally limits itself to countries or
regions within countries.

The study of labor encompasses a variety of subfields ranging from
demography — which also stands as an independent subject of its own,
outside economic history — to migration, education, and especially wages
and the impact of changing wage rates on economic growth. Demography
is too vast a subject to cover in these few pages, but for those interested in
Europe there are chapters on demography, or on labor more generally, in
the various volumes not only of the *Cambridge Economic History of
Europe,* but also in another set of studies, not mentioned thus far, the
Fontana Economic History of Europe under the editorship of C. M.
Cipolla, which appeared in paperback in six volumes between 1974 and
1978. Labor in particular countries attracts the interest of radicals and
reformers, from F. Engels, a German businessman, to E. P. Thompson
and E. J. Hobsbawm.[27] One of the few studies that are comparative is by
P. N. Stearns.[28] One difference of insight is that between the quasi-
Marxist model of Sir A. Lewis that large numbers of unemployed or
underemployed labor stimulate growth through holding wages down and
profits up, such profits being reinvested, and that of H. J. Habakkuk
which ascribes vigorous growth in the United States to high wages which
stimulated labor-saving invention.[29] Wages were high in the United States
since artisans could readily quit industry and farm. The Lewis model was
one of growth with unlimited supplies of labor,[30] the Habakkuk model,
growth with unlimited supplied of land. High wages brought about by

taxation on items in the cost of living in Holland were widely held to have contributed to relative economic decline in that country after 1672 or 1700 or 1730.

One point made by a few economic historians is that labor should not be treated like a commodity, analyzed in terms of markets with demand and supply and market-clearing prices in the form of wages. An early study in this direction is the one by K. Polanyi;[31] another, by W. M. Reddy, emphasizes the difference in bargaining power between employers, who normally can find many to work at the prevailing wage, and employees, for whom the alternative to accepting a particular job is frequently unemployment.[32]

Historical study of capital formation, outside its statistical estimation, raises a number of questions: whether capital formation is widening or deepening in the production process, in the first case keeping up with the supplies of labor and land, in the latter increasing the capital/labor ratio and in the usual case embodying the latest technology; whether investment abroad starves domestic industry of capital it would be glad to have, or not; whether shortages of capital more generally held back economic growth in some cases, or growth produced profits which produced capital. In a well-known study of Germany in the first half of the nineteenth century, K. Borchardt insisted that the widely expressed complaint of a capital shortage was illusory, for when growth picked up capital grew.[33]

The position of the entrepreneur as a distinctive element in the development process was first underlined by J. Schumpeter, following whom a center for the study of entrepreneurship was established at the Harvard Business School. Questions about the role of the entrepreneur became salient particularly over British economic decline in the late nineteenth and early twentieth centuries. The question was whether the loss of dynamism could be blamed on a class of businessmen who were ready, after a certain success, to move into élite circles such as the weekending classes, pubic figures who served in Parliament or as justices of the peace. The contrast was sometimes made with France, where successful businessmen sent their sons to the *grandes écoles* for professional training whereas in Britain the sons of the rich were more usually pushed into the public schools, and Oxford or Cambridge, for education in the classics, philosophy, or modern greats, regarded as suitable backgrounds for politics or the civil service. A number of economic historians defended the British entrepreneurs of the period, pointing to bottlenecks in missing resources or technology; the counterargument held that vigorous entrepreneurship broke bottlenecks rather than sitting while waiting for others to lead the way. One particular brand of entrepreneurship in Germany, studied by J. Kocka, was bureaucratic, patterned after military life. Prussian monarchs were among the first in Europe to bureaucratize government, combining tax collection with management of royal domains.[34] Junkers moved easily between military and governmental bureaucracy, and in a number of cases, from one or the other to business.

Comparative economic history deals also with sectors of production — agriculture, industry, services, including transport, trade, and finance. Technological change features in each of these sectors, plus institutional creativity in evolving forms of land tenure, industrial organization, and bank instruments. Agricultural productivity was conditioned by tradition (under feudalism for example), and by system of inheritance, whether dominated by primogeniture or equal inheritance. Development of property rights to sell and bequeath agricultural land was furthered by cadastral surveys, undertaken by royalty so as to determine whom to tax for what land. Clear title of property produced a strong incentive to develop it, leading D. North to make private property rights the center of his institutional theory of economic growth.[35] Exceptions of counter-examples can be found, however. In Spain and other arid agricultural areas, to function well irrigation had to be organized communally, as demonstrated by T. Glick among others;[36] maintenance of dykes against the North and Baltic seas was another task, undertaken cooperatively in Holland, Germany, and Denmark; French tax farmers and Dutch regents turned their offices into hereditary property, which in both cases proved dysfunctional. The former system was overturned by the Revolution, which resulted in the guillotining of 28 *officiers et financiers.* The hereditary system in Holland, where even the widows and small children of rich merchants were elected regent of several provinces after the death of husband or father, was reorganized only after the occupation of the country by the French and the establishment of the Batavian Republic.[37]

Comparative historical studies in services are abundant, especially in trade, transport, and banking. Trade turns, of course, on comparative advantage, which is guided to a considerable degree by the relative abundance or scarcity of factors of production. It is also affected by trade policy, in which P. Bairoch has had a keen interest. Issues include the appropriateness in given circumstances of export-led growth or import substitution; the success or failure of mercantilist policies, studied in the classic work of E. F. Heckscher.[38] A strong view expressed by F. List and again by B. Semmel is that free trade is a policy adopted by an industrial leader to dissuade other countries from following it into industry by making a market for their agricultural products.[39] There are other dimensions: the comparative profitability of trade in luxuries and bulk necessities — the so-called Mother trade of Holland in which Dutch flute ships brought grain, timber, and naval stores from the Baltic to Amsterdam and Rotterdam, as against silk, spices, and wine from the East, the Eastern Mediterranean, and the Iberian peninsula, and sugar, tobacco, dyes, and cotton from colonies in the New World.

The line between government and private enterprise — official navies and merchant fleets — was muddled in time of war by privateering. Large ships in distant trade had to defend themselves with heavy guns, while lightly built vessels were often protected by naval convoys. Treasure ships were also convoyed, or in the British case, specie was carried by naval vessels. Technology gradually made ships larger and more maneuverable, leading them, however, to outgrow some ports upstream of shallow rivers or estuaries. National rivalries in fishing and whaling were particularly acute in cod fishing off Newfoundland and Nova Scotia in Canada, leading the Canadian, H. Innis, to develop a theory of economic history, based on the characteristics of "staples" in trade. Jean-Baptiste Colbert, Finance Minister under Louis XIV, was a great mercantilist, interested in the navy, the merchant fleet, and building *de novo* or reconstructing ports on the French Atlantic coast.[40]

A major factor in a country's trade was the vigor of its merchants — not storekeepers or even wholesalers, but those engaged in "distant trade." Spain had few such merchants because of aristocratic values which disdained commerce; at the height of Spanish trade with the New World, Seville and then Cadiz were filled with Dutch, British, French, and a few German merchants. German merchants were limited in number, outside the Hanseatic cities; according to F. Braudel, because they had been ruined by the Thirty Years' War from 1618 to 1648. A brisk historiographic industry has grown up around the slave trade, with vigorous debate as to whether captains of slave ships were solicitous or careless of their human cargo, and whether the fortunes made in the slave trade and in using slaves, mostly for sugar in the West Indies, financed the British industrial revolution.[41]

The studies edited by R. Cameron on comparative banking were mentioned earlier. In part, their inspiration came from A. Gerschenkron's hypothesis that the role of entrepreneurship in the British industrial revolution was taken up on the Continent nearby — in France, Italy, and Germany, by banks, and beyond them by government.[42] It is of interest that the findings on the role of banking differed between the first volume and the second.[43] The first volume covered England, Scotland, France, Belgium, Germany, Russia, and Japan, and more or less confirmed the Gerschenkron view that banks could drive industrialization. The second volume, dealing with Austria, Italy, Spain, Serbia, Japan (a revised view),

Louisiana, and the United States, failed to support it. The exercise inspired, or should have inspired, anxiety over drawing conclusions from comparisons that are narrowly based, and even from those covering a substantial number of cases.

Another field of interest in international comparisons is urbanization, to which P. Bairoch has contributed.[44] An early entry was H. Pirenne's study.[45] The popularity of the subject is attested by the books of J. de Vries, and covering a longer time period, of P. M. Hohenberg and L. H. Lees.[46] Within countries, cities tend to fall into two patterns, the log-normal in which cities arrayed by size slope downward in a straight line on a logarithmic scale, and a primary distribution, in which single cities such as London, Paris, Vienna dominate smaller ones by a wide margin. Financial centers tend to arrange themselves by a Darwinian process into a hierarchical pattern, with the leading center sometimes in the political capital, sometimes split off as New York/Washington, Toronto/Ottawa, Zurich/Berne.

The history of government belongs mostly to political science, but government performs a number of economic functions which are not usually left in private hands. Adam Smith listed three: national defense, the administration of justice, and public works too large to be undertaken privately. The borderline between public and private functions has wavered throughout history, especially in education, health, housing, and provision of minimal levels of living. Some public goods have included the setting of common standards and their enforcement by checking on the length of yardsticks and the accuracy of weight scales on a continuous basis, and occasional intervention in times of market crisis, ranging from crop failure to bank failures which threaten to spread. A primary government responsibility is the provision of a stable money of account, making the gold standard, inflation, deflation, and foreign-exchange disorder subjects of compelling interest to economic historians. The economics of war comes under the heading of defense (or offense), and branches off into various aspects of crisis, in the finance of armament, inflation, and financial reconstruction when peace is restored, including payment of indemnities, sometimes assisted by international lending. War in particular poses questions of taxation, debt, and default, with ensuing financial crises, and pressures producing both financial innovation and financial breakdown. Leading works are too numerous to list without neglecting scores of great cogency.[47]

In every field of scholarship, one issue is whether to try one's hand at a well-worn topic, perhaps with revisionist notions to distinguish one's efforts from those of others, or to find some small neglected corner of the universe so as to ensure a monopoly product. As already mentioned, four well-worn topics stand out: the British industrial revolution, the French Revolution, the German inflation of the early 1920s, and the world depression of the 1930s. Concerning the first, a revisionist flurry asserted that the changes in British industry from 1770 to 1830, which spread to the Continent mostly after the Napoleonic Wars, were evolutionary, not revolutionary. The issues are put forward in the book edited, with a penetrating introduction, by J. Mokyr.[48] I know of no definitive economic study of the French Revolution, since most scholars who tackle it are immersed in the political issues. On the Great Depression of the 1930s there is, first, M. Friedman, and A. J. Schwartz's chapter 7 of their book, though that focuses exclusively on monetary policy in the United States;[49] then my own book, and P. Temin's and B. J. Eichengreen's studies.[50] The German inflation is treated, among many, in C.-L. Holtfrerich's and G. D. Feldman's studies.[51]

The need to rewrite earlier histories is a function of new data, new theories, and different approaches. An illustration of rewriting to accommodate new theories is furnished by J. Viner.[52] He sought to test the price-specie flow mechanism in balance-of-payment adjustment, working through gold flows, and found it largely confirmed. With the development of Keynesian income analysis, G. M. Meyer, in a 1953 article, reworked the analysis and found that income changes brought about by British investment in Canada explained some of the features of the capital transfer that J. Viner could not account for. Still further illumination came with J. C. Ingram's incorporation of a Harrod-Domar growth aspect which explained how exports could grow when prices in Canada were rising (1957).

The elaboration of the Viner thesis on Canada's borrowing took place in successive stages, as each theoretical advance pushed the analysis further. Many differences in interpretation take the form of debates. Among the most famous was one that started when R. M. Hartwell challenged the view of E. J. Hobsbawm that the level of living had declined with the British industrial revolution. One British publishing house produced a series of Debates in Economic History, mostly on British topics, but including one on Venice in the sixteenth and seventeenth centuries, edited by Brian Pullan.[53] In the level-of-living debate in Britain, the possibility that average real per capita incomes were unchanged or even declined through the "hungry" 1840s, until the sharp rise in the 1850s, poses a question in economic development whether it is justified to condemn one generation to low income for the sake of their descendants.

Much international economic history searches for similarities in behavior from country to country in areas like trade, industry, finance (both private and public), public goods, institutional development, and the like. While such an economic historian as E. E. Rich warns against looking for the laws of economies in history, since "if they exist, they are far from simple,"[54] others claim to find them in Engel's law of consumption, Gresham's law that bad money drives out good, the law of one price, and the like. A salient issue is the difference between a "law" which almost always holds, and a model, like the Lewis model of growth with unlimited supplies of labor, mentioned earlier, which helps the understanding of many situations but is not universally true.

Looking for similarities in the history of economic behavior is one task of history; looking for differences is another. Economic theory suggests that the fall in the price of wheat in Europe that took place after 1880 as a result of the advent of railroads to bring grain to ports, and steamships to carry it from outlying continents to Europe, should lead either to liquidation of wheat farming, as in Britain, or to protection through tariffs, as in France and Germany. But other responses are possible, demonstrating the complexity of the human condition in the aggregate. In Italy, hundreds of thousands emigrated to the New World, largely the United States and Argentina, contrary to the assumptions of international-trade theory which postulates "fixed factors of production." And in Denmark, a dynamic instead of a static response led to a switch from exporting grain to importing it. With the aid of the cream separator and the producers' cooperative, Danish farmers turned from cattle grazing and exporting grain, to exporting meat and dairy products which used grain as inputs.

Some divergent responses to similar stimuli are rooted in social factors. In the nineteenth century, Germans emigrated in periods of poor business; French did not. The French emigration to Algiers in the 1840s was mostly from the Alsace and Lorraine provinces that were quasi-German.

Other differences in response are connected to the outcomes of war. Countries victorious in war may suffer relative stagnation, as victory solidifies the positions of old men in power, whereas defeat is likely to sweep them aside in favor of new men, younger, more experimental, less hidebound. The insight comes from M. Olson's study as he tried to explain the economic buoyancy of Germany and Japan after 1950 or so, compared with the United Kingdom and the United States.[55] Similar differences can occur within a single country in ostensibly similar cases of defeat. In Germany, defeat in 1918 failed to dislodge the Junkers, industrialists, labor leaders, peasant farmers, or civil servants, whose struggles to avoid the burdens of reconstruction and reparations led to hyperinflation that exploded in November 1923. The defeat of 1945 saw the destruction of the Junker base by Russian and Polish occupation of former German territory up to the Oder-Neisse line, labor unions and agricultural groups ruined by Hitler, and industry and civil service discredited by unambiguous defeat which could not be explained away by an assumed "stab in the back."

In the *Perspectives* volume (III) of F. Braudel's *Civilization and Capitalism,* the author says that "the world is the only valid basis of history." The world is also complex, with, in economics, laws, models, similarities and differences. P. Bairoch understands this well as shines forth from the title of his latest work, *Economics and World History: Myths and Paradoxes.*[56]

NOTES

1. C. P. Kindleberger, *Economic Response: Comparative Studies in Trade, Finance and Growth* (Cambridge, 1978).

2. R. Cameron, *A Concise Economic History of the World. From Paleolithic Times to the Present* (New York, 1989).

3. F. C. Spooner, *Risks at Sea: Amsterdam Insurance and Maritime Europe, 1766–1780* (Cambridge, 1983).

4. E. J. Hamilton, *American Treasure and the Price Revolution in Spain: 1501–1650* (Cambridge, 1934).

5. L. Reynolds, *Economic Growth in the Third World* (New Haven, Conn., 1986).

6. W. Fischer (Hg.), *Geschichte der Weltwirtschaft im 20. Jahrhundert* (München, 1973–1984).

7. R. Cameron, ed., *Banking in the Early Stages of Industrialization* (New York, 1967); *Banking and Economic Development* (New York, 1972); D. Spring, *European Landed Elites in the Nineteenth Century* (Baltimore, 1977).

8. E. L. Jones, *Growth Recurring: Economic Change in World History* (Oxford, 1988).

9. W. W. Rostow, *The Stages of Economic Growth* (Cambridge, 1960); *The World Economy: History and Prospect* (London, 1978).

10. A. S. Milward and S. B. Saul, *The Economic Development of Continental Europe 1780–1870* (London, 1973); *The Development of the Economies of Continental Europe 1850–1914* (London, 1977).

11. A. S. Milward, *The Reconstruction of Western Europe, 1945–51* (Methuen, 1984).

12. C. P. Kindleberger, *A Financial History of Western Europe,* 2d ed. (New York, 1993).

13. F. Braudel, *The Mediterranean and the Mediterranean World in the Age of Philipp II,* 2 vols. (New York, 1966).

14. I. Wallerstein, *The Modern World System,* 3 vols. (New York, 1974–1989).

15. J. Clapham, *The Economic Development of France and Germany, 1815–1914,* 4th ed. (Cambridge, 1953).

16. C. Wilson, *Anglo-Dutch Commerce and Finance in the Eighteenth Century* (Cambridge, 1941).

17. J. A. Van Houtte, *An Economic History of the Low Countries: 800–1800* (London, 1977); J. Mokyr, *Industrialization in the Low Countries, 1795–1850* (New Haven, 1976).

18. F. Crouzet, *De la supériorité de l'Angleterre sur la France: l'économique et l'imaginaire, XVII–XXe siècles* (Paris, 1985); P. O'Brien and C. Keyder, *Economic Growth in Britain and France, 1780–1914* (London, 1978); C. P. Kindleberger, *Economic Growth in France and Britain: 1851–1950* (Cambridge, 1964).

19. P. Bairoch, "European Trade Policy, 1815–1914," in P. Mathias and S. Pollard eds., *The Cambridge Economic History of Europe* (Cambridge, 1989), 8:1–160.

20. R.-H. Bautier, *The Economic Development of Medieval Europe* (London, 1971); J. Day, *The Medieval Market Economy* (Oxford, 1987); H. A. Miskimin, *The Economy of Later Renaissance Europe 1460–1600* (Cambridge, 1977); Center for Medieval and Renaissance Studies (U.C.L.A.), *The Dawn of Modern Banking* (New Haven, Conn., 1979).

21. J. de Vries, *The Economy of Europe in an Age of Crisis, 1600–1750* (Cambridge, 1976).

22. T. Aston, ed., *Crisis in Europe 1560–1660* (New York, 1967).

23. W. O. Henderson, *Britain and Industrial Europe, 1750–1870* (Liverpool, 1954).

24. D. S. Landes, *The Unbound Prometheus: Technological Change and Industrial Development from 1750 to the Present* (Cambridge, 1968); N. Rosenberg, *Perspectives on Technology* (Cambridge, 1976); J. Mokyr, *The Lever of Riches: Technological Creativity and Economic Progress* (New York, 1990).

25. P. M. Hohenberg, *Chemicals in Western Europe, 1850–1914: An Economic Study of Technical Change* (Chicago, 1967); D. S. Landes, *Revolution in Time: Clocks and the Making of the Modern World* (Cambridge, 1983).

26. W. N. Parker, *Europe, America and the Wider World,* vol. 1, part 3 (Cambridge, 1984); W. N. Parker and A. Maczak, eds., *Natural Resources in European History* (Washington, 1978).

27. F. Engels, *The Condition of the Working Class in England in 1844* (New York, 1958); E. P. Thompson, *The Making of the British Working Class* (New York, 1963); E. J. Hobsbawm, *Labouring Men. Studies in the History of Labour* (London, 1968).

28. P. N. Stearns, *Lives of Labor: Work in Maturing Industrial Society* (New York, 1975).

29. H. J. Habakkuk, *American and British Technology in the Nineteenth Century* (Cambridge, 1962).

30. W. A. Lewis, "Economic Development with Unlimited Supplies of Labour," *The Manchester School of Economic and Social Studies* 22(1954): 139–91.

31. K. Polanyi, *The Great Transformation* (New York, 1944).

32. W. M. Reddy, *Money and Liberty in Modern Europe: A Critique of Historical Understanding* (Cambridge, 1987).

33. K. Borchardt, *Perspectives on Modern German Economic History and Policy* (Cambridge, 1991), chap. 2.

34. J. Kocka, *Unternehmungsverwaltung und Angestelltenschaft am Beispiel Siemens, 1847–1914* (Stuttgart, 1969).

35. D. C. North, *Structure and Change in Economic Growth* (New York, 1981).

36. T. Glick, *Irrigation and Society in Medieval Valencia* (Cambridge, Mass., 1970).

37. S. Schama, *Patriots and Liberators: Revolution in the Netherlands, 1780–1813* (New York, 1977).

38. E. F. Heckscher, *Mercantilism* (London, 1934).

39. F. List, *Das nationale System der politischen Ökonomie* (Stuttgart, 1841); B. Semmel, *The Rise of Free Trade Imperialism* (Cambridge, 1970).

40. J. Konvitz, *Cities and the Sea: Port City Planning in Early Modern Europe* (Baltimore, 1978).

41. E. Williams, *Capitalism and Slavery* (London, 1964); B. L. Solow and S. Engerman, eds., *British Capitalism and Caribbean Slavery: The Legacy of Eric Williams* (Cambridge, 1987).

42. A. Gerschenkron, *Economic Backwardness in Historical Perspective* (Cambridge, 1962).

43. Cameron, *Banking in the Early Stages of Industrialization; Banking and Economic Development.*

44. P. Bairoch, *Cities and Economic Development from the Dawn of History to the Present* (London, 1988).

45. H. Pirenne, *Medieval Cities, Their Origins and the Revival of Trade* (Princeton, 1969).

46. J. de Vries, *European Urbanization, 1500–1800* (London, 1984); P. M. Hohenberg and L. H. Lees, *The Making of Urban Europe, 1000–1950* (Cambridge, 1985).

47. But I am moved to cite, partly because of recent exposure: R. Ehrenberg, *Capital and Finance in the Age of the Renaissance,* 2d ed. (New York, 1928); R. Roover, *The Rise and Fall of the Medici Bank, 1397–1494* (New York, 1966); P. G. M. Dickson, *The Financial Revolution in England: A Study of Public Credit, 1688–1756* (New York, 1967); R. Nurske, *The Course and Control of Inflation after World War I* (Princeton, 1946); S. A. Schuker, *The End of French Predominance in Europe: The Financial Crisis of 1924 and the Adoption of the Dawes Plan* (Chapel Hill, 1976); and G. D. Feldman, *The Great Disorder: Politics, Economics and Society in the German Inflation, 1914–1924* (New York, 1993).

48. J. Mokyr, ed., *The Economics of the Industrial Revolution* (London, 1985).

49. M. Friedman and A. J. Schwartz, *A Monetary History of the United States, 1867–1960* (Princeton, 1963).

50. C. P. Kindleberger, *The World in Depression, 1929–1939,* 2d ed. (Berkeley, 1986); P. Temin, *Lessons frm the Great Depression* (Cambridge, 1989); B. J. Eichengreen, *Golden Fetters. The Gold Standard and the Great Depression, 1919–1939* (New York, 1992).

51. C.-L. Holtfrerich, *The German Inflation 1914–1923* (Berlin, 1986); Feldman, *The Great Disorder.*

52. J. Viner, *Canada's Balance of International Indebtedness, 1900–1913* (Cambridge, 1924).

53. B. Pullan, ed., *Crisis and Change in the Venetian Economy in the Sixteenth and Seventeenth Century* (London, 1968).

54. *Cambridge Economic History of Europe,* vol. 4 (1967).

55. M. Olson, *The Rise and Decline of Nations* (New Haven, 1982).

56. P. Bairoch, *Economics and World History: Myths and Paradoxes* (London and New York, 1993).

13

Historical Economics

It is probably useless to ask the oldest generation of economists where the profession is going. They are too apt to urge turning the clock back as they provide apologies for their own lives. M. M. Posten once wrote that economic history is for economists in their dotage. The same may perhaps be said of methodology, as graying elders bewail the directions that youth is taking the profession. Nevertheless, while recognizing the advances that have been made in the science in the last half century, and at some risk of sounding querulous, I join Professor Rechtenwald in addressing the question of which should be the most productive lines of inquiry in the decades ahead.

My vote runs for attention to economic history, or more accurately historical economics, to fact, and less to mathematical theory that spins derivatives from axioms and hypotheses, runs regressions to prove relationships that presumably hold good in great numbers of circumstances and can be used for policy determination. Medicine, like economics, has produced great advances in specialized fields — from pediatrics to geriatrics — but there remains a social need for the general practitioner to administer to the whole person, and not just his or her life-passages and parts. The same is true for economic science. And the cultivation of comparative economic history should not be neglected.

Since the marginalist revolution of the 1870s, the cutting edge of economics has lain in its possible resemblance to celestial mechanics. Man is rational, knows his own mind, possesses all needed information, and maximizes his welfare. Such a monumental figure as Alfred Marshall made room for the analogy with biology, a trend which has been strengthened lately by chaos theory. This stresses the unpredictability of

This is more or less the English version of a paper that was first published in German under the title "Geschichte und Okonomie," in Horst Hanuson and Horst Claus Rechtenwald, eds., *Okonoische Wissenschaft in der Zukunft* [Economics in the future] (Düsseldorf: Verlag Wirtschaft und Finanzen, 1992), pp. 225–30. The "more or less" is called for because I mislaid the English original and have reproduced this from a draft that probably was not much changed. Reprinted with permission of Verlag Wirtschaft und Finanzen.

mutations, some of which take off on their own and change the economic paths followed by individuals, groups, and nations. Most recently there has been a reaction against comparing economics with physics, suggesting that rather it resembles rhetoric. It uses metaphor, analogy, anecdote (well chosen so as to be representative), plausibility, seeking to persuade rather than to demonstrate conclusively. This school calls for the rejection of positive modernism that would test economics by its capacity to predict, asserting that prediction has failed (as is clearly the case in at least some fields such as monetarism, Keynesianism, and flexible exchange rates). But it is a mistake to throw the baby out with the bathwater. Economic analysis is highly successful in many fields, especially those in which partial-equilibrium analysis can be applied: if this, then that, other things being held more or less equal. As long as most of the necessary conditions can be impounded in *ceteris paribus,* economics works well. General equilibrium with loops, feedbacks, critical distances among variables (as in meteorology), and long strings of variables is more difficult. It calls for intuition, feel, and insight, as McCloskey holds. In this view economics should be a conversation in which the participants seek to present plausible stories, and to persuade one another. One way of gaining insight and plausibility in my judgment is to consult economic history. Let me illustrate.

The theory of rational expectations plus the axiom that economic actors maximize their personal welfare suggests that there can be no bubbles leading to financial crises. Markets for assets and for goods and services will adjust prices in accordance with well-known economic models. Fundamentals will dominate. In Friedman's view there can be no destabilizing speculation on Darwinian reasoning. Those who buy on rising prices and sell on falling will lose money and fail to survive. It is readily understood how axioms and hypotheses can lead to these conclusions, but acquaintance with economic history should show that they are untenable, or at least that the past is replete with economic episodes that contemporary observers called bubbles, and identified with destabilizing speculation. One line of endeavor is to explore the theory more deeply and to decide what factors have been left out — imperfect or asymmetric information, different degrees of experience or intelligence among the participants. Another reaction, frequently and in my opinion wrongly used, is to deny the facts and alter their description.

Theorems are statements of relationships that always hold true, and that can be contravened by a single counterexample. Economic laws are rather general tendencies that permit a wide number of exceptions. Some laws contradict one another: Say's law that supply creates its own demand can be opposed by Keynes's law that demand creates its own supply. Both may be true (though not simultaneously) with the appropriate necessary conditions: Say's law with barter and a Walrasian auctioneer; Keynes's law with an adequate supply of unemployed resources. In one historical case I know, merchants taking their textiles to Caen and Gilbray in the eighteenth century returned home with a sizable percentage of the cloth they had taken to be sold — ranging from 14 percent in 1761 to 50 percent in 1750 in Caen, and 58 percent in Gilbray in 1781. The proportion brought back ran regularly from 25 to 30 percent. Keynes's law fails to work under conditions of full employment when increases in demand lead not to supply but to inflation. Again there is Hume's law — that imports beget exports and exports imports through the price-specie-flow mechanism, the foreign-trade multiplier, or both. This works well at times, for example following Britain's repeal in 1846 of the Corn Laws, along with the timber duties and the Navigation Acts. On other occasions it fails, as persistent disequilibrium in balances of payments testifies.

Gresham's law provides an interesting test. The neo-Austrian free-banking school of monetarists is not fearful that Gresham's law would create havoc if any person or firm were allowed to issue his or its own money. It hypothesizes that instead of bad money driving good into hoarding or export, good money would drive out bad. Sellers would indicate the kind of money they required for their products, and would insist on good money. That surely is a possibility, and there is at least one historical example early in the millennium when private minters competed with one another in France and Spain to have their money accepted. A theorist confronting such a difference as to how Gresham's law might work with how it typically has been known to work in economic history should examine the necessary conditions not ordinarily accounted for. Markets generally fall into one of two categories — either sellers' or buyers' markets. In a sellers' market, the seller has the edge and can denominate the money in which he wants to be paid. In buyers' markets, on the contrary, the buyer makes the choice. Price is of course a critical consideration, but the money used is not irrelevant. Since most cases of Gresham's law involve bad money driving out good, there may be something of a presumption that buyers' markets generally prevail over sellers'. A general-equilibrium theorist may postulate one money, and dispose of the problem in that fashion. Attention to fact, however, makes that assumption problematic. When money consisted of precious and other metals, it was necessary to have coins of different value — gold, silver, and copper simultaneously — for transactions of different natures and sizes: international trade, urban purchases, and rural payments, respectively. Gold was too valuable for use by peasants, copper too bulky for international payments. In the modern world of paper money transactions typically involve national money and one other in use in international transactions. To save costs, international traders maintain stocks of both, which opens up the foreign-exchange market to Gresham's law.

Economic laws must make room for exceptions. This makes suspect their use for prediction, as called for by positive economics. Generalizations of the sort of regular cycles — Braudelian for 150 years, Kondratieff, 50 to 60, Kuznets 20, Juglar 9, Kitchen 39 months — are helpful in telling economists what to look for but not much help in forecasting. I have more (but little) faith in stages of economic development — Rostow's preconditions, takeoff, drive to maturity, and high-level consumption — but nothing on economic sclerosis, or Gerschenkron's "big spurt" which is analogous to takeoff except that it makes room for the substitution of one or more actors for others — for example, banks or government for entrepreneurship. More reliable in my opinion is the Gompertz, logistic or S-curve, regarded by an MIT metallurgist colleague as the "curve of material transformation." Again, such patterns are useful in guiding search for patterns, but new mutations or nuclei can give rise to another spurt out of the old.

Economic history requires a study of institutions which are sometimes produced endogenously, sometimes left over from earlier circumstances. Most theorists, particularly those that profess rational expectations, assume that institutions adapt to changing conditions. If so, they can of course be ignored. Institutionalists tend to believe that the cake of custom involved in institutions dominates economic outcomes. Each is possible. It calls for the skills of the anthropologist, sociologist, the political scientist among others to formulate a general rule on the question. R. C. O. Matthews has tried to work out an economic theory of institutions, surely a worthy undertaking.

Martin Shubik mentioned to me privately that his title at Yale as Professor of Mathematical Economics and Institutions rests on a recognition that his specialty, game theory, requires rules of the game. These are mostly shaped by institutions, often rooted in historical development, leading him to read economic history. Terence Gorman notes that the great economists of our generation — he mentions Arrow, Hahn, and Samuelson — have a wide, and perhaps deep, knowledge of economic and general history. Arrow and Solow contributed papers to a symposium on the role of economic history in the training of economists. When Gorman was at the London School of Economics, however, he tried to put forward a program in economics that he thought optimal — combining technical economics, mathematical and econometric, with economic history, but without success, as he says, because of the single-mindedness which is the besetting sin of much modern economics. Teachers concentrate on their own specialties, and joint honors students feel like outsiders everywhere. Commenting on the Gorman attempt, Michio Morishima, who believes that the mathematization of economics since 1940 has lost all sense of balance, doubts whether economics and history can be taught simultaneously: "Heaven does not bestow more than one gift, and those who like history tend to dislike mathematics." He sees a need to construct theories, and modify and improve them, in accordance with historical development.

There is much to be said for letting 1,000 flowers bloom. If the fertilizer of economic history cannot be applied in the course of early education, there may be merit in encouraging economists to get their feet wet in history at a later stage when they are not so driven to conform to the ruling mathematical method.

Economic history should be comparative. The single true observation does not contribute a great deal unless it is substantiated by similar behavior at other times and/or places. It may do better, however, than the stylized fact assumed to conform to the needs of a theory.

I conclude with a relevant quotation from that paragon of economic common sense, Walter Bagehot:

> Political economy is an abstract science which labors under a special hardship. Those who are conversant with its abstractions are usually without a true contact with its facts; those who are in contact with its facts have usually little sympathy with and little cognizance of its abstractions. . . .

Part 3

Personal History

14

Some Economic Lessons from World War II

This essay is based on memory, not scholarly research — though I include a few references from books on my shrunken shelves — and on the writer's experience in and after the war in the Office of Strategic Services (OSS) in Washington, the Enemy Objectives Unit (EOU) of the Economic Warfare Division (EWD) of the U.S. Embassy, London (on detached service from OSS), in G-2, 12th Army Group, General Omar N. Bradley, commanding, on the European continent, and from June 1945 to July 1948 in the Department of State in Washington, as an economic adviser on German reparations, as chief of the Division of German and Austrian Economic Affairs (GA), and as adviser for the European Recovery Program (ERP, commonly known as the Marshall Plan).[1] No attempt is made to produce a unified treatment of the economic problems of war and postwar. Instead, the essay consists of a series of separate, largely economic, points that seemed important at the time and in retrospect, some based on personal experience, some analytical, many recalled from hearsay. The points are numbered for reference.

Lessons of this sort may not be relevant in any future war. If the war involves hydrogen bombs, for example, the damage would be orders-of-magnitude higher than in World War II, which for the most part in Europe used 500-pound high-explosive bombs. There is a possibility that in a future war between more or less evenly matched forces, nuclear bombs would be treated as poison gas was in World War II, too dangerous to use, as likely to backfire, resulting in mutually assured destruction. The question involves game-theory problems which I am not competent to discuss. The lessons I have in mind are local in time and place to U.S. experience in Europe, 1943–48. They may nonetheless have suggestive value.

This essay was originally commissioned by the Industrial College of the Armed Forces in 1994.

1. Total War

In ordinary parlance "total war" means one in which civilians on the home front are exposed to bombing, shot, and shell. To an economist, a mobilization appropriate to total war is that allocation of man- and womanpower that makes it impossible to increase a country's fighting value by transferring an individual from the home front to the military. In effect, such a transfer would reduce the value of the war effort on the home front — the production of materiel, for example — by as much as military capabilities would be increased in the armed forces. The United States in 1945 was far from being mobilized to this extent. Moreover, Germany, which thought at length in terms of total war, was also far from being fully mobilized, largely because of its strong prejudice against using women in industry or in the armed forces, rather than keeping them confined to *Küche, Kinder,* and *Kirche* (the kitchen, children, and church). Early *Blitzkrieg* victories gave the Wehrmacht access to additional manpower in the persons of prisoners of war (POWs), displaced persons (DPs), worker battalions provided by German allies and conquered nations, plus German Jews and others corralled in concentration camps. This last group was literally worked to death as far as most of the men were concerned. In a visit to a concentration camp at Kohnstein, near Nordhausen, in April 1945, I learned that worker rations were meager: a strong man could last six months before dying under the regime, a thin or weak one no more than three.[2]

If the British did well balancing the manpower of the home and military front overall, they bungled badly within the armed forces, as among ground, sea, and air forces. If I have the numbers broadly right, they ended the war with two million men and women in the Royal Air Force (RAF) who could be brought to bear against the enemy only with great difficulty as the war on the ground proceeded, and only 14 ground divisions (roughly 200,000 men), including Canadian troops.[3] The error lay in accepting too readily the strategic views of 1920 analysts of air power, such as Duhet and Seversky, who thought that the next war would be won by bombing attack on the enemy's economy, battering it to bring it to its knees, without much in the way of specificity as to how this would be done. I come to the issue below in discussing strategic bombing. The air force appealed to youth more than the infantry, in the United States as in Britain. At the end of the war, if my recollection is not wide of the mark, both air forces were refusing volunteer recruits (probably about to be drafted), to force numbers into the infantry.

A point about the relative attraction of the air and ground forces was made to me by Colonel Richard D'Oyley Hughes, A-5 (Plans) of the U.S. Strategic Air Forces (USSTAF) in Britain. Hughes had been a lieutenant in the British infantry in France in 1918, later served 10 years in a British regiment in India before moving to the United States. He noted that once an airman gets into his bomber he no longer can exert his will. Flying formation, the group is led by the captain of the lead plane, and except in the case of mechanical failure or damage by enemy fire, the other planes follow him. In the infantry, on the other hand, each private must apply his own willpower to get out of his foxhole and go forward in an attack. The highest rate of casualties in the military has always been company-grade officers in infantry regiments.

One further economic lesson on manpower. A distinguished labor economist, Professor Eli Ginzburg of Columbia University, served during some part of the war as manpower adviser to Secretary of War Robert P. Patterson. Ginzburg observed that promotion in the medical corps depended upon the numbers of enlisted personnel an officer had under him, which led the ambitious among officers in hospital units to hoard manpower. He suggested, if I have the theory correct, that a better criterion for promotion would be the ratio of bed-patient days to manpower in the command. Control had to be applied to make certain that medical doctors would not keep patients in bed beyond the time appropriate to their medical problem. With the numerator controlled, however, the ratio could be raised by shrinking the denominator, by sloughing off orderlies and clerical bodies. While all this is hearsay, I was given to understand that this change in procedure produced enough numbers to man another division, or perhaps it was only a regiment, as men and women excess to basic hospital needs were turned out.[4]

2. Strategic Bombing

Two models can be used to describe a highly industrialized economy. One is the input/output table, listing producing industries down the left-hand tab, with the rows for each industry showing the use of its products according to columns representing both industries using the outputs of other industries as inputs, such as components, materials, and fuel, plus final use in consumption, exports, government, and the like. The input/output table was perfected in 1947 by Professor Wassily Leontief, then of Harvard, for which he won a Nobel Prize in economics. As a general notion it went back to Léon Walras, a French economist at the end of the nineteenth century, who produced a *Tableau économique*. It was intuitively understood before Leontief by those who recommended bombing a particular industry in enemy territory as a means of bringing the economy to a halt by depriving the user industries, including the military, of the selected industry's output. This was the rationale for bombing such basic industries as ball bearings and oil, and for recommending bombardment for many other industries, such as carborundum grinding wheels, needed for polishing metal. It was early observed that various industrialists in the United States were enthusiastic about the bombing of their own industry in Germany, not for the self-interested reason that they would hope to knock out a postwar competitor, but because it is human nature for people to believe that their own industry or profession is of critical importance to society at large.

The second theory holds that the basic resource of an economy is labor. If an economy is wounded in any particular, reallocation of labor to that spot, like white corpuscles gathering at a flesh wound, will heal it. Like input/output, from which it differs, this view of a given economy is valid. The apparently conflicting notions that an economy is highly specialized in an intricate pattern, and that it is all essentially reducible to labor, can be reconciled in theory by introducing the time dimension. In the short run, an economy is brittle; in the long run malleable. Given the attacked economy has enough time, it can repair bomb-damaged industry, no matter how concentrated, provided it has or can obtain the manpower.[5] This puts a premium on sustained attack in a narrow time frame. But the attacking forces also need time, to repair damaged aircraft, rest crews, replace combat losses and crews coming to the end of their quota of missions — 25 in bombers. In the early "blooding" stages of operations, some missions are directed to easy targets, not heavily defended, such as the submarine pens at St. Nazaire which the Navy wanted bombed continuously, but which were defended by yards of reinforced concrete that was impervious to 100- and 500-pound bombs. The attacked economy was also protected by weather, which made pinpointed attacks on specified targets often impossible because of cloud cover and because concentrated periods of clear weather were rare. In a famous week of February 1944, with a Siberian "high" holding promise of a week of cloudless weather, Major General Fred Anderson, commanding USSTAF in the temporary absence of General Carl Spaatz, ordered a week of attack on prime targets deep in Germany. He ordered the medical officers at all levels not to allow crews to stand down for battle fatigue (I forget the exact term). His rationale was that the air forces were morally bound to force themselves to the limit when they had the opportunity, as the ground forces would have to do on D day and thereafter, without the luxury of relief from operations for combat fatigue.[6]

I come to the choice of industries for strategic bombing presently.

First, however, note the contrary theory of winning the war by area bombing attacks on population centers. The choice was made partly because the RAF decided that it was unable to tackle precision targets in daylight, as their planes would be shot out of the sky. The American air force had confidence in the B-17, or Flying Fortress, thought capable of defending itself against enemy fighter aircraft as it flew above the effective range of antiaircraft fire (*flak*). Air Chief Marshall Arthur Harris of RAF Bomber Command believed an invasion of the Continent unnecessary, as Germany would surrender and the war would be won by the wholesale bombing of cities. EOU thought that this strategy involved all hammer and no anvil. As it happened, the German government was content to let residences such as urban apartment houses be destroyed without much in the way of effort to repair them or build new.[7]

EOU analysis ran in terms of "depth" of an industry behind the fighting front — in this case the ground fighting consequent to the invasion of the Continent — and the recuperative powers of an industry following successful attack. Such industries as steel and electric power lay too deep to be worthy of attack despite the thoughts of Albert Speer and the afterthoughts of USSBS. In the winter of 1943–44 all the steel that would be used in defending against the invasion had already been produced. Electric power stations were both difficult to destroy and had the "cushion" of standby local power at most industrial plants producing army equipment.

EOU did underestimate the depth of ball bearings behind the fighting front. Assembly plants for aircraft, tanks, trucks had inventories which could be drawn down. Assembly procedures could be reorganized to incorporate bearings in the completed weapon at the last possible moment, bearings which had been hand-carried from the bearing plant to the assembly point in cars driven by otherwise useless salesmen, a preview of today's Japanese practice of just-in-time.[8]

The attack on German aircraft was a failure insofar as it did not prevent rising numbers of aircraft being produced. In an unanticipated way, however, along with ball bearings, it was a resounding success as the German air force (GAF) chose to defend against these deep penetrations, and in the course of so doing, lost command of the air over the invasion battle by running out of pilots, not aircraft.[9] This was serendipity, to be sure, something that could not be counted on. War and life in general do not lack this sort of luck. I have been told that the P-47 with its radial Pratt-Whitney and Curtiss-Wright engines was designed for high-altitude fighting, while the P-51 with a liquid-cooled Allison engine was intended for use at low level. The latter proved vulnerable to ground fire, which might pierce the engine casing and drain the coolant;

the P-47 could lose one or more cylinders to ground fire and keep flying with little performance loss. The two swapped intended roles, with a great gain for military effect.

I suspect that the German air force had to defend against the B-17 and B-24 daylight raids deep in Germany or lose the moral support of the Nazi command and of the German populace. In any event, command of the air on D day, in June 1944 was critical to the success of the invasion. A strong case can be made that it was won by General Fred Anderson in February 1944 with his willingness to spend his air forces. It is conjectured by many — and strongly hinted in Wistar's novel — that General Spaatz would have been unwilling to suffer such losses, on the theory for which admirals are sometimes criticized, of preserving a fleet in being rather than risking its loss.

As the day of invasion drew near in the winter and spring of 1944, the U.S. strategic air forces needed another target system, and chose oil. This had limited depth behind the fighting front. The German Ardennes offensive in December 1944 revealed that the Wehrmacht was short of gasoline: trucks were using gasogene fuel (charcoal converted into gas), artillery was hauled by horses, and plans called for capturing American p.o.l. (petroleum, oil, and lubricant) dumps. There was a difference of opinion on the Allied side whether U.S. heavy bomber forces should be kept on their strategic mission — say, oil — or be reallocated to invasion support by attacks on the French railroad system, discussed below under tactical bombing. W. W. Rostow has written a book on this — *Pre-invasion Bombing Strategy: General Eisenhower's Decision of March 25, 1944* (Austin: University of Texas Press, 1981). The interesting question, to which I do not know the answer, is whether or not the German effort to put a number of synthetic oil plants — Bergius hydrogenation or Fischer-Tropsch — underground would have succeeded, given more time, and how much more time.[10]

It was a surprise to the Research and Analysis Branch of OSS that the U.S. air forces did not have a well-worked-out plan for attacking the German economy, but relied on British intelligence. Since this followed a different bombing strategy — area night instead of daylight pinpoint bombing — British target information did not exactly suit American plans. General William ("Wild Bill") Donovan, a hero of World War I and a New York lawyer, started OSS on the theory that the U.S. military would leave gaps in intelligence and in special operations, and that he could create an organization to fill them in advance of knowing what they actually were. Secret Intelligence (SI) and Special Operations (SO) performed in ways I neither knew about nor could evaluate if I had known. William Casey wrote a book on SI in Europe before his death, published by Henry Regnery in Chicago. Research and Analysis, made up of academics, had geographical divisions, populated largely by historians and geographers, and an economics division, organized into sections dealing with enemy materiel, manpower, industry, agriculture, plus possibly another which does not come to mind. R & A as a whole is discussed in Barry M. Katz, *Foreign Intelligence: Research and Analysis in the Office of Strategic Services, 1942–1945* (Cambridge, Mass.: Harvard University Press, 1989). EOU in London was drawn largely from the enemy materiel section of the economics division of R & A, plus some personnel from the separate Board of Economic Warfare (BEW), an agency patterned after the British Minister of Economic Warfare.

British night bombing of cities was thought by some to harm German morale, perhaps on the home front, certainly on the battlefield where soldiers and sailors would worry about families at home. Others thought it strengthened the will to resist. I know of no definitive settlement of the question. Some targets like the massive raids on Hamburg in August 1943 were undertaken to test the effectiveness of radar targeting, which worked especially well along the waterfront because of the clear definition it gave between land and water. This raid luckily hit and badly damaged a plant making something like tank transmissions. This was not purposeful but a bonus. Many American soldiers thought it was a conspiracy by international corporations that the I. G. Farben plant at Hoechst, a landmark on the highway from Wiesbaden to Frankfurt-am-Main, escaped evident damage. Two reasons held: chemicals were not on the USSTAF list of target-system priorities; and second, the RAF had difficulty identifying Frankfurt-am-Main and its outlying industrial regions because of the Taunus hills shielding them from approaching radar.

In due course, the RAF developed special squads. One attacked the Dorpe and the Moehne dams in the Ruhr, with spherical bombs that were spun at high speed in the bomb bay so that on release they would skip along the surface of the water, jump over the nets that the Germans had strung to protect the dams from torpedo attack, and sink when they hit the dam, exploding below the surface. The dams were destroyed, thousands of tons of water were let loose, but actual damage of military consequence was minimal. The physical, not economic, success of the attack had a strong positive effect on British morale, however, which may have been its purpose. The German people may have found the exercise depressing.[11]

Another special squad was used in the war to attack transport targets — see below on tactical bombing — at night, with 2-, 3-, and 4-ton bombs, the last, one to a plane. Guide aircraft would lead the way and illuminate the sky over a wide area. The monster bomb or bombs would be brought in in a low-flying aircraft—below ordinary flak—and hover over the target, so to speak, at a minimal altitude to be sure of a direct hit. I recall one use against the approach to a Loire bridge. I assume that deep penetration into Germany was impossible with so much weight.

3. Tactical Bombing

Support of the invading ground forces from the air, apart from parachute drops and some bombing of fortifications which was not highly effective, concentrated on trying to drive back the railheads from which German troops coming to the beachhead to repulse the invasion would detrain. Air superiority meant that German divisions moving to the battle by road were vulnerable to Allied fighter strafing. One general, Bayerlein of *Panzer Lehr* (tank training division), lost three drivers as he escaped by diving into the ditch with only seconds to spare, seconds unavailable to the drivers who had to stop the car and get out from behind the wheel on the side away from the ditch.

The salient operational question was how to drive back the railheads. In this there was a wide difference of view between the British, and especially Solly (later Lord) Zuckerman, scientific adviser to Air Chief Marshall Arthur Tedder, deputy to General Eisenhower, and EOU. Based on experience observed in Sicily and Italy, from which EOU thought he drew the wrong lessons, Zuckerman recommended bombing the French railroad system at freight classification yards—called, in English, marshaling yards. Great damage could be done to these installations, thick with freight cars, locomotives in their turntable sheds, coaling facilities, water towers. Italian workers had been slow in cleaning up and repairing those damaged in the southern campaigns, especially at terminals where there was no through traffic. EOU, on the other hand, believed in bombing bridges, particularly those with spans above 110 feet—shorter ones could be repaired with "Bailey bridges," which were standard Army transport equipment. The USSTAF/EOU plan was to isolate the lodgement area by knocking out all the bridges on the Seine from Rouen to Paris, later a series of bridges over the Loire, and maintaining rail-line cuts, principally by damage to viaducts and embankments between the two river systems. Destruction of the bridges along the Seine worked into the cover plan, feinting that attack might be launched by the 3rd Army under General George Patton in the Pas de Calais, by hindering the lateral movement of German forces in both directions. The early attack on Seine bridges was accompanied by others on other rivers to the east and south to disguise the pattern. Those on the Loire were not attacked systematically until after D day.

Zuckerman, favoring marshaling yards, claimed that bridges could not be destroyed from the air. I believe that there was even a SHAEF order against attacking them. Someone in an ORS (Operations Research Section) of a fighter wing had heard of the dispute, and persuaded his commanding general to practice bridge attacks. On May 8, 1944, if I have the date correctly, less than a month before D day, his commander, one General Smith, directed a squadron of 14 fighter-bombers against the railroad bridge over the Seine at Vernon. Six planes aborted; the remaining eight attacked and dropped the bridge into the river. In retrospect, the target may have been chosen with luck as the railroad track, while it crossed the river, did not connect with the rail system east of the Seine, and may, on that account, not have been strongly defended. In any event, the success of the attack brought about a change of tactics; the bombing of bridges picked up sharply. By D day, the Seine system of rail and road bridges down to the city of Paris had been destroyed.[12]

Bombing attack on a marshaling yard does great damage, like those on apartment houses, but for little military effect. These yards are a poor place to stop through-running, as they hold the largest number of parallel tracks anywhere in a rail system. Most yards could be repaired for getting troop trains through in a matter of hours. In one briefing in London before Air Chief Marshall Sir Trafford Leigh Mallory of the British tactical air forces, and other high British and American brass, Zuckerman, a civilian, produced some British railroad executives and asked them how they would like to have 2,000 tons of bombs dropped on their principal marshaling yard. None seemed to welcome the idea. As a mere captain in the high-level assembly, and at a strong disadvantage against a civilian, I asked the group how long, after such an attack, it would take to get a series of trains through. The answer was "a few hours."[13]

A certain amount of literature has grown up around the debate. Rostow's book referred to earlier contains a report on the success of the railroad attack, written by me on June 16, 1944, as I returned to EOU from the British 21st Army Group headquarters to which I had been detached for several weeks before, during, and after the invasion, later to transfer to G-2 of the American 12th Army Group. Zuckerman's autobiography (*From Apes to Warlords* [New York: Harper and Row, 1978]) contains a series of disparaging remarks about the EOU group, to which I responded in *Encounter* in November 1978, with Zuckerman replying in June 1979, and Rostow joined in in August/September 1980, all in the same British periodical. Katz's book, *Foreign Intelligence,* called the debate "inconclusive" (pp. 121–22), but this, as might be anticipated, is not the way I see it.

The debate ran basically between slowing down rail traffic and interdiction. Cuts on rail lines, from sabotage or bomb attacks, in open running or in concentrated areas like marshaling yards, took hours or at most a day to get trains through. Destruction of a bridge span over 110 feet in length needed roughly three weeks to restore traffic. The success of the interdiction attacks, and of bombing in general, has the disability that it is sometimes kept up too long. The 9th Air Force, under the command of General Hoyt Vandenberg, wanted to keep bombing rail and road bridges after the Allied armies had broken out and through German land defenses and needed the bridges for their own use, as persuasively demonstrated at Remagen on the Rhine. Vandenberg, not the most brilliant of the air force generals, kept urging his A-2 section to produce programs for more interdiction well after they had become thoroughly dysfunctional.[14]

4. Intelligence

Too little attention has been paid to Polish intelligence in World War II. It is applauded for stealing and delivering to the British an Enigma machine for encrypting military messages, thus giving an enormous assist to British cryptography in producing ULTRA. But the spread of Polish workers over Germany, and good organization, produced a torrent of documents, photographed surreptitiously in German war plants and elsewhere. The difficulty was that the photographers could have little sense of what was useful and what not, so that the recipients had to wade through piles of paper to find useful information — the proverbial problem of the needle in the haystack. In EOU we had one lucky find when, following a quick dismissal of a document, a second thought led to its retrieval and reexamination: a production schedule for a Focke-Wulf 190 part — a *steuerknupfel* (steering coupling for the joystick), with scheduled deliveries to various plants which represented in fact the production schedule of that fighter plane.

ULTRA was of course a wonderful source of intelligence so long as the German forces were at great distances from central headquarters and forced to rely on radio, the messages of which could be intercepted, decoded after a considerable learning experience, and distributed to units with an imperative need to know. The list was kept short to limit the risk of detection. There was a danger, however, of relying too trustingly on a single intelligence source. After the August 1944 break-through, with German forces back on their own territory and land lines available, ULTRA dried up, and failed to yield more than one or two hints, easily ignored, regarding the German Ardennes offensive of De-cember 1944. In addition, a rich source of intelligence such as ULTRA tends to make its recipients lazy. Two contributors to the book *Code-breakers: The Inside Story of Bletchley Park*, Sir F. H. Hinsley and Alan Stripp, eds. (Oxford: Oxford University Press, 1993) criticized Field Marshall Bernard Montgomery for not relying on it sufficiently, hesitat-ing when he had full knowledge of the weakness of the opposing Rom-mel force. At the same time, RAF intelligence relied upon it excessively, and misinterpreting some of the messages, could on occasion be led astray.

EOU in London was not privy to ULTRA for the understandable reason of security, and was therefore forced to rely on every possible intelligence source — pilfered documents, especially those from Polish intelligence, aerial reconnaissance and photographic interpretation, prisoner-of-war interrogation, detritus from shot-down enemy aircraft or overrun tanks, guns, trucks. ULTRA signals led AIC (3), if I have the RAF intelligence unit designation correctly, to believe that the Focke-Wulf plant in Bremen was operational (in its convenient location for bombing from Britain) and deserving of attack. Polish documents sug-gested that it had moved to Marienbad in the east. EOU sought com-parative aerial cover of the Bremen plant, with a request to AD (I) Medmenham for interpretation of the plant's activity. This revealed that some planes that looked active in a single aerial photograph had been stationary over time (see Constance Babington-Smith, *Air Spy: The Story of Photo Intelligence in World War II* [New York: Harper and Row, 1957], pp. 182ff). A request to the British intelligence unit in charge of prisoner-of-war interrogation to sort through the crowd of German POWs captured in North Africa and find those who had worked in the Focke-Wulf plant in Bremen produced nothing. A number of such were singled out, but were brought to London for questioning in a body, and readily determined among themselves what they had in common and refused to talk on that subject. Interrogators liked to be asked pointed questions on which they can zero in. On the Continent after the Ardnennes offensive had been stopped, and thousands of prisoners rounded up, a unit was asked to ascertain how various divisions had been brought to the jumping-off site by rail, questioning those with some knowledge of and interest in routing. The interrogators were thor-oughly bored with grinding out the order-of-battle information they had been trained in putting together, and tackled the task with enthusiasm.

In the war, EOU and later R & A, OSS, developed an intelligence method for estimating enemy materiel production from the serial numbers on captured enemy equipment. Initially, during the planning phase of the attack on German ball-bearing production, EOU learned of an RAF depot which contained large numbers of salvaged parts of German aircraft shot down in the battle of Britain. On weekends, the staff would visit the depot, wash bearings of a given size with gasoline to penetrate the oil and grease, and take down the serial numbers, with, where possible, which was true in a sufficient number of cases, the identification of the company and plant that produced them. The work was continued at first by an economist who, born in Russia and having worked for a time in Berlin for the U.S. Embassy, was a clerk in the U.S. Embassy in London and later an analyst at Rand in Santa Monica, Oleg Hoeffding. Next a group from OSS, Washington, led by Richard Ruggles, later a professor of economics at Yale, specialized in national-income analysis, took it on. After the Ardennes offensive members of the team toured the battlefield with cameras specially designed with a frame to hold the lens at the appropriate distance from nameplates inside tanks. The technique came to be known as the numbers game.

Not everyone is aware why military equipment and its components are numbered. The numbers are needed by producers, assemblers, maintenance personnel, and the like to be able to identify the correct part for the correct model. The issue is general. The secrecy that would handicap an enemy in the matter would at the same time handicap the home forces. I vividly recall the consternation of a major in counter-intelligence in G-2, 12th Army Group, on learning that some G-4 high-up laundry outfit was broadcasting in clear to lower units where to go to pick up laundry, and in the course of it giving away the U.S. Army order of battle. The lower units, however, presumably needed to have instructions.

5. The Resistance

French and I presume Belgian and Dutch Resistance were heroic in risking life to collect intelligence and especially to sabotage German military installations. It was nonetheless a regret that their efforts could not be better focused. In bombing strategy and tactics it would have been useful to have sabotage on the ground coordinated with bombing from the air. In tactical bombing, for example, we should have liked to have the Resistance concentrate on the few lines emanating from Paris between the interdiction systems of the Seine and Loire bridges, but could discover no channel by which to direct their scattered and rather random efforts. Later in July 1944 when the Falaise-Argentan gap was being closed and remaining elements of the Wehrmacht were being supplied by barge down the Seine — difficult to bomb or strafe — a sabotage effort to sink barges was needed. The command chain from armies to intelligence at higher headquarters to liaison with those trying to direct the Resistance was too rubbery. The Resistance did its best with targets of opportunity rather than a systematic set linked to bombing plans. Their efforts doubtless produced considerable benefits in delaying transport and cutting landlines, which helped to force German communication to radio and expose itself to ULTRA. Overall efficiency, however, was not high.

6. Operations Research

World War II produced the first formal use of operations research, as far as I am aware. The 8th Air Force in Britain had a unit, as did the 15th Air Force in Africa, then Sicily, then Italy. While I was not then and never have been a practitioner of operations research, nor a student of its methods, I was struck during the war by a difference of result achieved by the two units, a difference based on different techniques, which, whether still troubling operations research or not, remains a methodological issue in social science in general. The question was how a heavy-bomber squadron should bomb a target under conditions of good visibility: each plane's bombardier sighting the target through his Norden bombsight, and releasing when he had the target squarely in the crosshairs, or all releasing as a body when the lead bombardier gave the word. Deductive theory, used by the 8th Air Force ORS unit, called for independent sighting, anticipating that the bombs would fall in a Gaussian or normal curve of error around the central value of the target. The 15th Air Force had tried this method for a period and found that the scatters were far more skewed in practice than could be explained by the 8th's theory. It ultimately concluded that heavy bombers flying in close formation could not aim independently, as if they were flying singly at a distance from one another in their target approach, as the theory called for. All except the lead plane were in fact flying with great turbulence because of the air stream over the wings of planes in the formation, and this made accurate bombing by all but the leading aircraft impossible. The 8th Air Force ORS had left a critical variable out of its calculations. The same happens frequently in economics when high theory proceeds without empirical testing.

7. Spare Parts

I am unaware of an economic or industrial literature on spare parts before the war. Afterwards, at Nuffield College, I ran across a scholar named Cole, first name lost to memory, the son of G. D. H. Cole, the socialist economist who had given his extensive library to Nuffield College. Cole was a student of locomotives and buses, and interested, among other things, in the question of how to handle spare parts. Need for spare parts for maintenance and repair inhibited railroads and buses from improving their park of equipment incrementally, adding new and better models a few at a time. This would have required a bewildering array of spares for a variety of older models. The existence of a second-hand market in which obsolescing equipment could be sold off helped, as older ships, locomotives, trucks, and the like could be sold to others, often abroad, to make room for newer models on an efficient scale. Bristol buses in particular were sold both to Scotland, where bus companies were thrifty and not especially model-proud, and to India where they were poor, in both cases accompanied by an array of spare parts. As is well known, British youth, and some who extend the interest into later life, collect serial numbers of locomotives and try to amass a complete set. The same was true of Bristol buses. Cole told me of one ardent collector, who, missing some numbers in his collection, made trips to Scotland and to India to fill in the gaps. In the latter instance he found that an Indian company, failing to understand the purpose and importance of spares, had assembled the supply on hand into a new and complete bus. This presented a philosophical question whether he had or had not found a bus which belonged to his Bristol collection.

From OSS, Washington, a colleague in the military supplies section, Harold J. Barnett, and I made a trip to Fort Knox, Kentucky, to learn what we could about the care of tanks. We were told that unless it fell off a cliff or caught fire from a hit, a tank was immortal in the sense that a new engine, transmission, suspension, gun, or tracks could be added to the armored frame as the old was damaged or wore out. A hit by an armor-piercing shell that did not result in fire might kill the crew, but the tank would still survive with damaged parts replaced. The hole could be papered over as the chance of another hit in the same place was negligible.[15]

One source of spare parts was cannibalization of obsolete or depreciated equipment. An economist who later made his mark as a member of the Federal Reserve Board of Governors, Sherman Maisel, spent the greater part of his war in the air force at a depot which was destroying fully depreciated heavy bombers. On his initiative, despite being only a lieutenant or captain, he made sure that the Norden bombsight, each costing hundreds of thousands of dollars, was removed from planes before they were broken up. The parallel, of course, is with the yards of auto-wrecking companies which collect spare parts for sale to owners of obsolete models no longer supplied by dealers or the automakers.

One further anecdote on tanks. En route stateside in mid-June 1945, I spent a night in London in an officer billet before going on to Prestwick for the flight to the United States. My temporary roommate was a major in ordnance. I asked whether he had had a satisfactory war. He answered no. During the war his work was designing tank suspensions. Every time he succeeded in getting a suspension appropriate for a given tank, other part specialists in the unit would proceed to design a more powerful and heavier gun, more impenetrable armor, a more powerful engine, each and all of which added weight, rendering his suspension inadequate and forcing him to return to the drawing board.[16]

Continuous changes in design produce greater problems than spare parts for maintenance. They slow production. *Planning in Wartime: Aircraft Production in Britain, Germany and the USA* (London: Macmillan, 1991), by Sir Alec Cairncross, records

> a universal tendency to underestimate the cost of programme changes in lost output . . . Innovation was indispensable to air supremacy. But there was a point at which the gain in quality was insufficient to counterbalance the loss in output. (30)

Cairncross also attacks the proliferation of aircraft marks and types: 42 types of aircraft in production in 1940, 32 main types of airframes in November 1943, with many different marks of any one type, for example, at least twelve marks of the Spitfire (p. 31). He concludes the discussion by saying that the Stirling was three times as expensive in labor costs and casualties (two scales that should perhaps be consolidated using cost-benefit-analysis), and that the Buckingham and Warwick bombers were just mistakes.

8. Some Military Decisions and Actions of Academic and Practical Interest

When the Allied armies broke through the German lines in France in August 1944 with the Argentan-Falaise gap closed, the principal constraint on early victory was the limited supply of gasoline which could be brought from Britain to the advancing army units. A gasoline pipeline hastily thrown together from lengths of fire hose proved difficult to protect from marauding French with ice picks and pans, and had in any event a meager throughput. Jerry cans hauled by the Red Ball express used considerable of the gasoline they could carry, reducing the net. The question is still unsettled in my mind whether there was enough gasoline available to provide one of the two Army Groups, Montgomery's or Bradley's (the latter with Patton as its far-ranging attacker). Each wanted the whole supply. It was a mistake to divide it between them, stopping both halfway. Economists deal in trade-offs; lawyers seek compromises. Some cases, however, call for what economists call "corner solutions," all for one or the other. As a diplomatic general, Eisenhower divided it. Perhaps a diplomatic necessity; a military error.

In August 1944, I happened for some intelligence purpose to be sent to London from Eagle Tac, 12th Army Group's forward headquarters. There, gaining the information I was after, now forgotten, I looked up Colonel R. D. Hughes, A-5 (Plans) of USSTAF, the man who had directed the work of EOU. We talked of what the strategic air forces could do at this stage of the war, and agreed that the answer was to carry gasoline. Hughes waited on General Spaatz, who somewhat reluctantly agreed, but stated that he did not want the 12th Army Group G-4 (Supplies) to ask the help from his A-3 (Operations), but required a personal request from General Bradley to him, General Spaatz. The separate services were proud, and General Spaatz, I was told by Hughes, did not take kindly to having his units assigned to a service role. When I got back to 12th Army Group, then at Chartres, I was taken by General Edwin Sibert, the G-2, to General Bradley and told the latter of the evident need for a direct approach to General Spaatz. General Bradley was thoroughly irritated, but agreed. In the event, I was later told, the B-24s, which were the only planes with a bomb bay suitable for carrying the five-gallon jerry cans, needed runways for landing longer than those available at forward airfields. I am unable to weigh the force of this explanation. It seemed plausible, however, that if the services had been enthusiastic about cooperating, instead of worrying about prestige, more could have been done to carry gasoline to Patton by air.

The foregoing comes from personal experience, however untrustworthy memory may be over a half a century. A similar story was told me during the war by Colonel William Jackson, a distinguished Wall Street lawyer (senior partner of Carter, Ledyard, and Milburn), ranking officer in G-2, 12th Army Group, under General Sibert, who in Washington in a different unit had tried to persuade the Navy to operate in a certain way in the war against German submarines (details lost). He got nowhere with a series of direct approaches to the Navy at his level. Persuaded as he was of the efficacy and importance of the operations he had learned of, he sought an interview with General George C. Marshall, head of the Joint Chiefs of Staff, and after some maneuvering, obtained it, probably because of his earlier civilian distinction. He tried to persuade General Marshall to ask Admiral King, the naval commander in chief, to undertake the operations in question. General Marshall listened to his plea, but declined to raise the matter with the Admiral, on the ground, Jackson told me, that Admiral King would find such a request intrusive.

I must be careful not to give an impression that social scientists have answers for all or most of the problems that arise in wartime. Occasionally they were inordinately misguided. I heard a story that some agricultural experts went to Winston Churchill, the prime minister of the United Kingdom, and said that with submarine warfare at its effectiveness (before the help in locating them from ULTRA) and the need for transporting materiel and troops with limited shipping, it would be necessary to slaughter the cattle in Britain and convert pasture to arable to grow grain. Churchill is reported to have answered "Nonsense," disposing of that idea. Some economists thought that the ideal way to conduct the war was to give General Eisenhower in Europe, and General Douglas MacArthur in the Pacific, notional budgets representing large sums of money. The budgets would be allocated by the importance of the theater, and the generals would bid for ships of all classes, tanks, guns, landing craft, and the like, in effect producing a series of markets with prices reached for each kind of equipment, representing its military value in relation to strategic goals. The idea is basically nonsensical. After the war, some economists teaching elementary economics liked to compare the feeding of New York City using markets with the supply of the "far shore" (in Normandy) from Britain, using planning. This last was a brilliant exercise in which planners worked out the kinds and amounts of troops and supplies which would be warehoused where in western Britain, their path and timing to the embarkment area before D day, what was loaded in what ship when, with provision, once the battle had been joined, to alter the schedules to make up for critical losses and unanticipated needs by snaking specific items through the vast columns moving in preordained order to the head of the queue. It was a remarkable achievement in logistics, which I have heard discussed but seen no study of. New York, on the other hand, is fed, clothed, and supplied daily without planning, except for public utilities and infrastructure, through a series of complex markets operated fairly automatically—another remarkable achievement. Research which compared and contrasted the two might produce insights.

Another problem of World War II that I had no contact with and heard little about what was worked on by at least two distinguished economists of my generation, Richard Bissell and Max F. Millikan. This was the supply of the United Kingdom from the United States. This must have been a planning operation like that of the supply of the Far Shore from the English side of the Channel. A continuous question that had to be settled at high levels was how much shipping to devote to feeding the British people on the one hand, and to transporting troops and materiel on the other. The problem changed before, during, and after D day, and with the ebb and flow of the submarine campaign of the German navy. British authorities were naturally concerned not only with the flow of goods for civilian needs, but with building and maintaining stockpiles against an adverse turn in shipping losses. In their interest in getting military supplies in place, Americans viewed that issue more optimistically. The question is doubtless addressed in the official war histories on both sides. I am not up on them.

9. The Postwar Settlement

It is an open question, with evidence on both sides, whether governments learn from history. The classic case of failure to do so is the Maginot Line, built by the French to escape another invasion by German armies, like that of 1914. On the other hand is U.S. experience with the United Nations, the United Nations Relief and Rehabilitation Agency (UNRRA), Lend-lease, the Bretton Woods institutions, and the Marshall Plan which avoided in great measure the economic and political turmoil of the U.S. refusal in 1919 to join the League of Nations, and later insistence on collecting war debts from its Allies. I come to the connected issue of German reparations shortly.

Wartime planning that produced Lend-lease and the Bretton Woods institutions (the International Monetary Fund and International Bank for Reconstruction and Development, a.k.a. the World Bank) had an impressive payoff. There was much more postwar planning that did not. In 1941 and the first half of 1942, I served as secretary to the American side of the Joint Economic Committee of Canada and the United States, consisting of Professor Alvin H. Hansen of Harvard, chairman, a high official of the Department of State, whom I forget, Harry D. White, undersecretary of the Treasury, William L. Batt of the Office of Production Management (on leave from SKF, the Swedish ball-bearing company), Jacob Viner, a professor of economics from the University of Chicago, and a Canadian at birth, plus others. The Committee's initial task was to introduce government officials in the two countries to their counterparts, after which the Committee was asked to leave and let the separate functional groups go ahead on their own. The Committee then turned to postwar planning. The Canadian secretary, Alexander Skelton from the Bank of Canada, and I wrote a study of several hundred pages which was promptly filed and forgotten, never again heard of. In the State Department, Leo Pasvolsky, an economist from the Brookings Institution, had a staff working on postwar planning. I am unaware that it had any impact on the White or Keynes plans which resulted in the Bretton Woods agreements, negotiated primarily by the Treasury, and when I was in the Department of State after June 1945, I never saw anything of its product or thought. Planning, of course, went into the making of Joint Chiefs of Staff directives, one of the most famous of which was J.C.S. 1067 on the occupation of Germany with its strong slant of deindustrialization. But General Lucius D. Clay, commander of the Office of Military Government, U.S. (OMGUS), wrote in his memoirs: "advance planning was of little use since action has to be dictated by experience" (*Decision in Germany* [Garden City, N.Y.: Doubleday, 1950], p. 5). In reading about the work or the Economic Section of the War Cabinet in Britain, I find it surprising that as early as November 1941, before the U.S. entry into the war and a reasonable prospect of winning it, the Section devoted much of its time to thinking about postwar unemployment, balances of international payment, control of industry, international trade, and financial relations (Sir Alec Cairncross and Nita Watts, *The Economic Section, 1939–1961: A Study in Economic Advising* [London: Routledge, 1989], esp. chap. 7).

In what follows, I treat two aspects of the postwar settlement of which I have some personal knowledge, the question of German reparations and U.S. policies on foreign investment in German property.

The German Reparations Settlement

Roosevelt, Churchill, and Josef Stalin met at Yalta in the Crimea in February 1945 to discuss, among other things, the postwar treatment of Germany. The Soviet Union proposed a reparations bill of $20 billion, half to be paid to the Soviet Union and eastern countries, the remainder to be divided among the western Allies. Mindful of unhappy attempts to collect reparations from Germany in money after World War I, Churchill repudiated the suggestion. To effect compromise, Roosevelt proposed that the three countries establish a Reparations Commission to meet in Moscow shortly after the war's end, and consider the Soviet plan as its first order of business. The Commission met at the end of June, but was unable to agree. The question was then transferred to the Conference among the heads of state of the three powers which met at Potsdam, outside Berlin, from July 17 to August 2, 1945. There the western powers were faced with a *fait accompli,* the fact that Soviet troops had removed a large volume of capital equipment from German industrial plants, and even light and plumbing fixtures, as war booty ("war trophies" in literal translation from the Russian, connoting battle flags and weapons). War booty in Anglo-Saxon law is limited to property to which armed forces have title, and does not extend to private property. On the other hand, American and British forces removed a small amount of highly technical equipment, such as that from the optical works at Jena, and evacuated a number of scientists. In addition, the western continental allies were entitled, again under Anglo-Saxon law, to restitution of identifiable Allied-owned property removed by the Germans and surviving the war. Far more restitutable property belonged to the Dutch and Belgians than to Soviet peoples, since the two countries were overcome without prolonged fighting, whereas war on the eastern front had left scorched earth.

In the circumstances, President Harry Truman and Prime Minister Clement Atlee, both new in their positions and anxious to return to duties at their capitals, hastily cobbled together a settlement under which reparations would be handled largely on a zonal basis. The Allied Control Council, with France added as a fourth occupying power, was charged with producing an agreement, setting out a level of industry for the four zones of Germany, treated as a single unit, which would provide the German people in future a standard of living no higher than that of the surrounding countries. German capital equipment in excess of that needed to support that standard of living would then be removed as reparations. The Soviet Union and its eastern associated powers would receive equipment moved from the Soviet zone of occupation, plus a small percentage of that available from the more highly industrialized western zones. The western allies established an agency to divide western reparation removals. Key to the plan in American and British eyes was the provision that the four zones would be treated in this and other respects as a single economic unit. A "first-charge principle" was expressly set out that the proceeds of exports from any zone would bear as a first charge the payment for imports into any zone. There were other provisions dealing with German property abroad that proved troublesome but need not detain us.

This hurried solution proved quite unworkable. The Soviet Union quickly became disenchanted with thousands of pieces of equipment and fixtures loaded on flatcars, unused and increasingly unusable, and shifted its demands to reparations out of current production. The United States was strongly opposed. American and British armed forces had been feeding not only their own troops, while French and Soviet armies lived off the land, but were feeding the German populace in their more highly industrialized part of the country. The United States had insisted on the first-charge principle to avoid a situation similar to that after World War I, where Germany borrowed money in various forms from the United States, later inflated away or repudiated, to pay reparations to France and Britain. These loans were private, not governmental, to be sure. But if the Soviet Union were to take goods out of Germany when Britain and the United States were forced to bring food and supplies in, the two countries would in effect be paying reparations to the Soviet Union. The Level of Industry agreement was a nightmare type of economic calculation, especially as the commanding generals from time to time interfered in amateurish fashion on their own.[17]

Other reparation settlements after the war, by Japan with countries in Southeast Asia, with Israel by Bizonal Germany, paid mostly in prefabricated housing, and by Finland to the Soviet Union, were more successful. The Finnish experience, made painful by the fact that the Soviet Union demanded payment in goods of sorts that Finland had not previously produced in any quantity, proved to be a strong force for the industrial development of that country, in contravention to views expressed by some who favored acceding to Soviet demands for reparations out of current production.[18]

Postwar Direct Investment in Germany

When, after the war, I became the chief of the Division of German and Austrian Economic Affairs in the State Department, one problem was whether or not to permit American businessmen, some still in uniform, to begin to enter into private business arrangements with German concerns. Under the strict terms of the Trading with the Enemy Act of 1917, still in effect, such contacts were forbidden. As the American authorities became concerned to restore the German economy, the act had to be set aside for contracts between German exporters and foreign buyers. A certain amount of looting by Allied soldiers went on, which the Army had difficulty in containing, if it in fact had wanted to. Soldiers would buy large quantities of cigarettes from the United States to be used to buy all sorts of goods, cameras, binoculars, pianos, even in one case a yacht which a naval officer planned to sail back to the United States. A particular problem was what economists call direct investment, that is, investment not in the securities of a company but the company as a whole, or a majority ownership. Since German companies were anxious to gain the protection of the American flag against a plant being taken under the reparation provisions of Potsdam, many were willing to sell.

U.S. companies saw simple bargains or in other cases were interested in replacing plants which had been destroyed in the war or gutted by Soviet depredations. In due course, the economists in the State Department deemed it important to wait. Many German plants had been destroyed. Some of the survivors had belonged to Jews driven into exile but were acquired by Aryan owners under the Nazi regime; when these were restored they would constitute foreign-owned property. Other things equal, foreign-owned plants would be taken for reparation removals only after comparable German factories. If foreigners were to buy up German plants under existing conditions, the proportion of foreign ownership of German industry would be markedly increased as compared with prewar, which would be politically damaging to the democratic purposes of the Allies in the longer run.

In formulating a program for a temporary moratorium on foreign investment in Germany, the economists were intuiting a theory in economics, developed fully only some years later, that came to be known as "the theory of the second best." This states that if the best course of action is unavailable, the second best should be used. In most cases this comes down to saying that if markets don't work in existing condition, don't use them. The best course, to be sure, would be to restore the conditions that would enable the market to function efficiently, in the German case, among other things, the monetary reform which was realized in June 1948. With that in place, the moratorium on foreign investment in Germany was lifted.

Under ordinary circumstances, a somewhat recondite economic theory is not readily understood and welcomed by leading government officials. In this case, understanding was readily achieved. Secretary of State James Byrnes came from South Carolina, the Undersecretary, William L. Clayton, from Texas, General Clay of OMGUS from Georgia. These Southerners quickly understood when the moratorium was presented to them as a means of restraining carpetbagging. The experience is not without relevance to U.S. policy today in the states of the former Soviet bloc and Haiti.

Property problems abound in war. For a glimpse of some of them, see my *The German Economy, 1945–46,* op. cit., esp. letter no. 8 of August 8, 1946.

NOTES

1. I happened belatedly to read Albert Speer's *Inside The Third Reich: Memoirs,* translated from the German by Richard and Clara Winston (1970,

paperback edition; New York: Collier Books, 1981), which provides confirmation on a number of points set out below. Rather than rewrite the paper, I have included a series of footnotes for Speer's remarks.

2. For a description of this visit see my *The German Economy, 1945–1947: Charles P. Kindleberger's Letters from the Field* (Westport, Conn.: Meckler, 1989), letter no. 170 of April 19, 1945, with the estimate noted on p. 205. Speer notes that factory managers told him that many prisoners of war sent to work in factories were undernourished and weak. At the Nuremberg trial a Pasteur Institute professor described the starvation of workers. A Gauleiter friend of Speer's told him not to accept any invitation to inspect a concentration camp, never (1981, pl. 370, 374).

3. Speer states that jealousy among the German armed services made it impossible for the army to avail itself of hundreds of thousands of young soldiers redundant in the air force (1981, p. 379).

4. German armed forces were overmanned throughout, according to Speer. In a memorandum of July 20, 1944, he wrote that of 10.5 million men conscripted, only 2.3 million saw active service in the field. The German system maximized the number of independent units, each of which wanted self-sufficiency, with separate services, separately equipped, separate headquarters, etc. (1981, p. 382).

5. Discussing the American air force attacks on synthetic oil which began in the spring of 1944, Speer states that with high priority for repairs, the industry had 150,000 skilled workers in two months, many drawn from other armament industry, and 350,000 by the late fall of 1944 (1981, p. 351).

6. An overly dramatic novel (*Command Decision,* by William Wistar Haines [Boston: Little, Brown, 1947], later a movie of the same title with Clark Gable), was based on this week, despite the usual claim to being entirely fictional. Haines had been an intelligence officer with the 8th Air Force. In 1994, J. Kenneth Galbraith, in *A Journey through Economic Time: A Firsthand View* (Boston: Houghton Mifflin), called the concentrated attacks of the week "a striking example of economic error," presumably because, while aircraft production was knocked down by a third, it recovered quickly, Speer called the situation after the February week critical, but observed that there was no follow-up, and that the attack had been divided between aircraft assembly and aircraft engines, with the latter more vulnerable and difficult to disperse.

7. Speer writes very little about area bombing of cities until he comments on the destruction of Berlin in the spring of 1945. Earlier he stated that the air raids had shown that life could continue in orderly fashion, even in the worst bombed cities. The orderly German populace continued to pay its taxes even when bombs had destroyed the Treasury's records (1981, p. 255).

8. After the attack on Schweinfurt, German armament plants first used up their stocks of spare bearings — enough for six to eight weeks — and then hand-carried daily output from the bearing plants to assembly units, often in knapsacks (Speer 1981, p. 285).

9. Speer attributes the incapacity of the German air force to resist the allied

invasion of June 1944 to lack of pilots brought about by the shortage of fuel for training, caused by the attacks on synthetic oil plants (1981, p. 405). He wanted fighter aircraft diverted from the front ("where experience showed it would be wiped out") to resisting bomber attack on armament plants (ibid., p. 406). Hitler at one time ordered a halt in production of fighter aircraft in favor of flak, but Sauer and Speer disobeyed (ibid., p. 408).

10. In April 1944 the Todd organization was ordered by Hitler to construct six underground industrial sites, and promised to complete them in six months. Speer was ill at the time. He later said that it was easy to predict that they would not even be started in six months (Speer 1981, pp. 336–37).

11. Speer attached much greater importance to these attacks, saying that nineteen bombers tried to attack the whole German armament industry by destroying the hydroelectric plants of the Ruhr. But a footnote states that immediate power and water needs of the Ruhr were supplied after the attack of May 1943, and that the diversion of seven thousand men from the Atlantic Wall to repairing the Möhne and Eder areas repaired the dam in time for the fall rains which would guarantee the water needed for the summer of 1944.

12. Speer in a footnote follows an American source in stating that the Seine rail and railroad bridges were destroyed in bombing attacks starting on D day. This mistake in timing should perhaps not undermine his credibility, since his concern was with the economy, not tactics in the field.

13. On the eastern front, Speer advised against bombing the Russian railroads on the ground that the German railway network was much more complex and damage to railway sections could be repaired "in a matter of hours" (1981, p. 283).

14. Speer describes the chaos of railroading in the Ruhr in the fall of 1944 with traffic blocked for six weeks and railroads exhausting their coal stocks, steel plants and hospitals out of coke, jammed marshaling yards preventing supplies getting to the front for the Ardennes offensive. A page later, he discusses the army's lack of gasoline, owing to the bombardment of oil-producing facilities, adding that tank train cars had to be improvised to carry daily production up to the front (1981, pp. 4414, 4416, 4417). In the spring of 1945, he devoted much of his energy to countering Hitler's scorched-earth policy, justifying protection of bridges and plants by saying that the Wehrmacht would need to have them available when it retook the offensive.

15. But spare parts had to be provided in abundance. On the long lines for the German attack on Russia, supplies could not keep up with the armies, and spare parts had long been used up (Speer 1981, p. 238).

16. Similar troubles affected German tank design. The Panther was designed for speed as a lightweight tank but in the course of a year Hitler insisted on adding so much armor as well as larger guns that it ultimately reached 48 tons — the weight at which the Tiger tank had started. It, the Tiger, had gone up in weight from 48 to 75 tons (Speer 1981, p. 224).

17. See B. U. Ratchford and W. D. Ross, *Berlin Reparations Assignment: Round One of the German Peace Settlement* (Chapel Hill, N.C.: University of

North Carolina Press, 1947); Sir Alec Cairncross, *The Price of War: British Policy on German Reparations, 1941–1949* (Oxford: Blackwell, 1986); Sir Alec Cairncross, *A Country to Play with: Level of Industry Negotiations in Berlin, 1945–46* (Gerrards Cross: Colin Smythe, 1987); C. P. Kindleberger, "Toward the Marshall Plan: a Memoir of Policy Development in Germany, 1945–47," chap. 11 of C. P. Kindleberger, *Marshall Plan Days* (Boston: Allen and Unwin, 1987).

18. Kindleberger, *Marshall Plan Days,* chap. 12, "Finnish War Reparations."

15

Legislating the Marshall Plan: A Memoir

I

This "memoir" is confined to the legislation for the Marshall Plan because I left the Department of State on July 31, 1948. In the Department I had worked mostly on German economic matters, but on June 25, 1947, as *Foreign Relations of the United States—1972* reminds me, had been named executive secretary of the Department's Committee on the European Recovery Program. "Memoir" is in quotation marks as I have no papers from the period after returning from the Council of Foreign Ministers meeting in Moscow, where I had been a lowly staff member, at the end of April 1947. Some later papers are at hand, however, one on "The Origins of the Marshall Plan," written in July 1948, another an excerpt from an oral history for the Truman Library, which are gathered with later writing in a book, *Marshall Plan Days.* Recollections after the event are notoriously unreliable, and some written in timely fashion suffer from the limited perspective of one below top echelons. To piece out this account, therefore, I have read, largely reread, memoirs, biographies, or historical accounts—Forrest Pogue on Marshall, Walter Isaacson and Evan Thomas, *The Wise Men,* Dean Acheson, Charles Bohlen, Clark Clifford, the Dulles siblings, George Kennan, Walter Lippmann, James Reston, and Senator Arthur H. Vandenberg, although my recollections do not always square with their accounts. At an advanced age—I remind myself of the Civil War veterans one saw in Memorial Day parades in the 1920s—I have been unable to do original research in archives, beyond the single volume of *Foreign Relations of the United States* that I own. For this periodical—and at considerable scholarly pain—I have suppressed my normal proclivity of giving citations for every statement.

This essay is the original version of a paper that was published in truncated form as "In the Halls of the Capitol: A Memoir" in *Foreign Affairs* 76, no. 3 (May–June 1997): 185–90. Reprinted by permission of *Foreign Affairs.* © 1997 by the Council of Foreign Relations, Inc.

II

History is a fable agreed upon. Before starting on the legislative history of the Marshall Plan, I address three aspects of its fabulous character which have troubled me over the last half century: one, the speed with which Ernest Bevin, British Foreign Minister, responded to Secretary of State Marshall's speech of June 5, 1947; two, the widely neglected role of Assistant (later Under-) Secretary of State for Economic Affairs, William L. Clayton; and three, the claims of others than General Marshall to authorship of or responsibility for the program.

On the evening of June 4, 1947, as I rode home in a car pool with Clifford Durr, William Livingston, and Leonard Miall, the BBC Washington correspondent, Miall showed me a press release he had just picked up at the State Department's new building on 22nd Street, N.W., in Washington, D.C., where I worked. It reproduced Secretary Marshall's Commencement Address at Harvard University the next afternoon. Miall said he had already called in a broadcast, "American Commentary," usually given by Joseph Harsch of CBS and the *Christian Science Monitor,* but that this looked significant enough to warrant doing another. I read the release and said yes. He then did another "American Commentary" the next day at noon, June 5, with some hesitation over the timing because of not having a firm release time for the speech. This commentary was broadcast in Britain at 10:30 P.M.

The world believes that Ernest Bevin, Foreign Secretary, heard the broadcast and responded immediately. As I remember it, Miall and I waited several days before we detected a response. The British Embassy in Washington had mailed the speech. The *Times* (London) carried only a Reuters paragraph or two. Malcom Muggridge had a full story in the *Daily Telegraph,* as did René McColl of the *Daily Express,* which, after having heard the broadcast the night before, Bevin may not have seen. In recent letters and telephone calls, Miall tells me that Bevin went to the Foreign Office on June 6, in great excitement, where Sir William (later Lord) Strang suggested they call the British Embassy to find out what was up. Bevin said no. "Apparently," however, they did call the British Embassy in Paris. Then the Foreign Office packed up for the weekend and called Georges Bidault, the French Foreign Minister, on Monday, June 9, when Bevin and Bidault agreed to meet eight days later in Paris on June 17. This response was regarded by me as leisurely, but by the rest of the world as immediate, and was so characterized by Acheson in his memoirs, and by Clayton, thanking Bevin for his speed, as reported in *FRUS.* In economic history we have a concept of the "counterfactual," what would have happened in the absence of an event.

My counterfactual was an open response on Friday, June 6; in this case, June 9 was slow. Older and more sophisticated people understood that diplomacy moves slowly as a rule, so that Monday, the 9th, was fast. A British history, *The Semblance of Peace,* by Sir John Wheeler-Bennett and Anthony Nicholls (1972), scolds me for attacking Bevin for tardiness. Sorry.

Acheson and Reston claim that Acheson tipped off Miall, Muggridge, and McColl to the forthcoming Marshall speech. Reston even complains that he was not made aware of it by Acheson, whom he used to interview frequently, so that the *New York Times* carried only a few paragraphs on the speech on an inside page. But Acheson and Reston are muddled on this. Miall, Muggridge, and McColl invited Dean Acheson to lunch on Tuesday, June 3, as they had done earlier in May in connection with the Delta, Mississippi, speech, but Acheson told the British group nothing about the proposed Marshall speech, which text he may not have seen. All of this is trivial but says something about memories when the documentation is sparse or nonexistent, a point that George Kennan, with copious documentation in his *Memoirs,* makes repeatedly in the few blank spots.

In *The Wise Men* Isaacson and Thomas celebrate the contributions to the Golden Years of postwar American foreign policy of six graduates of private preparatory schools, five in the east, three Episcopalian, and the Big Three Ivy League universities — Dean Acheson, Charles Bohlen, Averill Harriman, George Kennan, Robert Lovett, and John McCloy. One need not derogate from the reputations for wisdom of this list, although the contributions to the Marshall Plan of some did not match those of Marshall, Acheson, William L. Clayton, and Lovett. Marshall needs no praise from the journalists Isaacson and Thomas. Memoir after memoir speaks of him in awed and reverential tones, occasionally preceded by the remark that the author, e.g., Bohlen, does not believe in hero worship. He surely was wise.[1] Clayton did not attend an eastern preparatory school, or Yale, Harvard, or Princeton, but he was wise too. His role in the formulation and development of the Marshall Plan has been widely neglected except in Pogue's biography of Marshall, and Acheson's *Present at the Creation.* Some readers may like content analysis, or statistics such as economists are wont to produce. Pogue's index has 16 references to Clayton, Acheson's 19, my *Marshall Plan Days,* 21, *Foreign Relations of the United States, 1947,* volume 3, on the European Recovery Program alone, two plus pp. 230–446 with the designation *passim,* meaning throughout. In contrast Kennan refers to Clayton four times, Lippmann twice (once simply as an old friend),

Bohlen once, Reston once. Acheson's admiration for Clayton was un-
bounded. "Will Clayton," he wrote, "was one of the most powerful and
persuasive advocates to whom I have listened, qualities which came
from his command of the subject and the depth of his conviction."[2]

Lastly, why the *Marshall* Plan? The memoirs are full of possible
alternative designations. In "Origins of the Marshall Plan," I recorded,
not seriously, that Joseph Harsch wanted to have it called the Miall Plan
because of Miall's strategic broadcast to Bevin; Eleanor Lansing Dulles,
an economist who failed to capture my admiration, suggested it should
be called the Bevin Plan because Marshall threw a wild forward pass
which Bevin caught. Issacson and Thomas write that Acheson was more
responsible for the Truman Plan of March 1947 then Truman, and for
the Marshall Plan of June than Marshall. When the Marshall speech was
submitted to the White House for clearance, Clark Clifford, the Truman
political adviser, proposed to the President that he, the president, deliver it, and that it be called the Truman Plan. Truman thought that such
a step would lead Republicans to defeat it, whereas they would hold
back from voting against Marshall — by no means an accurate forecast.
Reston twice wanted it called the Acheson Plan, and John Foster Dulles,
who recognized that it was Marshall's idea and claimed that he supported it riding back from Moscow at the end of April, the Vandenberg
Plan. Ronald Steel, Lippmann's biographer, claims that Lippmann
called for massive new aid to Europe in newspaper columns of March 20
and April 5, 1947, suggested to Kennan, whom he saw at James For-
restal's urging, that Europe be asked to draw up a plan, and laid out the
essence of the Marshall Plan in a column a week later on May 1. Acheson's Delta speech was drafted April 23, tested May 1, revised May 6,
and delivered May 8. As far as I have explored — not far — no one called
it the Clayton Plan, but Acheson observes that Clayton wrote two memo-
randa on the agonizing economic troubles of Europe (each on the airplane rides), one on March 5, en route to Tucson for a short rest, the
other returning from the Economic Commission of Europe organization
meeting in Geneva late in May. The latter memorandum and the Policy
Planning Staff memorandum of George Kennan were the building
blocks of the Harvard speech, cobbled together by Bohlen, department
Counsellor, at Marshall's request. In Acheson's view, the second Clayton memorandum was the first to give a concrete outline of what proved
to be the Marshall Plan. At one point, Reston holds that Acheson was
the principal architect of U.S. postwar foreign policies, especially the
Truman doctrine and the Marshall plan, that in the latter had considerable help from Clayton, Kennan, and Bohlen.

III

Once the Europeans had begun to respond to the Marshall initiative, the U.S. executive branch sprang into action. On June 19, the Policy Planning Staff under Kennan's directorship proposed a series of committees to study the feasibility of such a program for the United States. On June 22, President Truman convened a meeting in the White House with Senators Arthur Vandenberg and Tom Connally of the Foreign Relations Committee and Senate majority and minority leaders William White of Maine and Alben Barkely of Kentucky, along with secretaries Marshall, John Snyder of the Treasury, Clinton Anderson of Agriculture, and Julius A. Krug, plus Acheson, who was returning to private life on June 30, and Robert A. Lovett, his successor as Undersecretary of State. Appointment of three committees was discussed and announced the same day: one on the adequacy of U.S. resources for the planned undertaking, under Krug, another on the macroeconomic (inflationary) implications of the program, under Edwin G. Nourse, chairman of the Council of Economic Advisers, and one on the program generally, chaired by Secretary of Commerce W. Averill Harriman, and made up of distinguished citizens outside government. At my level one had respect for the exalted leaders and members of these committees, but knew that the work would be done down the line, as it happened, by Tex Goldschmidt of the Interior Department for the Krug Committee, Walter S. Salant of the Council of Economic Advisers staff for the Nourse, and Richard N. Bissell for the Harriman. I kept in touch with each, and was especially impressed by Bissell's work, the first real application of national-income accounting and Keynesian analysis to a major peacetime problem that I had seen.

On June 25, as mentioned earlier, the Department set up a Committee on the European Recovery Program, which *Foreign Relations of the United States* says in a footnote "prepared a substantial corpus of background and operating materials." This committee, as I remember it, grew out of an informal study group that had met Tuesday and Thursday evenings in late May and early June under the chairmanship of Assistant Secretary of State for Economic Affairs, Willard L. Thorp. *FRUS* states that a Working Party on European Reconstruction, drawn from the economic side of the Department under Thorp, met on June 23 to consider "ways and means of implementing the European Reconstruction [sic] Program." The Policy Planning Staff addressed Thorp on June 24, asking for a series of background studies relating to certain items of the European economy.

In due course, the State Department organized itself more formally. At the top under the Secretary was Undersecretary Lovett with a special assistant Lt. Col. (later Lt. Gen.) Charles ("Tic") Bonesteel, and at more or less the same level, Paul Nitze and Lincoln Gordon. Below these was the economic staff of the Department, buttressed by economists on assignment from other departments and the Federal Reserve Board, with committee and country committees and a small coordinating group in the middle. The task, as it developed, was to estimate the amounts of aid needed by the sixteen participating European countries (after the Soviet Union and its satellites dropped out) for four and a quarter years from April 1, 1948, to June 30, 1952.

Assistant (later Under-) Secretary Clayton for Economic Affairs was dispatched to Europe to explain American intentions, having his first of several meetings with Bevin and other members of the British cabinet on June 24. In London, Paris, and throughout his meetings with European statesmen, Mr. Clayton kept emphasizing that any program prepared in Europe and approved by the executive branch of the U.S. government had to meet with Congressional approval. This approval, moreover, would have to come in two stages, authorizations proposed to the Senate by the Foreign Relations Committee and to the House of Representatives by the Foreign Affairs, the second, appropriations of funds, which bills fell into the jurisdiction of the Senate Finance Committee, Eugene Millikin of Colorado, chairman, and the House Appropriations Committee headed by Congressman John Taber from upstate New York. The process was time consuming.

First, the Europeans who had organized themselves into a Committee on European Economic Cooperation (CEEC) would prepare a plan, then the Americans would render "friendly assistance," not implying endorsement, but only help in preparing the material in a form appropriate for submission to Congress. Then Congressional authorization, finally appropriations.

In early September the CEEC had drawn up a program which called for American assistance of almost $30 billion over four years, consisting of $19.9 billion for the European deficit with the United States and $8.3 billion for net imports from the rest of the American continent. Clayton in Paris was joined by Bonesteel and Nitze to make clear in a friendly fashion that this was too much. In his second May 27 memorandum, Clayton had given the round number of $6 or 7 billion a year for three years. In a *New York Times* column on May 24, 1987, Reston, celebrating the fortieth anniversary of the Marshall speech, claims that he wrote these amounts in the *New York Times* and on May

25, 1947, got a telephone call from Senator Vandenberg saying that he must have been misinformed since Congress would never appropriate that amount of money to save anybody.

One item that was eliminated was the money to buy goods outside the United States — so-called offshore purchases. This had been discussed over the summer but not decided. Early European suggestions had included the idea that American aid would be extended to European colonies. This too was dropped.

A number of other policy issues were discussed in the American government over the summer of 1947: whether the program should consist of commodities and services, or cash, or both; what if any conditions should be placed on "counterpart funds," monies accumulated by aided governments in local currencies from selling commodity aid in national markets, i.e., whether to limit the purposes for which they could be used; how hard to push on policy matters such as balanced budgets, tight monetary policy, and cooperation among the participating countries, extending as far as customs union, or a less precisely defined concept of economic integration. One requirement of the CEEC program deemed of paramount importance to the Congress was that European countries would be self-supporting without outside aid at the end of the multiyear program.

In commodities, the U.S. government had been concerned with increased European coal production and its efficient distribution as early as July 1945. Enormous added pressure came from the harsh winter in Europe in 1946–47 — the worst in a century — that led to a miserable harvest and tied up rail transport in Britain for months on end. The Policy Planning Staff under Kennan asked Thorp in June for estimates of European needs in coal, electric power, steel, agriculture, food, inland transport, and shipping plus shipbuilding. Talking in London on June 25, Clayton spoke of fuel, food, and fiber, presumably especially cotton in which his business experience had focused, and later of the three "fs," which might have been extended to four with fertilizer. Bevin suggested that the British Commonwealth could contribute rubber and wool, this for a brief moment when he was thinking in terms of a preliminary large American grant to Britain to enable it and the United States together to help the reconstruction of Continental Europe.[3] Other early European lists mentioned timber, food, especially dairy products, dried fruit (Cripps), fertilizers, steel, fiber, transport machinery (a British Aide-Memoire), consumer goods (Monnet in France). In the event the U.S. interdepartmental staff produced a program listing 26 commodities and commodity groups, both provided by the United States and exchanged among the participating countries, sixteen in number, over 4¼ years, laid out in so-called Brown Books. At one point I could have recited the entire list of 26, starting with "bread grains, feed grains . . . " but without a visit to National Archives in Washington or the Truman Library in Independence, Missouri, where my copies are on deposit, I cannot.

The commodity approach has considerable deficiencies from the viewpoint of economic analysis. First, provision of commodities was held to correct balance-of-payments deficits, independently determined, but without the aid, there could have been no deficits on the assumed scale. Aid determined the deficits more than vice versa. Secondly, the notion that American surveillance of the commodities it provided was necessary to ensure their efficient use, as bankers are supposed to do, involves the fallacy of misplaced concreteness. Not just U.S.-provided steel should be used efficiently, for example, but all steel — U.S. provided, home produced, and steel imported from other countries. Third, any attempt to forecast balances of payments long in advance is almost certainly destined to be wide of the mark. The good harvest of 1948 following the miserable one of 1947 made agricultural imports proposed for 1948 excessive. The Korean War was another factor throwing estimates off course, and there were, and will always be, many more.[4]

However deficient from the viewpoint of economic analysis, the Brown Books involved a tremendous effort on the part of many economists and secretaries, working weekends, late at night, and often all night. They impressed the Congress. In November Senator Vandenberg wrote his wife: "the preparations the State Department has made of this next showdown [after Interim Aid] are amazing. I have never seen better work. Indeed they overwhelmed us with documentation. I got the report of the Harriman Commission . . . It is a magnificent piece of work. But it is three inches thick . . . " Isaacson and Thomas believe that the Brown Books were the work of Paul Nitze, who, with Lovett, had borrowed calculators from the Prudential Life Insurance Company for the Pentagon. I had thought an early computer, in the Pentagon to be sure, and cannot recall a Nitze role in the production of the numbers, as contrasted with the presentation. The same writers state, " 'Never before had Congress been bombarded with such propaganda,' grumbled Congressman John Busby of Illinois. It worked."

In the summer of 1947, it became clear that the CEEC would not finish its task in time for the U.S. government to prepare its submission to the Congress soon enough to be acted on before the end of the year. First there was the need to provide a supplement to the United Nations Relief and Rehabilitation Agency (UNRRA) which had had two tranches; the first voted at Hot Springs in 1944, the second in London in the summer of 1945 as Clayton and staff returned from Potsdam. The second experience, with the United States providing more than 80 percent of the aid, having only one vote in 17, and the Soviet Union, the United Kingdom, and Canada holding out for changes of their own, persuaded Clayton of the need for a new course. In his memorandum of May 27, 1947, his final sentence read, in italics, "We must avoid getting into another UNRRA. The United States must run this show." To wind up the program, however, Post-UNRRA Relief was sought for Austria, Italy, Hungary, Greece, and Poland, though help for the last country did not survive a political (?) decision by Department of Agriculture officials that the Polish people were not really hungry. These monies — $350 million — were authorized in September 1946. In December, the British said they could no longer go on feeding their heavily populated zone of occupation in Germany, and wanted a Bizonal Agreement in which relief costs would be spit 50-50 between Britain and the United States, requiring an increase in American appropriations for Government and Relief in Occupied Areas (GARIOA). Things got no better in 1947. As Secretary Marshall was preparing to leave for the Council of Foreign Ministers meeting in Moscow, Britain informed the United States that it could no longer support the economies of Greece and Turkey — leading President Truman and Undersecretary of State Acheson to put forward the Truman doctrine and a proposed budget of aid of $400 millions. The Marshall Plan of June 1947 was intended to end this series of rescue operations, but in the deal in getting it under way, one more emergency intervened as France and Italy, both with strong local Communist parties, ran out of money. This called for a limited down payment called Interim Aid as legislative action on the Marshall Plan was postponed until the next year. Undersecretary of State Lovett testified for two weeks in a special session of the Congress called for November 1947. Pogue in his biography of Marshall states that Lovett was treated roughly, and that he observed that although the Congress did not directly attack sin, it thought the State Department furnished an adequate substitute. Isaacson and Thomas note that Lovett was more successful at stroking Congress than Acheson, who, they claim, had to feign friendliness to Vandenberg, for example, as Lovett did not.

IV

Dean Acheson has written that while Vandenberg did not furnish the ideas, the leadership, or the drive to put over the Marshall Plan, he did make the result possible. Acheson's early description of the senator was mocking: "a severe cyclonic disturbance caused by hot air. . . . producing heavy word fall." In time, however, Acheson came to have great respect and considerable affection for Vandenberg. This evolution was closely connected with Vandenberg's metamorphosis from a strident isolationist, who voted for the Neutrality Act of 1938, for example, to an internationalist, largely as a result of Pearl Harbor. Vandenberg was a candidate for the Republican nomination for president in 1940, the isolationist beaten out by the one-world Wendell Wilkie, who lost in the election to Franklin Roosevelt. He contemplated briefly running for the nomination in 1948, but decided he would rather work for a bipartisan — often expressed as unpartisan — foreign policy in the Congress where the danger lay rather than in the White House.

Republicans won both the House and Senate in 1946, and Senator Vandenberg moved into the seat of chairman of the Foreign Relations Committee, previously occupied by Senator Tom Connally of Texas. In that capacity he had the leading voice on foreign policy. Senator Robert A. Taft of Ohio, chairman of the Republican Steering Committee and important member of the Senate Appropriations Committee, packed a considerable punch and had a considerable followership. Vandenberg's son writes that the father expected some degree of trouble with Taft, and thought that the presidential election the next year — when Thomas Dewey won the Republican nomination — must be "what was biting Robert." Taft finally voted for Interim Aid.

Both House and Senate had regular staff to analyze executive draft legislation on the European Recovery Program, a special House Select Committee on Foreign Aid, with William Yandell Elliott, a Harvard professor of government, as staff director, and a special committee in the Senate, in addition to the staff headed by Francis O. Wilcox, chaired by Christian A. Herter, a former Congressman and later Governor of the Commonwealth of Massachusetts. I confess I retain no recollection of the roles played by these committees. In addition many Congressmen and Senators went to Europe in the interval between the end of the regular session and the special session in November called to deal with Interim Aid. *FRUS* contains aides-mémoires by U.S. Embassy staffs on meetings in Paris and Rome of members of various Congressional committees. These report, however, the remarks of the European officials rather than the questions posed by the legislators, and are not as helpful as they might have been.

In 1948 began a series of hearings on the European Recovery Program led off by General Marshall who testified before both the Senate Foreign Relations Committee and the House Committee on Foreign Affairs on January 18. I have no memory of these beginnings. When the Foreign Relations Committee approved the Economic Recovery bill, with minor amendments, I was assigned by the Department to attend the full Senate debate, and to be available with statistics and analysis, in case any were needed. I sat in the last row of the Senate chamber on the Republican (right-hand) side, directly behind Senator Jenner of Indiana and Senator McCarthy of Wisconsin, whom I considered, perhaps partly with hindsight, evil. Observing the Senate all day long for two weeks in February 1947 was an educational experience that I wish could be made available to all young men and women.

Impressions retained: the two members of the Committee on whom Senator Vandenberg depended mostly were Henry Cabot Lodge, Jr., of Massachusetts and H. Alexander Smith of New Jersey. Smith seemed to me far more intelligent and knowledgeable about the issues, but Taft was far more effective in the debate. Smith's voice was low and hesitant, Lodge's loud and confident. In each case, effectiveness was measured less by what was said than how it was said.

Senator Joseph H. Ball of Minnesota had had an epiphany the opposite of that of Vandenberg, moving from a strong internationalist position early in his senatorial career to a skeptical isolationism. Like some then, and a few revisionists since, he felt that proper fiscal and monetary policies would have obviated the necessity of American aid. The formulae of Professors Frank D. Graham, Friederich Lutz, and Jacob Viner of Princeton University, Gottfried Haberler of Harvard, and Oxford University Reader in International Economics, Roy Harrod, approximated "balance the budget, control the money supply, and devalue the exchange rate." Ball was more precise. He said that no aid would be required if the European countries would balance their budgets and depreciate their exchange rates to the purchasing-power parity — the rate which would restore the relationships among national price levels at some early time when payments were in more or less balance. Here, I thought, was something for which I might be needed, if the Foreign Relations Committee was not fully cognizant of the theory. I waited for Francis Wilcox to stroll back to me and ask for enlightenment. He failed to stir. Senator Vandenberg rose to his feet and demolished Ball by asserting that the purchasing-power-parity theory was the work of John Maynard Keynes and we wanted none of that. I suspect I was the only person in the room aware that the theory had been propounded not by Keynes, but by the Swedish economist Gustav Cassell after World War I.

The most interesting confrontation was between Taft and Vandenberg. Some years later, a book of John F. Kennedy, written with (or by) Theodore Sorenson, called *Profiles in Courage,* included Senator Taft among the six courageous persons profiled. I did not think he showed much courage in this debate. Rather than claiming that Europe did not need help, or that the United States could not afford it, or that Europe should take care of its own problems — this last the isolationist position I believed he really held — he said he was for the program but that the amount should be cut. Instead of $4 billion for the first full year, the number should be $3 billion. Again Vandenberg produced the effective riposte "When a man is drowning 20 feet away, it's a mistake to throw him a 15-foot rope." There were still many isolationists in the Senate, who attacked the program as helping socialism, or a WPA for Europe. Some, like Taft, ended up on the winning side in the end, having voted against in the preliminaries. The motion to cut the authorization for twelve months from $4 to $3 billion lost 56 to 31; in the final vote the bill passed 69 to 17. The margin of victory in the House for the program was slightly higher in percentage terms, 329–72.

After authorization, appropriation. My recollections of this process are limited, and relate mostly to the House Appropriations Committee under John Taber. Isaacson and Thomas have an account of how he pilloried Paul Nitze when Nitze made the initial presentation of the Brown Books, going down each item, line by line, coming ultimately to pulse peas, and asking Nitze, a financial expert from Wall Street, how they were cultivated. A wobbly answer failed to satisfy. Taber stormed out of the room, telephoned Lovett, saying that all this was unsatisfactory. Lovett, according to this account, asked Taber how many rivets there were in the wing of a B-29, drew a blank, and followed up by saying that it was a mistake to ask inane questions.

Some government witnesses at the commodity and country level were superb. Failing memory permits me to mention only two. Louis Lister, a coal expert, had the Appropriations Committee eating out of his hand. Walter Levy, a petroleum economist, fascinated the committee members by converting tons of oil production a year, used in Europe, to barrels per day, the practice in the United States, in his head. The trick was to multiply the first number by 50 to get the second. One item in the Brown Books on fish drew from Taber the question whether it referred to dried cod (klipfish in Norwegian parlance), or fish in brine. On hearing the answer, both, the Congressman was gratified, saying that at home (in Auburn, N.Y.) his family kept a small barrell of mackerel in brine in the cellar each year.

Personal recollections are few. Sitting among the spectators at a Senate Appropriations hearing, I drew a sharp rebuke from Senator Kenneth Wherry when I laughed silently at some economic *bêtise* he perpetrated. I escaped trouble on another occasion when testifying in defense of the country "residuals" in the Brown Books, imports allowed for beyond the 26 commodities and commodity groups. The 26 usually accounted for 80 percent or so of total estimated imports, but in the

Belgian case, only 55. In preparing for the ordeal I pushed more deeply into the Belgian case, and found that in 1946 and 1947 other imports had been substantial but included some indefensible items such as luxury automobiles and silk stockings. Luckily Taber ignored the Belgian estimates. It had happened that Belgium finished the war in some financial comfort because of regaining its gold supply in a suit against France where the Germans found it, and renting out facilities to the American armies between the end of August 1944 and V-E Day in May 1945 — this on reverse lend-lease, paid by the United States in dollars.

I am unable to repress two remarks this last brings up. First, American commodity experts wanted more of their commodity for Europe, country experts more aid for "their" country. Second, the "residual" was a necessity for the estimators, because if new information required revision of one of the 26 commodities or groups, we could not change the total because that would have undermined whatever confidence the Congress had in the estimates. Just change the residual in the opposite direction.[5]

With the Czech crisis of March 1948, the tenor of the debates changed and became more anti-Soviet. Forrest Pogue recounts how General Marshall's speeches throughout the country took on a Cold War slant. The President addressed the Congress which passed the Economic Cooperation Act. Despite Truman's earlier expectation and the anti-Soviet sentiments of many Republican legislators, the final vote recorded a significant number of "nays."

V

Dean Acheson wrote that Senator Vandenberg had a legislative trick he used consistently, which was to find exception to draft legislation in some minor respect, move to amend it in this particular, and when the amendment was accepted, pronounce the bill satisfactory. In Acheson's account, this dealt in the ERP case with a small role for the United Nations. But the Congress shaped the legislation in other respects, and in some less positive ways. With my help, a newspaper columnist, Holmes Alexander, wrote up two: one, a requirement pushed by lobbyists for the milling industry that most or all of bread grains be shipped as flour on the alleged ground that the country needed to keep the chaff as chicken feed (at a time when Europe did not raise chickens on any considerable scale); and two, a provision that U.S. commodities be shipped half in American bottoms. In later appropriations, if my memory serves, this restriction was extended to apply separately to each receiving country so that countries with a substantial merchant marine, like Greece and Norway, could not pick more than half of their aid to make up for the deficiencies of countries with limited fleets. In his second memorandum of May 27, 1947, but a part not incorporated in Marshall's Harvard speech, Clayton had written: "Europe must be equipped to perform her own shipping services. The United States should sell ships to France, Italy and other maritime nations to restore their merchant marines at least to prewar levels. (To do so we shall have to lick the shipping lobby, fattening as it is on the U.S. Treasury.)"

The treatment of counterpart funds had been a subject of serious discussion between the Executive Branch and the CEEC during friendly assistance. Its solution was an agreement that the monies should belong to the recipient government, but that their use required agreement by the U.S. mission in the country. The purpose of the restriction was to guard against inflationary spending by using the funds to cover deficits. In the event, the requirement was helpful in cases where a finance minister wanted a lever to use against spending-happy cabinet colleagues, insulting to countries like the United Kingdom which thought their adherence to sound monetary and fiscal policies was equal to that of the United States, and awkward in such a country as France which had tied itself up in its own restrictions and sometimes needed some counterpart cash to achieve a desirable purpose under the Monnet Plan. I recall a later visit from Cambridge to Washington in 1949 or 1950 when purist younger officials in the Economic Cooperation Agency, like Richard Bissell and Arthur Smithies, wanted to deny an application of the French government, with the strong likelihood that another French cabinet would fall, only to be overruled by their boss, Paul Hoffman, and the Secretary of State — Acheson? — at the time.

Counterpart funds looked to the Congress as an opportunity to get something, not for nothing, to be sure, and with some ambiguity as to whether it was for the United States, the budget of the Department of State, or the Congress itself. Some part of the counterpart funds, the Congress insisted, should belong to the United States and be used by it at its own discretion, within, of course, the general laws of the country involved. The State Department objected that this was not aid but selling U.S. goods against local currency, even if that was inconvertible. In the end the State Department yielded to the extent of agreeing to 5 percent of counterpart funds belonging to the United States. Some was used to buy or build embassies and ambassadorial residences, much to entertain visiting congressmen.

An important issue in the legislation was how the act would be administered in the United States and abroad. Congress was strongly opposed to having the State Department in charge, and insisted on a separate Economic Cooperation Administration, with its own missions abroad, though necessarily in close communication with the local U.S. embassy. A tricky question was how the ECA would deal with Germany, and the imperious American Pro-consul, General Lucius D. Clay. This was settled by bringing in the ERP central mission in Paris under W. Averill Harriman. But Senator Vandenberg could not accept a transplanted State Department official as ECA head. President Truman asked him to accept Acheson: Acheson suggested to him Clayton. Vandenberg vetoed both. He wanted a businessman from outside government, and acceded to Paul Hoffman, the automobile manufacturer, who had been a member of the Harriman Commission.

One, or possibly another, positive contribution of the Congress to the final legislation came in the preamble to the Economic Recovery Act, in which the participating countries were urged to join in a United States of Europe. European integration had been discussed in the executive branch before the draft legislation was presented, and with the CEEC, as already mentioned. In the final analysis, however, the State Department held back from adding this political gloss to a program aimed at economic recovery. Congress lacked such delicate inhibition, however, and a year and a half later Paul Hoffman gave a widely noted speech urging European economic integration, now scheduled in the 1989 Maastricht treaty for half a century later.

Vandenberg's heroic efforts in behalf of the European Recovery Program seem not to have earned him much political capital. He told Acheson that support of a nonpartisan foreign policy did not win Democratic votes, and after the Foreign Relations Committee had published a summary of its work in the 80th Congress, he noted sardonically that Truman campaigned for election in 1948 claiming that the 80th was the worst Congress in history.

VI

I stop here. Sometime in the second quarter of 1948 I was laid low with a kidney stone and kidney colic, spent a week in hospital and another recuperating in Florida. With only one week of vacation in 4½ years of service, including the army, I had promised my wife I would leave the government if my normal weight of 160 pounds fell below 140. It did and I did. In addition to making good on a promise, like all the world I thought that Truman would lose the 1948 presidential election and I did not want to serve in the State Department under Dulles as secretary.

Looking for a teaching position, I gave a seminar at Princeton defending the Marshall Plan and was shot down by Graham, Viner, Lutz, with the same result later at Yale where Viner happened to be visiting and attending. Richard Bissell, who had been teaching at M.I.T. before coming to the Harriman Committee, told me that there was an opening there. I was not asked to give a seminar, got the job. As a lame duck and needing income until the new payroll kicked in, I wrote the memorandum "Origins of the Marshall Plan" in a lighthearted vein, turned away from Washington at the end of July. The total experience was serious, however, and exhilarating.

NOTES

1. Acheson says that General Marshall's most impressive attribute was self-command. Late in the historiography, however, Clark Clifford recorded that on one occasion Marshall almost lost it. In May 1948, after Britain had yielded independence to its Palestine mandate, Truman called a White House meeting to discuss whether the United States should immediately recognize the new country — days later known as Israel, — a move firmly opposed by the State Department. General Marshall asked the President why Clifford, a domestic adviser, was present in a discussion of a foreign-policy matter. Truman: "I invited him." After Clifford had spoken at some length on the issue, Marshall came close to *lèse-majesté,* saying to the President: "If you follow Clifford's advice and if I were to vote in the election, I would vote against you" (italicized in Clifford's memoir).

2. In one important respect, Acheson may have gone too far in his admiration of Clayton. President Truman announced the cancellation of the wartime Lend-lease program on August 21, 1945. According to Acheson the decision had been taken two days earlier on the advice of Undersecretary of State Joseph Grew, and Leo Crowley, the Foreign Economic Administrator, and was reached without considering the consequences which were "most far-reaching and harmful. If either Clayton or I had been there, I cannot believe it would have been taken." But the decision was made on the heavy cruiser, U.S.S. Augusta, taking the President and Secretary of State James F. Byrnes — a man notorious for not consulting staff — to the Potsdam Conference on the German occupation, which met from July 17 to August 2. When Clayton and Emilio G. ("Pete") Collado arrived in Potsdam by air, Byrnes told them of the decision. Collado protested vigorously with example after example of the harm that would ensue, once, twice, three times. Byrnes said to Clayton: "I do not want to see that man again." This is a strong memory of the story told to me by Collado for whom I was working at the time to backstop the economic members of the U.S. delegation at Potsdam.

3. Mr. Clayton indicated that the special relationship between the United

Kingdom and the United States had been put to one side for the purpose of the program, and that Britain was just another European country. A September 4 memorandum by Kennan for the Policy Planning Staff paints the English position "as tragic to the point that challenges description. Her problems . . . are deep-seated and grave . . . " and "I am inclined to think that there is no satisfactory solution for England's long-term problem . . . than closer association between England, Canada and the United States."

4. On a later occasion when I was preparing a program for the annual convention of the American Economic Association, I asked William R. Cline of the Institute for International Economics in Washington to discuss long-range forecasts in international economics, suggesting that he look particularly at the Brown Books, a task I have been unwilling to undertake myself. He evaded that particular assignment, choosing to measure, among other forecasts, projections of the dollar shortage on which I had written later, and a Brookings forecast of the U.S. balance of payments in 1968, made in 1963. His overall conclusion that long-term forecasts are rarely right because of a tendency to project conditions of the past into the future is surely correct.

5. We estimators had a joke to the effect that the Pentagon calculators (or computer) would probably spout $5.3 billion—the amount asked for by the Executive Branch for the first fifteen months—every time they were asked a question for the next several years.

16

From Graduate Student to Professional Peer: An Appreciation of Carlos F. Díaz-Alejandro

On several occasions when I have been on the same platform with a former student I have found it impossible to resist telling a story I first heard in a class in Logic at the University of Pennsylvania in the spring of 1929. In Ancient Greece a young man wanted to learn sophistry and went to the agora; he asked a renowned sophist to give him lessons, cautioning, however, that he had no money for tuition. The older man said that was not a problem and that the two could draw up a contract providing that when the young man won his first case he would pay his teacher. The lessons were duly delivered and absorbed. Years went by, however, and the young man did not practice sophistry. In due course the old teacher needed money, as old teachers will, and took the young man to court. He said, "Learned judge, you decide. If you decide in my favor the young man must pay me. If, on the other hand, you decide in his favor, he will have won his first case and by the terms of the contract, he must pay." But the young man had been an assiduous student and countered with the following: "Learned judge, if you say I won I don't have to pay, and if you say I lose I shall have lost my first case and don't have to pay."

I do not recall how a logician would solve this case, and perhaps never learned. Its use, of course, is to protect me in the case that a student outshines me. That only shows what a good teacher I am.

The story goes deeper, however, as it illustrates how the hierarchical relationship between teacher and student evolves into one of the equality of professional peers. This metamorphosis seems to me to be a good scaffolding within which to build my memorial of my dear student, advisee, thesis writer, colleague, critic, and friend, Carlos F. Díaz-

This essay originally appeared in Guillermo Calvo, Ronald Findlay, Penti Kouri, and Jorge Braga de Macedo, eds., *Debt, Stablilization and Development: Essays in Memory of Carlos Díaz-Alejandro* (Oxford and Cambridge, Mass.: Basil Blackwell, 1989), for the World Institute for Development Economics Research (WIDER) of the United Nations University. Reprinted with permission of UNU/WIDER.

Alejandro, with whom I have had an active interchange at the personal
and professional level for twenty-nine and a half years. The attempt runs
the risk of excessive intrusion into the account by me. I shall do my best
to limit this. I do not claim the pattern is general. I have been and am
warm friends with many of my graduate students, but with few to the
same extent as with Carlos. Fortunately I am of Anglo-Saxon and not of
Latin origin and can keep this account unemotional at least to some
degree. But I apologize in advance for any offense on either score.

The first item in the "file" is a letter form Carlos dated 12 December 1956, asking for an application form for admission to graduate
school. The file is one kept on all graduate students so long as they are
being closely followed and includes a mass of material: correspondence
dealing with admissions and fellowship aid, records of courses taken,
grades, general examinations and orals, copies of correspondence about
the dissertation and job hunting, letters of recommendation for jobs,
fellowships, and the like. Some instructors dealing with a student, current or past, turn the correspondence over to the central file. Others do
not. When correspondence is kept in a personal file, or discarded in an
occasional effort to slim one's accumulation of paper, the graduate file
stops. The last item is a letter from Minnesota dated 23 October 1967,
addressing me as Professor Kindleberger. The few letters retained in my
personal file pick up in 1981 where I am addressed by nickname. I am
certain that an abundant exchange took place meanwhile. In addition, I
have on my shelves volumes of *Festschriften* and symposia to which we
both contributed, and two of Carlos's contributions to symposia at MIT
with which I was associated. My last contacts with him in the spring of
1985 were at the March meeting of the American Economic Association
Executive Committee which he attended as a member of the Committee
on Honors and Awards, at a meeting at the Council on Foreign Relations on 28 April when I spoke and he introduced me, and at the memorial service in Boston for Paul N. Rosenstein-Rodan on 10 May 1985, at
which he gave one of the eulogies.

The early entries in the graduate student file are of interest. His
home address is given as Havana, Cuba, where he was born on 18 July
1937, forty-eight years less one day before his death in New York City.
He spent one year of college at Leicester Junior College, Leicester,
Massachusetts, before transferring for three years to Miami University
in Oxford, Ohio. The letters from Miami University were fulsome in
their praise: "One of the best minds of all students that I have taught"
(Delbert Snider); "the best student I have seen at Miami University in
seventeen years" (George W. P. Thatcher); "one of our best economics
majors — ever" (Paul M. Vaile). All emphasized his agreeable quality:

"very personable," "modest," "completely honest with himself and others," "mature concerns," and the like. At the time the admissions procedure of the department required a statement of the purposes that the applicant hoped to serve if admitted for the doctorate program in economics. Carlos's statement, received with his application dated 21 January 1957, included the following excerpts, some prescient, others geographically wide of the mark:

> For the last three years my main interest could be best referred to as "Political Economy." I am very hopeful that sound and dynamic economic policies could do a great deal toward improving the general standard of living of my country Cuba. This fact has weighed heavily in my decision to select Economics as my career. Furthermore, I am quite interested in government and politics in general . . .
>
> I would like to . . . have a general knowledge in all fields of Economics and mastery of the principles governing economic development and growth, and the governmental policies which would be appropriate to facilitate them . . .
>
> After receiving my Ph.D. degree, I hope to find employment in the Department of Economic Research of the Cuban National Bank. Later on, I would like to formulate, or help to formulate, the policies of that institution and those of the government . . .

Later, on the MIT departmental admissions committee, I was disposed to mark down candidates who wished to do good in the world, below those who were primarily curious as to how the economy worked. Had that standard been applied in the case of Carlos Díaz-Alejandro, it would have resulted in a misallocation.

The MIT program in economics started out connected with industry and was called "Industrial Economics," a term that startles one today when looking at old forms. Carlos's career as a student of economics got off to a fast start with A's in micro and macro, A−'s in international economics and mathematics for economists, and an A+ in economic history. In the second term he recorded two A+'s (a grade that most of the faculty did not mete out), one in economic history from W. W. Rostow who was new, and one in fiscal policy, I believe from Richard Musgrave who was filling in; he was given A's in the second part of micro and in mathematics for economists and another A− in international. Having written off most of his minor in management on the basis of business courses at Miami University, he had time in his second year to take more theory, statistical theory, reading courses in economics, and mathematics in the math department, both in the spring of 1959 and in the spring of 1960 when he was working on the thesis. In graduate courses in linear algebra, methods of applied mathematics, and probability, competing against graduate students in mathematics, he received C's.

The general examinations were taken in May 1959. Grades on these are not communicated to students, except in the vaguest terms, so that professors record what they really think, the better to evaluate students later for letters of recommendation when MIT's reputation is at stake. The average grade has been somewhere between Fair+ and Good−. Carlos received Excellent on the international written, Excellent− in theory and in "fluctuations" (macro), and Good+ in development. On the oral he had Excellent in international, and Excellent− to Good+ in theory and in development, for an overall grade of Excellent−. A typed comment on the form, that sounds like me, reads:

> Good flow of language. Occasionally too much. No facts on international trade, but handles those supplied very well, Flubbed external economies. Consensus is that he will make an excellent economist and that with some experience to check the poor ideas the flow will stand him in good stead.

On 11 June 1959, a letter to Professor Snider at Miami University said that MIT was trying to institute a policy of writing people who had recommended students to give an account of their progress. "It is very easy to do this about Carlos F. Díaz." His grades in courses and the general examination were detailed, as was his having won a Ford Foundation fellowship to write his dissertation on Brazilian [*sic*] experience with devaluation, a topic suggested by Alexandra Kafka that would "make an important contribution to a subject that has just about been exhausted theoretically and where empirical research is very much needed. In short, Mr. Díaz stands out at MIT in an outstanding class of graduate students, and we predict a successful career for him in economics." Knowledgeable economists will be aware that the dissertation in the end dealt with Argentine experience. How the Brazil reference crept in, by error or if the topic was later changed, is lost to me.

At this stage the file turns to two topics: job search and dissertation writing. An attempt to wheedle a fellowship in Demography out of the Population Council for the second year goes back to February 1958 and is too honest to have been effective, saying that his interest in demography was secondary. In December 1959, a note to Carlos talks of a luncheon with J. J. Polak of the International Monetary Fund (IMF) who both had an interest in recruiting Carlos and a suggestion about the relevance of Mexican experience for the absorption doctrines that Carlos was studying in Argentina. In 1960–61 I was on sabbatical, from which I brought back exchanges of letters of May and July discussing firstly the content of the thesis, but secondly and more important, whether Yale University would regard the thesis as finished as deemed necessary for him to start there as an assistant professor. In October 1961 a letter to him discussed how he could get portions of the thesis published. Perhaps the topic was too narrow for publication in the series that the MIT department was trying to get started for outstanding theses. I suggested sending it to the DiTella Foundation in Buenos Aires to see if they would be interested, or to the International Finance Section at Princeton where Professor Machlup might be interested in it for the support it gave him against Sidney Alexander (not much) in the clash between the elasticity and the absorption approaches. It appears from correspondence of July 1962 that he had shortened it too much for the Princeton series which seems to have turned it down, and now needed to loosen it up for the MIT series that accepted it in principle. Some correspondence in the file expresses the doubt of one professor that the thesis was of broad enough interest to merit subsidized publication, but apparently the commitment had already been made.

The program that Carlos joined at Yale was that of the Growth Center, headed originally by Lloyd G. Reynolds and later by Gustav Ranis. The idea was to work out a set of statistics to be collected by different researchers on a comparable basis, with each then writing a monograph on a separate country. Carlos was assigned to Argentina, and after a year of preliminary research in New Haven, went off thence. He had not finished the revision of the dissertation, but thought that this could be better done after his year in Buenos Aires.

The flight of Batista and the takeover by Fidel Castro in 1959 had given him both anguish and notoriety. After his first year at MIT he had gone to Havana, on 11 August 1958.

> I am enjoying a pleasant summer, dividing working hours almost equally between the beach and my father's business. I have managed to do some reading, but the heat has taken all ambition out of me.

A letter from him dated 13 May 1961, when I was on sabbatical, largely about the thesis, remarked: "I have retired from my public life as a speechmaker. As a matter of fact I loathe to discuss politics, especially Cuban politics. Now I am against Castro, but with little hope." A letter recommending him to a department of economics as late as 30 November 1964 sums up his Cuban connection in these terms:

He is a native Cuban, and he took the Castro Bay-of-Pigs business seriously and hard, disturbed over the policies of the two governments and unhappy at seeing his country torn up.

Ten days later a letter to another university adds slightly to this picture:

A Cuban, he was pro-Castro for some time, changed at about the same time as Pazos, who had a strong and good influence on him.

That letter goes on to make an economic point, " . . . He is likely to be underpriced now, as contrasted with three years from now. And he is very good indeed, one of the stars of the best class we have had at MIT in my sixteen years. _____ is after him, but he tells me that he might stay another year or two at Yale. First class, or as we used to say at O.S.S., *Erste Klasse.*"

These letters of November and December 1965 were a prelude to a flurry of letter-writing in 1966. On 1 February I wrote to Professor Powell who had asked for an appraisal as Yale contemplated a reappointment after a three-year stint.

Professor Díaz-Alejandro is a very much sought-after young man. For one thing, he is clearly the top young man in the Latin American field. I understand that he has this year, at the completion of his first appointment from Yale, received seven offers of appointment. But Díaz-Alejandro is more than a Latin American economist: he is a distinguished theorist generally in the fields of international trade and economic development. I know nothing about his teaching ability, but judging by his interest, enthusiasm, energy and friendliness, I confidently estimate that it is of a high order. He is perhaps less dedicated to theory than B _____ , J _____ , M _____ and V _____ of my students, but in his own way he is every bit their equal in excellence.

(This last was offered in response to a specific request for comparisons.)

A month later Professor Powell asked for and received another letter as Carlos had received a good offer from another university, and Yale was preparing to appoint him an associate professor for a five-year term. The file has letters to Professor O. N. Brownlee at Minnesota, including perceptive remarks by Robert Solow:

During his years here, Díaz was one of our best and liveliest students. . . . The characteristic thing about Díaz is that his primary orientation is always toward policy, but unlike so many people with that interest he has a good analytical mind and uses it on policy problems. . . . You can be sure that Díaz will never turn out soft-headed stuff, nor will he turn out work that is remote from real life issues.

Combined with all this, he is an extraordinarily pleasant, alert and civilized person . . .

In the end, Carlos decided to go to Minnesota where he stayed until 1969, at which time he returned to Yale as a full professor. In 1983 he moved to Columbia. In the spring of 1985 I wrote more letters for him for Harvard and Princeton. When he died he had accepted an appointment to Harvard but had not moved to Cambridge. I leave to his curriculum vitae the many consultantships, members of commissions, boards, advisory committees, and the like with which he was associated, both in Latin America and in the United States.

Graduate students of course teach each other, but occasionally a teacher contributes to the process as catalyst. The file has a letter of 12 July 1961, addressed to Carlos that says in part:

> You will be interested to learn that I left your two chapters with Egon Sohmen who returned them to me with the following characteristically slashing remarks:
>
> "I enclose the two chapters (II and III) by Díaz. He is obviously a very competent man. Where I do not agree, of course, is his unquestioning acceptance of the view that devaluation must always increase the price level, hence lower the standard of living of the majority. I thought this had been disproved in the meantime. He lacks an understanding (so widespread, alas, a short-coming) of resource allocation and its consequences."

The last exchange in the file starts with a letter from me on 10 February 1967, saying:

> I got in a bit of a dispute with a student over your thesis. His paper, my comment and a letter from him are appended. I think it was OK of you to assume that there would be hoarding in the short run and that the substitution effect in the short run was unimportant. He does not. Would you judge whether this paper should have received an A? How do you like the thought that students are working away at your writings while you take your ease?

His reply to the last point on 14 March read:

> The thought of students working away at my writings makes me feel old and bloated.

On 23 March, he wrote a long and thoughtful letter to the student on the substance of the argument.

The paths from studentship to professional equality are many and varied, and my association with Carlos included acknowledgments in prefaces, inscriptions in presentation copies of books, conferences, his participation in my projects, mine in his, papers together in conference volumes and *Festschriften,* citations of him by me, my serving as a critic of volumes in which he was represented, and so forth, too many forms to summarize in orderly fashion. Some parts of the transition are observable in the material in my files and on my shelves.

When does a student call his professor by his first name? It depends, of course, on the brashness of the student and the warmth of the professor. Carlos seems to me to have been unusually shy. No letter in the graduate student file (up to 1967) uses my Christian name. One to the graduate student in 1967 refers to me as CPK which is an efficient compromise. Because of the gap between the graduate student file and the 1982 letters, I cannot tell exactly when he shifted. But evidence from the inscriptions puts it before March 1977.

This transitional progress in intimacy is mirrored with a lead in the inscriptions in the three volumes he gave me. *Exchange-Rate Devaluation* is mockingly presented:

> To the Chief Presbyterian
> from one of his apprentices,
> with respect and affection.
> Carlos F. Díaz-A.
> Minneapolis, April 13, 1966

The mockery is stepped up in the inscription in *Essays on the Economic History:*

> Tibi Professori Carolo Kindleberger
> exemplare magistro, magnanimo duci, viro honesto, anglosaxoni
> cultivato et cultivatori,
> Carolus Díaz-Alejandro
> maxima salutem dici tibique hoc donum praesentat.
> Datum ad Novum Portun
>   X, MCMLXX A.D.

For *Colombia,* the teasing is less formal:

> To Sarah and Charlie,
> from their populist step-son
>   Carlos F.
> Princeton, March 5, 1977

and for the reprint of "Latin American debt: I don't think we are in Kansas any more" (*Brookings Papers* 1984):

> To the Master CPK
> Abrazos
> Carlos Ⓕ

with the "F" circled and an arrow pointing to it to remind me that I had more than once addressed him with the wrong middle initial.

I suspect that teasing is a means of effecting the transition from the structured hierarchical relationship to one of equality. In particular I recall an episode when Carlos and Ronald Findlay cooperatively worked me over. I was giving a dinner seminar at Columbia, in some year I could perhaps reconstruct but it would be trouble, perhaps 1969, and was seated by Carlos, who had come down from New Haven. Memory does not suffice to indicate which took what role. One, say Carlos, took a piece of paper and wrote out an enormous mathematical expression, laden with integrals, complex fractions, exponentials, etc., concluding, "Therefore CPK is right." In reply, Ron Findlay drew a three-dimensional diagram replete with surfaces of various shapes tangent to one another, and curves, some through axes, others asymptotic, and so on, adding, "Therefore CPK is right." On occasion the mockery went public: His puff for the jacket of a book that he calls "a collection of Kindlebergeriana" reads in part "Aficionados of multinationals, scholars, teachers and other Kindleberger groupies. . . . "

To watch the maturing friendship of students is a lagniappe for the teacher, or caviar for the general. Jaroslav Vanek and the late Egon Sohmen roomed together in the mid-1950s at MIT and kept up a long friendship until Sohmen died in 1976. Ronald Findlay and Carlos Díaz-Alejandro saw a lot of each other in New York even before Carlos left Yale for Columbia.

They both came to Boston on 12 July 1971 and sat together I judge from the fact that their signatures on the flyleaf of a presentation volume are one under the other. But I especially envied my friend Max Corden who had them both at Nuffield College in the same term in 1977, if I remember correctly, when Corden, Findlay, and Díaz-Alejandro produced geometric international trade theory by the ream, month after month. A typical externality of this period is contained in a letter from Corden to me: "He was such a wonderful companion—we got to know him really well when he was at Nuffield College with Ronald—Dorothy felt like he was like a brother. And then, a really civilized economist. . . . " Many teachers, but especially I, have difficulty with depth perception among students, knowing who were contemporaries and knew each other and how well. With Carlos, the problem was not troublesome.

CPK as impresario: In the spring of 1969 I spent half the time in the Economics Department and half the time in the Sloan School of Management at MIT, in the latter capacity organizing a series of lectures on the multinational corporation that later appeared as a book (*The International Corporation* [Cambridge, Mass.: MIT Press, 1971]). Carlos contributed a lecture that appeared as "Direct foreign investment in Latin America." My preface states about Carlos:

> He brings to the troubled question of US investment in Latin America wide experience for a young man, a knowledge of history, and a well-honed kit of economic tools. But the heart of the matter is political. A long history of cavalier treatment of Latin American individuals, traditions, governments, and business by American businessmen corrupts attempts to keep the discussion on an economic level, and even then such legislation as the Hickenlooper amendment leads Latin America to believe that the United States turns economic disputes into political shows of strength.

Seven years later, a weekend conference at MIT's Sloan School on multinational firms emanating from small countries — to eliminate some part of the political element — resulted in Tamir Agmon and me editing *Multinationals from Small Countries* (Cambridge, Mass.: MIT Press, 1977). Carlos looked through the telescope from the other end, writing on "Foreign direct investment by Latin Americans."

CFDA as impresario: In 1982, Rosemary Thorp and Carlos planned the session on Latin American economic history during the 1930s at the 44th International Congress of Americanists, held in Manchester, England, and I was asked to sum up the various papers at the conclusion after Carlos had set the keynote in a paper entitled "Latin America in the 1930s." The papers appeared in Rosemary Thorp, ed., *Latin America in the 1930s: The Role of the Periphery in World Crisis* (London: Macmillan, 1984). By this time I was teasing him. His paper for the *Festschrift* in honor of Sir Arthur Lewis (Mark Gersovitz, Carlos F. Díaz-Alejandro, Gustav Ranis, and Mark R. Rosenzweig, eds., *The Theory and Experience of Economic Development* [London: George Allen and Unwin, 1982]) had been on "Latin America in the 1940s." I asked whether he was planning to do the economic history of Latin America decade by decade, with the more interesting decades assigned two papers each.

What I found especially flattering was that Carlos's interests seemed to evolve in the same direction as mine have done, though of course in a different region. He worked on trade and foreign exchange, on economic history, and ultimately on financial history, including financial crises. We moved in the same circles, and found ourselves writing for the same *Festschriften* — for Paul N. Rosenstein-Rodan, for Arthur Lewis, and for Robert Triffin. My records show that we attended four conferences together: on the frontiers for research in international economics in Princeton, on economic information in Kiel, on small open economies in Dublin (1979), and, as already mentioned, on Latin America in the 1930s, when Carlos gave the opening paper and I the closing one. My paper for Kiel was sent to Carlos for comment before the event as evidenced by its embellishment in footnote 33 by a reference to Jorges Luis Borges's short story, "The Library of Babel" (in *Ficciones* [Grove Press, New York, 1962]), provided by Carlos. The Dublin conference was difficult to place in time because there was no single volume and such papers as were published appeared separately. I pinned the date down by consulting my family photograph album which has several pictures of Carlos with me and Ronald Jones, and with Professor and Mrs. Dermot McAleese. In the course of the search I found two other snapshots of Carlos, one of him and me (and Jürg Niehans) at a party given by Rudiger Dornbusch on 8 January 1976, and another showing him with very long hair at some party in Budapest dated 29 January 1976 (the picture is cropped and some of the message on the reverse side is lost).

However, my greatest profit and pleasure came not from public occasions but from exchanging papers in draft, or reprints, and commenting freely in correspondence. It is regrettable that in retiring from MIT and taking papers home I disposed of most of these files.

A 1981 letter was kept as a personal treasure.

> Dear Charlie,
>   What a good "Life"!
>   Again I was amazed by how many of what I thought were my insights (in grad. school one learns more from fellow students than from faculty, etc.) came from you.
>   Also blushingly enjoyed pp. 243–244. [This passage refers to the distinction of MIT graduates in international economics and mentions Carlos along with Bhagwati, Branson, Chacholiades, Findlay, Jones, Hymer, Magee, Mundell, Sohmen, and Vanek.]
>   When I grow up I want a Life like that!

The 1982 correspondence between Stockholm and New Haven covered the 1930s in Latin America, financial integration, financial repression. The letter of 15 November 1982 gives reasons for leaving Yale for

Columbia, including pull factors: Findlay, Calvo, Bhagwati, Manhattan, and push factors: New Haven. My letter of 10 November starts:

> Dear Carlos,
>   You really believe in international multilateral balancing. I ask for comments on my paper. You provide them not. You ask for comments on yours, assuming, I guess, that you will comment on papers of others and they will do so for me . . .

The letter of 22 November 1982, commenting on the Edmar Lisboa Bacha and Carlos paper "International financial intermediation: A long and tropical view" (Princeton *Essays in International Finance,* no. 147, May 1982), which was not sent, starts out:

> Dear Carlos,
> I have finally caught up with your (with Bacha) Princeton essay which I like a lot. I cannot resist, however, one or two pot shots.

Typed across the head of the letter is "Not sent. But the essay is far too optimistic." I assume the reason for suppressing it was that there were too many niggling pot shots and that the total gave the wrong impression. In February 1983 there was a letter from him on my draft Zahid Hussain lecture, largely on French and British financial integration, which is all I know, in which he listed five criticisms from the point of view of a Moslem Punjabi. Point (e) starts, "Last but not least (remember my application to enter MIT in 1957!)," I did not, and did not have the application handy. Now that I do I cannot see what he meant. Nonetheless the remark suggests that inside every professional peer there is a student who sometimes reacts to a teacher.

After 1983 there is a gap until 1985. I had sent him for comment some draft lectures on international capital movements. He wrote or said hastily when we met in New York on 28 April, that it needed more on financial intermediation in the Third World lending instance. I asked what was meant, but there was not time in the larger group to explain. On 6 May 1985 came the last written communication from him in which he regressed for a minute to the role of student again:

> Dear Charlie,
> I was very impressed by your CFR session, and even awed. I worked during the morning on an eloquent and witty introduction, but so many of your old buddies unnerved me, and I ended up feeling and acting like a callow youth.

Then the professional friend takes over, answering my question:

> In the old days, Argentines bought Argentine bonds in London at arm's length. Today, Chase Manhattan lends to Argentina, and private Argentines have bank accounts with Chase . . .

The letter ends:

> Jerry Green [head of the Harvard Department of Economics] called to inform me that Bok approved my appointment. I await a call from Mike Spence [Dean of Arts and Sciences] to make sure they're not planning to ask me to teach Spanish five days a week. One never knows with that Imperial university.
>
> Abrazos
Carlos F

Sometimes the complimentary ending was spelled "Abracos" instead of with a "z," and sometimes it was accompanied by "Venceremos." In all that he wrote by holograph his liveliness and warmth shone.

It would be good to have a broad view of Carlos from *his* students. I was lucky enough to run into one, Michael Klein, who worked as his research assistant at Columbia when he was writing "Latin American debt: Not in Kansas any more." I asked him to write me a letter. He writes of Carlos's keen insights, wide-ranging knowledge, and his entertaining wit, "the enthusiasm, skill and joy that Carlos brought to the problem." But he referred to Carlos only as "Professor Díaz-Alejandro." José Antonio Ocampo wrote a dissertation under Carlos at Yale and became his peer, writing a paper on Colombia in the 1930s for the Rosemary Thorp symposium. Alas, too few can share that rite of passage.

His draft paper of April 1983, "Goodbye financial repression, hello financial crash," says on p. 7 "the financial history of Latin America remains to be written. . . . " I believe he would have written it. We are the poorer for our lack of such a history. Far more we are impoverished in spirit by the loss of the man.

The theme of the transition from gradate student to professional peer is, of course, only a peg on which to hang my appreciation for Carlos as an economist and as a person. Solow is right in emphasizing his concern for policy, rarely combined so effectively with strong analytical talent, a sense of history, and empathy for those left behind in the distribution of income and wealth. He and Corden are both right in pointing to his civilized nature. I had intended to call attention to the imaginative illustrations by his artist brother Ramon Alejandro for the frontispiece of *Colombia* and *Essays on the Economic History*—a brother he frequently visited in Paris. Michael Klein reminds us of his wit, and I should add, ability to turn an arresting phrase. I have left no room in this account for his courage as a Dissenting Member of the Kissinger Commission on Central America, on which he spoke eloquently and wittily in an interview in the *New Journal,* published at Yale (vol. 16, no. 4, 3 February 1984), an assignment representing still another facet of his complex personality, a sense of duty. Carlos was the paragon of Latin American economists and of economists generally, as student, colleague, collaborator, and friend.

In my drawer of stationery supplies is a mailing label for adhering to a large manila envelope addressed to Carlos at Columbia. I must have planned to mail him a paper, and then delivered it by hand. Its presence, now useless, is a poignant reminder of our present emptiness.

NOTE

I acknowledge with thanks the comments by Ronald Findlay and Barbara Solow on an earlier draft.

Index

STUDIES IN INTERNATIONAL TRADE POLICY

Studies in International Trade Policy includes works dealing with the theory, empirical analysis, political, economic, legal relations, and evaluations of international trade policies and institutions.

General Editor: Robert M. Stern

John H. Jackson and Edwin Vermulst, Editors. *Antidumping Law and Practice: A Comparative Study*

John Whalley, Editor. *Developing Countries and the Global Trading System.* Volumes 1 and 2

John Whalley, Coordinator. *The Uruguay Round and Beyond: The Final Report from the Ford Foundation Project on Developing Countries and the Global Trading System*

John S. Odell and Thomas D. Willett, Editors. *International Trade Policies: Gains from Exchange between Economics and Political Science*

Ulrich Kohli. *Technology, Duality, and Foreign Trade: The GNP Function Approach to Modeling Imports and Exports*

Stephen V. Marks and Keith E. Maskus, Editors. *The Economics and Politics of World Sugar Policies*

J. Michael Finger, Editor. *Antidumping: How It Works and Who Gets Hurt*

Horst Herberg and Ngo Van Long, Editors. *Trade, Welfare, and Economic Policies: Essays in Honor of Murray C. Kemp*

David Schwartzman. *The Japanese Television Cartel: A Study Based on* Matsushita v. Zenith

Alan V. Deardorff and Robert M. Stern, Editors. *Analytical Perspectives and Negotiating Issues in the Global Trading System*

Edwin Vermulst, Paul Waer, and Jacques Bourgeois, Editors. *Rules of Origin in International Trade: A Comparative Study*

Alan V. Deardorff and Robert M. Stern, Editors. *The Stolper-Samuelson Theorem: A Golden Jubilee*

Kent Albert Jones. *Export Restraint and the New Protectionism: The Political Economy of Discriminatory Trade Restrictions*

Alan V. Deardorff, James A. Levinsohn, and Robert M. Stern, Editors. *New Directions in Trade Theory*

Robert Baldwin, Tain-Jy Chen, and Douglas Nelson. *Political Economy of U.S.–Taiwan Trade*

Bernard M. Hoekman and Petros C. Mavroidis, Editors. *Law and Policy in Public Purchasing: The WTO Agreement on Government Procurement*

Danny M. Leipziger, Editor. *Lessons from East Asia*

Tamin Bayoumi. *Financial Integration and Real Activity*

Harry P. Bowen, Abraham Hollander, and Jean-Marie Viaene. *Applied International Trade Analysis*